Locating the Energy for Change: An Introduction to Appreciative Inquiry

Charles Elliott
Dean of Trinity Hall
University of Cambridge

INTERNATIONAL INSTITUTE FOR
SUSTAINABLE DEVELOPMENT

INSTITUT INTERNATIONAL DU
DÉVELOPPEMENT DURABLE

The International Institute for Sustainable Development
(IISD) is an independent, not-for-profit corporation head-
quartered in Winnipeg, Canada, established and supported
by the governments of Canada and Manitoba. Its mandate is
to promote sustainable development in decision-making in
Canada and around the world.

Copies are available for purchase from IISD.
Copies may also be ordered through IISD's online order form
at http://iisd.ca/about/prodcat/ordering.htm

Canadian Cataloguing in Publication Data

Elliott, Charles, 1939-

Locating the energy for change: an introduction to
appreciative inquiry

Includes bibliographical references.
ISBN 1-895536-15-4

1. Organizational change. I. International Institute for
Sustainable Development. II. Title.

HD58.8.E445 1999   658.4'06   C99-920073-9

This publication is printed on recycled paper.

International Institute for Sustainable Development
161 Portage Avenue East, 6th Floor
Winnipeg, Manitoba
Canada
R3B 0Y4

Tel: (204) 958-7700
Fax: (204) 958-7710
E-mail: info@iisd.ca
Internet: http://iisd.ca

Acknowledgements

As will quickly become apparent, this book depends on the cooperation of many, many people. At the risk of failing to acknowledge some, I would like to say a big thank you to the following:

- to Neil Ford at the IISD for making this volume available to a wider public

- to David Cooperrider and his colleagues at Case Western University for pioneering appreciative inquiry and sharing their findings so generously

- to my colleagues in the Cambridge Partnership for Organisational Transformation who have taught me so much, and especially to Mette Jacobsgaard with whom I shared much of the fieldwork reported in this volume

- to my colleagues in Trinity Hall, Cambridge for granting me leave of absence to do much of the fieldwork

- to Virginia Greany who helped read proofs against a tight deadline at considerable personal inconvenience

- to all those people and organizations that have undertaken an appreciative inquiry and shared the process and outcomes with me. Without them, this book could never have been written.

Joe Petrik edited the original manuscript and coordinated the layout and print production. Shannon Brown, Lael Dyck, Virginia Gonzales and Alison Patmore entered the edits to the manuscript. Don Berg designed the volume's cover and typeset the manuscript.

Charles Elliott,
Trinity Hall,
Cambridge.
17th March, 1999.

About the author

Charles Elliott, Dean of Trinity Hall, teaches economics at the University of Cambridge in the UK. He founded the Cambridge Partnership for Organisational Transformation to promote the practice of appreciative inquiry and has used it on three continents with groups as diverse as churches and prisons; African villages and multinational corporations; clinics and law firms.

He is married with three grown sons and a grand-dog.

Foreword

The International Institute for Sustainable Development (IISD) is publishing this book to introduce development practitioners to appreciative inquiry. This methodology can help them turn sustainable livelihoods from a theoretical concept into a practical approach. What's more important, it can help local people build improved, sustainable futures for themselves and their children, based on their strengths and achievements.

To date most applications of appreciative inquiry have taken place in the corporate world. Indeed, many of Elliott's examples come from executives who are positioning their businesses for the 21st century. But what works for companies can also prove valuable for communities, especially those that are struggling at the subsistence level, as Elliott demonstrates so effectively through his case studies from West Africa. Local people can use the appreciative approach to identify their current strengths, then plan an improved future, based on their understanding of the "positive present." I believe that appreciative inquiry is an exciting tool that local people can use to empower themselves and break free from poverty through their own vision and effort.

IISD has been working in poverty alleviation and empowerment since it was founded in 1990. We began by exploring the complex livelihoods of rural people in drought-prone areas of Africa to help us understand why five decades of development assistance had made such a small impact. IISD defines livelihoods as the activities, assets and entitlements that poor people use to survive. Unlike those of us who work for wages in developed economies, families struggling to live in the developing world usually depend on a number of activities. The father may herd goats and also pan for gold in a nearby stream. The children may peddle crafts in the street. The mother may grow food in a communal garden. None of it adds up to much, but by working together, family members can achieve a basic existence.

But can they ever prosper, and if so, will they prosper without diminishing opportunities for their children and grandchildren? For IISD a family's livelihood is sustainable when it can cope with stresses and shocks such as floods or low commodity prices, when it can maintain and enhance the family's capabilities and assets, and when it can preserve the natural resource base of the community for future generations. By 1995, through workshops and fieldwork, we had developed a framework that described the elements that produce sustainable livelihoods. They are:

- community adaptive strategies and local knowledge;
- enabling policies;

- appropriate science and technology; and
- access to credit and investment opportunities.

For us the first element is the most important. A community must understand what makes it strong if it is to participate effectively in decisions that affect local livelihoods. This knowledge can then be used to inform the other three elements to improve the overall community structure.

Our current challenge is to help communities participate effectively within this sustainable livelihoods framework by developing techniques and methodologies to help local people understand their strengths, analyze their options, plan effectively and participate more equally in decision-making. That's where appreciative inquiry can make a contribution. The current state of the art in poverty alleviation is the use of participatory methodologies to help local people identify problems, resource constraints and unmet basic needs. Development professionals then work in partnership with local people, implementing projects to fix the problems. Although this approach is logical and efficient, it can often disempower the community it is meant to help, by conditioning local people to view their village as a place full of problems that only outsiders can solve, and needs that only governments can meet. The problem-oriented approach can establish a sense of dependency in the community that seems insurmountable. As a result, community participation often dwindles when a project finishes and development professionals withdraw. Sustainability is difficult to achieve.

Appreciative inquiry starts from a fundamentally different—and more positive—point. It is designed to help local people identify their achievements. This process can be very empowering for people who have always considered themselves poor and disadvantaged. When they look for their strengths, they are often amazed to discover how resilient, adaptive and innovative they are. They have to be—poverty is a cruel and unforgiving circumstance. By focusing on their strengths they can use the "positive present" to build a shared vision of a better future, one that is grounded in reality. Appreciative inquiry creates a development pathway based on what is right rather than what is wrong.

But can appreciative inquiry help poor people protect and preserve their natural resource base, ensuring opportunities for future generations? Can it open up new income-generating opportunities? Can it enhance social conditions? Quite simply, we don't know, and we won't until we have more experience helping local people use appreciative inquiry and have evaluated its results more rigorously.

Initial indications, however, are positive. The appreciative approach encourages people to think deeply about the ways they would like to develop. What contributes to the well-being of their community? Material success? Cultural identity? A clean environment? Can they choose a development pathway that does not sacrifice some of these goals to achieve others? This holistic emphasis, this focus on gross national happiness rather than gross national product, fits well with a concept of sustainable development that integrates economic growth, environmental integrity and human well-being.

Charles Elliott is a pathfinder. He has used appreciative inquiry in corporate and institutional settings, then applied the lessons he has learned to community development in poor and remote regions of the world. It's up to us—community members, development professionals, corporate citizens and public servants—to widen that path into a well-travelled road to sustainable livelihoods.

Neil Ford
Program Director, Community Adaptation and Sustainable Livelihoods
International Institute for Sustainable Development
January, 1999

Table of Contents

Introduction:
A first glimpse of the appreciative mode

Consider these two true stories

Rosemary Willson is a successful New York publisher. Her marriage broke up three years ago and she has custody of her 11-year-old son, Joel. Despite Rosemary's determination to provide him with every material and emotional advantage, Joel is clearly having a hard time growing up as a lone child of a single parent. He has long had behavioural problems at school, has become truant and is truculent when challenged about this at home. He has never shown much affection for his caregiver, Joanne, though she is highly trained and does everything she can to win the boy's trust and regard.

Rosemary has decided the situation is now so serious that she must tackle it more systematically. She tells Joanne to keep a list of Joel's misdemeanours and to make sure to ask his teacher each day how he has behaved when she picks him up from school.

"He has to learn," says Rosemary. "I will go through the list with him every evening—quietly, methodically, thoroughly, explaining why what he has done is wrong or unacceptable. We will soon see a big improvement. He's a bright enough youngster; he just needs to have things pointed out to him in a consistent way. Once he sees that we are on to him, he'll change...."

Joel's behaviour has gotten no better; in some important respects, it has become worse since this list-and-tell regime was begun.

Two thousand miles to the South West, the Lakota people in New Mexico also have a delinquent youngster. He has been seen damaging people's cars and trucks in the car lot outside the store. When challenged, he has been rude and dismissive of the authority of the elders.

The whole clan is called together one evening and forms a large circle. The young man's father walks with him into the middle of the circle and then joins the other adults on the perimeter. The father begins to speak first.

"You are our first born, our most precious one. Your mother and I rejoiced the first time we felt you kick in her stomach. We ran from house to house, telling all these people that you were alive and well and strong. And so you were. You were born crying with a shout so loud they heard it three hundred yards away above the radio. How proud we were! How happy! You have always made us happy. Your first few steps—oh, how you fell over into a puddle. The look on your face! How we laughed...."

On and on, the father recounts, sharing the happiest memories of his son's life. No word of criticism is uttered. The father's task is to remind the young man of all that he means to the family, the clan, the people; of all the joy and happiness he has brought; of the delight his wider family have in him.

When he is finished, it is the uncle's turn. He is followed by the two grandfathers. The sky is darkening, the stars plainly visible. It will be long past midnight before they have finished. After the men, the women speak, in gentler tones, in softer cadence—for it is on them that much of the work, from first labour pains to saving enough for schoolbooks, has fallen.

Finally, the clan chief speaks. He summarizes all that has been said. He speaks slowly, with long pauses, as though searching for the deepest ways of saying what has to be said. His theme, from which he never deviates, is the same: the pride and pleasure this young man has brought to all the Lakota people; the living, the departed and those not yet born. Like all the earlier speakers, he never mentions the vandalism and the malicious damage, the shame, the anger, the futility, the mindlessness. All that is left unsaid, unhinted. The sole refrain is that this young man is a beautiful gift to the whole people, one of inexpressible value.

When the old man has finished speaking, he makes a small sign. The ring of people stands still, almost at attention, looking ahead of them at the young man in the centre of the circle. Then they melt wordlessly into the night.

Which youngster has the better chance of transformational change: the one whose faults are catalogued and reviewed each day? Or the one who has been ritually assured of his place in the hearts of all his people?

This contrast is what the appreciative approach is all about.

How to use this book

Before we go any further, it might be helpful to explain what this book seeks to do and how it does it.

Primarily, I want readers to both understand and feel what appreciative inquiry is and how it can be used to change organizations and communities. Feeling is as important as understanding, because the methodology teaches us that the energy for change comes from both the heart and the head. Appreciative inquiry takes the energy of the "positive present"—with the Lakota boy, the best possible interpretation of his meaning to his people—and uses it to build vision of a positive, desired future, one that is grounded in reality. It then helps people mobilize forces for change to turn that vision into reality—to help the Lakota boy grow into a responsible, fulfilled person.

Appreciative inquiry was developed at Case Western Reserve University in the early 1990s, primarily as a methodology to help corporations and institutions improve their competitive advantage or organizational effectiveness. I have used it in this context and found that it can produce dramatic results, as you will learn from the examples and case studies presented later on. More recently, I have applied it at the community level in developing countries. Here, appreciative inquiry appears to work equally well. It involves a significant shift in emphasis from local problems to local achievements, from participation to inspiration. By identifying and reinforcing positive and constructive actions, relationships and visions within a community, it encourages local ownership in activities that contribute to sustainable development and secure livelihoods at the village level.

Whether it is used to help a multinational corporation position itself for the 21st century or a community of nomadic herdspeople build new livelihoods, an appreciative inquiry usually proceeds through four stages:

- *Discovering periods of excellence and achievement.* Through interviews and storytelling, participants remember significant past achievements and periods of excellence. When was their organization or community functioning at its best? What happened to make those periods of excellence possible? By telling stories, people identify and analyze the unique factors—such as leadership, relationships, technologies, core processes, structures, values, learning processes, external relations, or planning methods—that contributed to peak experiences.

- *Dreaming an ideal organization or community.* In this step people use past achievements to envisage a desired future. This aspect of appreciative inquiry is different from other vision-creating or planning methodologies because the images of the community's future that emerge are grounded in history, and as such represent compelling possibilities. In this sense appreciative inquiry is both practical, in that it is based on the "positive present," and generative, in that it seeks to expand the potential of the organization or community.

- *Designing new structures and processes.* This stage is intended to be provocative—to develop, through consensus, concrete short- and long-term goals that will achieve the dream. Provocative propositions usually take the form of statements such as, "This community will do whatever is necessary to build a school and have a full primary cycle within the next year." Or, "This company will champion innovation by creating new teams that integrate marketing and product development more effectively." Or, "This village will protect what remains of the local forest and will plant one thousand trees over the next two seasons to ensure the forest's survival for future generations." Provocative propositions should stretch an organization or community, but they should also be achievable because they are based on past periods of excellence.

- *Delivering the dream.* In this stage, people act on their provocative propositions, establishing roles and responsibilities, developing strategies, forging institutional linkages and mobilizing resources to achieve their dream. New project plans will be developed and initiated, new relationships will be established and the group will proceed with vision and a renewed sense of purpose. As a result of the appreciative process, people will have a better understanding of the relevance of new initiatives to the long-term vision of the organization or community.

That's how it's supposed to work. In reality, of course, it never turns out quite the way you expect. My aim is to introduce the reader to the theory (modestly) and the practice (more extensively) of appreciative inquiry. Why? Because I have come to believe that it offers a genuinely new and rewarding way to tackle issues of sustainable change in a vast array of organizations and institutions—from the relatively simple to the hugely complex; from the corporate to the not-for-profit; from New York to the African bush. It is not organizational snake oil, a wonder tool that will solve every organizational ill from bankruptcy to hostile legal suits. Starting from a classically Cambridge position of skepticism, however, I have become convinced that the dynamic at the heart of appreciative inquiry cannot only transform organizational processes but also can do so in a way that becomes self feeding and therefore sustainable in the longer run.

To be more specific, appreciative inquiry is unusual in that it combines the five features that emerge again and again in discussions of organizational sustainability. They are as follows: (1) the incorporation of a wide range of stakeholders in assessing the past and planning the future; (2) transparency of organizational self-reflection; (3) the inclusive determination of decision-making criteria which include (4) non-quantifiable, non-financial elements that may crucially affect the long-term health of the organization; and (5) the wide dissemination of power and influence throughout the organization, as implied in (2) and (3).

How should readers use this book? Let me suggest the following guidelines:

- If you want to understand why appreciative inquiry works, read part 1. This section will introduce you to the psychological and social underpinnings of the methodology.

- If you want to learn how to conduct an appreciative inquiry, go directly to part 2. This section will take you through a typical appreciative inquiry, with all the untidiness, confusion, risk-taking and mixed emotions that will be familiar to anyone who has worked with organizations and communities.

- If you want to read about appreciative inquiry in action, turn to part 3. This section presents case studies of appreciative inquiry at work in organizational and community settings.

Naturally, I hope most readers will read all three sections, inevitably with variations in emphasis.

Part 1
Some theoretical soundings

Chapter 1
The appreciative approach

1. Learning and looking

Forty-five senior executives from corporations and public sector enterprises sat in the room. They had met each other before and so there was that pleasant hum of conversation, punctuated by an occasional burst of laughter, that tells you that the group is beginning to gel well. The morning session had been constructive, with a high level of participation and a sense of energy and constructive purpose. In a word, the group struck me as happy.

"Before we break for lunch," I announced, "here is a simple task I want you to perform individually. Take a sheet of paper, write at the top: "My organization is _____" and then write down 20 adjectives that you think most accurately catch the flavour of your organization. This is an exercise in immediate impressions rather than a heavy think-piece—so you have exactly two minutes. That is six seconds per word, so you'd better get moving. Start now."

Bear in mind that the work we had done earlier in the morning was highly unlikely to have contaminated the results of this exercise. It had been a review of recent legislation and did not encourage the executives to reflect on the organizational life of their companies in any way. Bear in mind too that these executives had been chosen because they were well integrated into their companies: they were not odd-balls or professional malcontents. If anyone might have been expected to take a positive, even rosy, view of their working environment, it was the group before me.

Yet when I came to analyze the figures, the results were as follows:

- Critical, negative or hostile words
  (e.g., chaotic; inefficient; inward-looking; lazy;
  poorly structured; over-bureaucratic; slow; careless; unaware)   72%

- Neutral words
  (e.g., mainstream; average; contented; unambitious)   13%

- Positive, affirming, approving words
  (e.g., creative, exciting, thrilling; cutting-edge; determined;
  satisfying; customer-oriented; high-tech; achievement-oriented)   15%

While it is true that I am not acquainted in detail with all the enterprises represented in that room, I know enough of them sufficiently well to be confident that that imbalance between criticism and approval is a gross misrepresentation. Allow for the fact that each executive may have been embarrassed about seeming

9

to boast about his organization, and that our culture, especially in its academic dimension, encourages critical responses more than it encourages praise. Even so the five-to-one ratio of criticism to affirmation in the off-the-cuff responses of those executives should surely make us stop and think.

What leads us to see the bad things, the dark underside, and ignore the positive and pleasing things, not only in our organizations but in all our relationships, experiences and environments? Why have our ways of looking at the world become so morose, "populated by aggressive and depressive moralists, problema-tists, "problemholics" and soft rigorists whose existential stimulus is no," or, in this context, "not good enough."[1] I shall answer those questions in many ways in the rest of this book. For the moment, here are two opening observations.

The first is that by taking issue with the tendency in our culture to highlight the deficiencies, I should not be interpreted as suggesting that all the news is good—anymore than the Lakota imagine that their young delinquent is a saint. Of course organizations have their failures; people have their faults; families have their dysfunctions; colleagues have their failings and incompetencies. The appre-ciative approach must never be interpreted as denying that or turning its back on the bad news. It is deliberately called the *appreciative* approach, not the affirma-tive approach or the positive approach or the uncritical approach. As we shall see appreciation in the sense that it is used throughout this book is about choosing the elements of a situation that we want to work with; it is not about a pollyan-naish refusal to recognize the fact that good and not-so-good are mixed in unequal proportions in everything we experience.

Related to that, the second point can be put like this: to a degree—and the appre-ciative approach is about enlarging that degree—we have a choice about what we see in each other, in our working environments, in our families and our most inti-mate relationships—just as the Lakota had the choice of what they saw in that young man. We even have a choice, one that many people find the hardest of all to exercise, about what we see in ourselves. I remember talking to someone I regard-ed with something akin to awe. He was successful, happily married with three interesting, well-adjusted children, thoughtful, sensitive and surrounded by friends to whom he meant a lot. Yet in his own eyes, he was a failure, a pariah, the perma-nent outsider, the leper whom no one wanted to know. That was the self he chose to see. When I suggested that his perspective on that self was seriously in conflict with the facts, he snorted: "You just buy the PR. I know the reality."

That, of course, raises the question. What reality? Whose reality? Let me illustrate the significance of that question from another exercise I sometimes have execu-tives do. Below are a couple of squiggles from a large bank of illustrations I have developed. I put one or more on a flipchart and ask each person to take a couple of minutes to decide what it represents. To motivate them, I will sometimes spin a yarn that a key attribute of a successful executive is being able to see the emergent shape of things to come in their organization, that this capacity to detect emergent shapes is rare and valuable, and so we are going to see who in this group has it. They all stare at the squiggles; tilt their heads first to one side then the other; squint; half close their eyes. (One man even stood on his head. Perhaps he will go far.) After a few minutes they begin to see—*or think they can see*—some emergent shape in the squiggle. For the two below, the most recent exercise elicited, among others, the following suggestions: for A—a cow, a skyline, a ship in a storm, a female body (inevitably), a cat and mouse; and for B—a galaxy, hair, a close-up of a carpet and a plume of exhaust smoke.

A   B

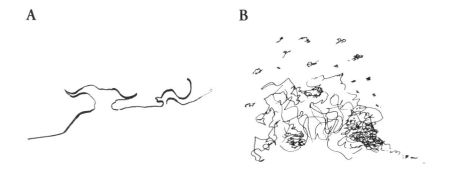

I then put them in threes or fours and get them to come to a consensus about what the squiggle *really* is. I am always surprised how much heat this exercise generates. People are quick to imagine that their interpretation of a random set of marks on paper is the right one; that they have seen reality and that their colleagues are somehow lacking in the percipience with which they have been richly and unusually endowed. The person who sees a cow knows with the rational part of his mind that that is one construction among many. But once he has selected that construction and announced it in public—"I see in this pattern a cow: I can see the horns, the rump, the suggestion of a tail and udders"—he will do his best to convince others that his interpretation of reality is reality—with the implication that their interpretations, however well articulated, are not quite in accord with the data presented by the squiggles.

What this exercise reveals is how readily we make and defend our versions of reality, sometimes on the back of very ambiguous data, or a very partial view of subsets of data. That itself raises some interesting and important questions about how we create reality. For the moment I hope I have said enough to convince you that the way we construct the data with which we are presented is, to a degree, a matter of choice. We can see a cow or a skyline. And having seen a cow, we can choose to replace that construction with a skyline or a ship in a storm. How we construct our environment is up to us.[2] (How free, intellectually and emotionally, we are to move from one construction to another; or what determines that A sees a cow while B sees a hippopotamus and C sees Mrs. Thatcher? That is a more difficult question to which also we shall have to return.) Another way of making the same point—but one that goes back at least to the 1960s in the United States—is to think of how we see hobos. We may see them as a nuisance, an embarrassment, an example of social deviance that ought to be eliminated or corrected. Or we might see them as an interesting example of an alternative way of life, an incarnation of a set of values that needs to be heard against the consumerist, success-oriented values of our own culture.[3]

We may *choose* as individuals how we see hobos—or any other social phenomenon. Much of our seeing, however, is a social process: we do not see as isolated receptors of data. Rather we see first as individual members of a group; and second, the interpretation of what we see is likely to be affected by the impressions and reactions of others. Those reactions may or may not be identical to ours. Most probably within any group there will be a range of reactions—as there is likely to be to a hobo or a jumble of squiggles. In this sense, we may need to *negotiate* with each other as groups about what we are, as a group, really seeing. "Reality is a negotiated interpretation."[4]

The appreciative approach, then, is about choosing (or negotiating) to construct our organizations *with an initial intentional empathy*—that is in a way that starts with the features that give joy, satisfaction, a sense of well being, delight. This is the appreciative framework of which Vickers spoke in the 1960s.[5] Those who write about corporate culture may sometimes adopt an appreciative standpoint, writing, for example, of how Tom Melohn turned around North American Tool and Die precisely by emphasizing the good things that he found in the organization and then carefully building upon them until they drove out, directly or indirectly, the bad.[6] In this book we shall be concerned less with culture *per se* than with strategies of corporate, organizational and community change that will certainly impact the culture, but which have as their goal more than a conventional change of culture. For what the appreciative approach seeks to achieve is the transformation of a culture from one that sees itself in largely negative terms—and therefore *is inclined to become locked in its own negative construction of itself*[7]—to one that sees itself as having within it the capacity to enrich and enhance the quality of life of all the stakeholders—a*nd therefore moves toward this appreciative construction of itself.*

This notion of choosing how to see our organizations suggests an addition to the already formidable array of metaphors for organizations.[8] As is well known, the management literature is full of metaphors that seek to illuminate the nature of organizational life. Two of the most obvious—though they have been around for a long time and criticized for nearly as long—are the organization as a machine and the organization as an organism. The machine image is classically Newtonian, inviting us to strip it down into little bits, clean up or renew the defective parts and put it together again. The organizational consultant becomes a super mechanic, and the organization is invited to see itself as a piece of clock-work—or even a complex circuit board.

Change the metaphor to organism and some new and helpful ideas are at least introduced. For example, you cannot strip an organism down. Interventions have to be minimal, they have to be quick and as painless as possible. By extension, notions like grieving, mourning, celebrating, healing, growing, maturing begin to have meaning and demand to be taken seriously. At least we are dealing with a family of metaphors that recognizes that organizations are about people. By implication this family also recognizes that people are more than bits of clock-work. They have emotions that interact with their physical and rational selves—for both good and ill.

Other metaphors have emerged in recent years, each of which gives a particular salience to features of organizational life. If we think of organizations as political systems, we are invited to look at the way power is mediated through the orga-nization; at the way alliances are formed; decisions taken; resistance mounted—and overcome. The metaphor of cultures encourages us to look at the ethos, the spirituality of an organization, that intangible set of assumptions, expectations, ways of being and doing that define the identity of this organization over against that one. Talk of organizations as flux and you make the whole concept much more dynamic. You emphasize change, instability, movement, a constantly shak-ing kaleidoscope in which no piece can be at rest for long. Flux points toward notions of the sea of energy at the heart of matter, naturally chaotic, but, once harnessed, an amazingly rich source of creative power.[9] The list could go on and on. Browsing through a representative cross-section of the recent management science literature, I jotted down no less than 17 metaphors. If you read a selec-tion of Chairman's reports, you would find them, and many more (some of them bizarre) in constant (and often unconscious) use: "Your company is lean and mean;" "a finely tuned machine;" "adopting a culture of outstanding service to the client;" "developing into a partnership of equals where each serves the com-mon good," and so on.

This plethora of metaphor is no accident. It comes about because different peo-ple choose—again more or less consciously—to see their organizations in partic-ular ways. *Why* they choose one way and not another is an interesting and much under-researched topic and one that we shall touch on again below. Clearly some people may have particular organizational or micro-political preference for one metaphor rather than another. A bully of a chairman is not going to choose a metaphor that emphasizes the interdependence of all employees. A company that sees itself under intense pressure from major institutional shareholders to increase the rate of profit is not going to choose a metaphor that emphasizes its good neighbourliness or its environmental sensitivity. A company that has just declared redundant half its workforce would be ill advised to start using metaphors that highlight teamwork and togetherness, though in the crazed world of corporate PR, even that is not unknown. I strongly suspect that much of the time, the choice of metaphor is haphazard, even barely conscious.[10] It is very seldom strategic and even more infrequently the result of careful participatory dialogue with all the stakeholders in the company—including suppliers and customers.

And yet the *power* of metaphor to shape the way we understand (at the intellectual level), relate to (at the affective level) and perform in (at the interactive level) our organizations is almost impossible to exaggerate. It is the function of metaphor to give us a handle on complex phenomena that would otherwise dissolve into unintelligible fragments. This *explanatory* function, however, is complemented by a *revelatory* function; that is, it is the nature of metaphor to surprise us with a glimpse of something we were not expecting; to point us in a direction we otherwise would not have thought of looking. This is a *poetic* function, not in a romantic or prettifying sense, but in the sense of making us look through a lens we would not have normally chosen and appreciating what we see through that lens. For example, when Gerard Manley Hopkins writes of the Clwyd Valley as "landscapes plotted and pieced—fold, fallow and plough," he has elided cartographic, textile and agricultural images in a way that enables us to see the Valley in a way that, once experienced, will never be forgotten.

In much the same way, once we have been gripped by an organizational metaphor—especially a fresh or well-chosen one—that lens determines the way we see the organization—and therefore of the way we relate to it, whether as employee or supplier or shareholder. As some of the case studies will bring out, many organizations, especially in the voluntary sector, are very intentional in the way they select their organizational metaphors because they find that the image of the metaphor is a powerful way of generating loyalty and understanding among all their stakeholders—and especially their donors (who are, in an important sense, their ultimate "customers"). As Willis Harman has put it, "By deliberately changing the internal image of reality, people can change the world."[11]

Now if the appreciative approach is to emphasize our capacity to *choose* how we see our organizations, we need a metaphor that constantly reminds us of that choice. One such metaphor I find helpful is that of text. Let's explore that a little.

2. Reading the text

Since Wittgenstein's work on language, there has developed a growing understanding of how language and the way we use it makes our world; that is, we can only experience, understand and communicate with others about the world (and even ourselves) through the use of language. Language is therefore the primary mode of contact with our reality, and the essential mode of checking that reality with others.

From that observation it is but a short step to see that any organization or community is the product of language. It functions in the same way as grammar functions; that is, it gives a common meaning to otherwise random or interrelated or confusing signs and symbols. But more than that, language is not just a *metaphor* for organization (though it is indeed a very important one and one to which we shall return in a moment). The whole process of organizing—that is working in complex relationships to achieve common, though often highly differentiated, tasks—depends critically upon there being a shared set of meanings between the various actors involved.[12] Consider the myth of the Tower of Babel. The whole (and surprisingly modern) point of that story is that once people can no longer *speak a common language* there is no way they can cooperate in any constructive venture. It is the ability to communicate, to construct a shared set of interpretations, symbols, assumptions, expectations, moral codes and ways of exercising authority and accountability that makes collaborative endeavour, in even the simplest task, possible.[13]

In this way we come to see that organization-as-language is *both* metaphor *and* reality. It is metaphor because there is more to organizations than language; and it is reality because organizations depend upon language; function in closely analogous ways to language; and respond well to being treated as though they were language.

To put the latter point in another, perhaps more helpful, way, think of organizations or communities as *text*.[14] Just as a literary scholar reads a text from many different perspectives—as narrative; as memoir; as history; as fiction; as self-disclosure by the author; as period piece; as original; as derivative from earlier sources—and holds all of these readings in his mind at once, so we can read an organization or community in very many different ways, recognizing that no one reading is any better than any other. Some might be more appropriate for particular purposes than others; some might appeal to some people more than others. But there is no one thing behind any reading that enables one reader to say, "Ah ha! That's it. That is the truth and everything else is less than the truth."[15]

Once we come to any group or organization as a text, we are then faced with three tasks—in much the same way as the literary scholar coming to a Shakespeare play is faced with three tasks. We can ask, what are the different ways in which this play can be read? Second, how are people (e.g., the actors) actually reading it? Third, what would be the most creative way to read it *at this time and in this place and this particular contemporary context?*

That last, notice, is a subjective judgement. You and I might not agree. You might want to read *Coriolanus* as an essay on ambition; I might want to read it as an anti-democratic polemic. (And if we were lucky enough to be producers of the Royal Shakespeare Company, the way we would present the play would be very different according to the reading we adopted. The product, then, would be determined by the reading.)

In exactly the same way, you and I might "read" the hospital as an organization in quite different ways. You might read it as a political battle field between the consultants and the administrators, with the patients consigned to walk-on parts that justified and occasionally heightened the tension between the two political adversaries. I might read it as a group of people with different skills, all under extreme pressure, all trying to squeeze a quart from a half-pint pot, and all seeing less than the totality of the picture. Equally, X might read an Indian village as inhabited by illiterates who were incapable of acting collaboratively; and Y might read it as the lowest unit in a hierarchy of structural violence that condemned the villagers to permanent poverty.

Essential to the appreciative approach is the realization that neither reading is "right" and neither reading is "wrong." There are many ways of reading the text. Part of the richness of the appreciative approach is to put us in touch with as many readings as possible. In this way we learn to honour the essential creativity of organizational life[16] and therefore to hold those readings together to enrich, first, a general (i.e., organization-wide) understanding of the plurality of ways of looking at the organization; and second to identify the sources of energy highlighted by each of the readings.

It may be thought that such a plurality of readings will only lead to anarchy and chaos. Isn't the plurality of readings I have been talking about only a recipe for disharmony? That question will answer itself in the course of this book, but let me give two "holding" answers in the meantime. First, many organizations get into a muddle precisely because they think they are all singing the same tune, while in fact the reverse is the case. Management, for example, think they have laid down a number of organizational parameters—objectives, style, programs, evaluative criteria—but these are so resented by the workforce that they are tacitly ignored. In this case, the management's song is different from that of the workforce, without management even being aware of it. On the other hand, a single song might actually produce underachievement because the management's instructions are so slavishly followed that much better ideas, and many creative improvisations, go by default. Or, to revert to the Indian example, an aid agency might read the village as needing a clean water supply and a credit union, while the villagers themselves need cash above all else. The result is familiar: the well gets dug as long as people are paid for digging it. Thereafter it is ignored—to the puzzled fury of the aid agency, itself incomprehensible to the villagers. The two songs never harmonize and will not begin to do so until each side tunes into the song of the other.

Second, it is the objective of the appreciative approach to listen to the best experiences of all stakeholders (that is, those that the stakeholders themselves read as *best*) and communicate the universalization of those experiences so that all stake holders will come to move in that direction. That is not over-riding other people's reading of the organization, but it is inviting them to listen to the most creative reading—the one that offers the greatest energy and fulfillment to all the stakeholders—and adopt it, or perhaps part of it, for themselves.

3. The organization as text

Once we think of the organization as text, we find ourselves naturally attuned to three features of its life that are commonly overlooked and yet which can be helpful in discovering the inwardness or ownmost possibilities of any organization.[17] The first is very obvious. It is language. The way people in an organization use language is a sensitive indicator of the quality of a wide spectrum of relationships. Here are three examples which speak for themselves. A major law partnership started writing to senior lawyers in other firms, not as *Dear Sirs*, but as *Dear Partner*. An engineering firm ceased sending its preemptory demands for payment to late-payers and replaced them with a carefully phrased letter that recognized the hard time the industry was going through and invited the late-payer to come in for a discussion of what the creditor could do to ease strain on their cash flow. Late payments fell by over 55 percent. A hospital replaced a notice to outpatients that simply said: "Wait here," with a notice that said: "We promise to see you as soon as we can. Please take a seat here until a doctor is free." The print bill might have risen fractionally, but patient morale soared.

So much is obvious. But what of the *grammar of the organization*? It is helpful to distinguish between the *grammar* and the *syntax*.[18] Syntax can be taken to be the rules of construction and word order that makes a sentence intelligible. Grammar is the larger concept that makes sentences mean what we want them to mean and which makes linked series of sentences convey precise concepts of sometimes complex meaning.

What, you may be wondering, has that got to do with organizations or communities? In my experience, it is not at all unusual to come across senior executives who have a close knowledge of the syntax of the organization, but who are unable to handle its grammar. That is to say, they know how the various bits of the organization fit together; they can manipulate the systems of committees, memos, departmental meetings, minutes and agenda; but they fail to grasp the grammar of the place with the result that they fail to understand its inner meaning. They can handle the instrument but they cannot play a tune. They can read

Shakespeare—as though it were the London telephone directory. They eat the menu not the meal; or they eat a gourmet meal and might just as well have eaten a bowl of dog biscuits. Let me illustrate.

Sir Richard was the chief executive of a well-known and highly prestigious concern. He was a meticulous chairman of all the functional committees below board level; an avid reader of papers and minutes; a tireless ingester of detail. He was good with people, too—kind, courteous, considerate. And yet he nearly brought the company to ruin because he had little feel for the wider vision, for, as one exasperated colleague put it, "what it all means." It was not that he lacked vision; it was that he lacked the bridge between the detail, which he routinely mastered, and the vision which he could expound fluently. He knew the syntax; he never internalized the grammar.

Let's translate that into a development context. It is not unusual for development workers to have mastered the syntax of their environment. They know its history, its social structures, its lineages, *ad infinitum*. But, perhaps because they are still trapped, in the deepest parts of themselves, in their own culture, they never learn its grammar. They remain an outsider looking in and can never even visualize what it might be like to be an insider looking out.

Now the appreciative approach, with its possibility of multiple readings of an organization—whether that be a corporation in New York or a tiny women's credit union in Rajasthan—encourages all the stakeholders to make explicit their own understandings of the grammar of the organization.[19] It helps them ask and answer the following questions: what gives meaning to what I am doing here? what gives meaning to our common endeavour? what *does* it all mean? and when is it most meaning*ful?* Clearly these are questions that go far deeper than issues of the use of language such as we briefly reviewed above—and yet the two interlock. For the meaning will shape the language and the language will shape the meaning. That is why a very important part of the process of appreciative inquiry is *active listening*, listening with an attuned ear to what is being said and to what is not being said; to how it is said; to the meaning that lies within, behind and between what is said. In that sense, it is akin to the best ethnography, which is precisely a disciplined attempt to learn the grammar of a social group.

Let me summarize these sections. I have argued that we all use metaphors in our understanding of any organization, and that those metaphors play an important part in shaping both our understanding and our behaviour. I have suggested that it is helpful to think of organizations as texts that can be read in many different ways, but which have, as constants, their syntax and their grammar. We thus have a hierarchy of levels of data: the syntax (roughly the procedures and rules); the grammar (how those procedures are given meaning); and the reading (how that meaning is interpreted or performed, or both.) I have suggested that each of these have to be taken seriously by anyone who wants to understand how an organization works, and that taking them seriously will involve intense active listening to what is going on in the organization.

4. Writing the text

When we think of organizations as texts that can be read in different ways, two questions immediately arise: who is writing the text? and who is doing the reading?

There are two sets of answers to the first question—a conventional one and one cast more in the spirit of the text metaphor. The conventional answer would be couched in the political systems mode of organizational analysis; that is to say we would look at who has what power over whom and at how that power is exercised.[20] Those are, of course, significant questions, and provide a perfectly sensible, though hardly exhaustive, reading of the organization.

The second set of answers would be to look at the way discourse about the organization is conducted: who talks to whom about what; how are reputations made and lost; who are the trend setters, the opinion formers, and the remembrancers? Who, in other words, writes the narratives out of which the organization's text is created?[21] And what happens when those narratives really come alive, like a first-rate theatrical performance?

This is a much less-well researched area. In a sense it is the ethnography of corporate (or village) gossip. But from that it does not follow that it is any the less about power. As Karen Brison has shown so illuminatingly in a Third-World village context, gossip *is* power.[22] Or to put it another way, gossip is one subset of a wider set of discourses that both reflect the distribution of power in an organization and shape that distribution. Let me illustrate that with some examples.

A & E, as I shall call them, is a medium-sized engineering company in the West Midland of England. In 1991 it appointed a new CEO from another company in the same general line of business. Inevitably telephones ran hot between the two companies as A & E people sounded out their contacts in the other company to try to get a bearing on the new CEO. Most of the feedback was fairly bland, even uninformative. One senior A & E executive, however, picked up that the new man was "a two-faced son of a bitch. He'll be all over you at first and then he'll knife you. That's his style of management—to show how tough he is, he kills off his best 'friends.' So keep him at arm's length. Don't let him get near you." The A & E executive took this advice himself—and passed it on to his closest friends, a tight-knit clique in the strategy and finance areas.

The new CEO found his feet very quickly and had little difficulty establishing working relationships throughout the company, except with the finance and strategy people. There he met, as he put it, "a firewall of resistance." Relationships were not just uncomfortable; they became dangerous to the long-term health of the company. It took a consultant several days of careful digging to get to the bottom of the problem and trace the cause of the resistance back to the conversation about the CEO's alleged two-facedness. When confronted with that, the CEO recalled an occasion on which, in his last job, he had indeed forced the resignation of a board member with whom he had worked closely and amicably for some years. He had done so, he now revealed, because the man had been involved in financial irregularities. It was unlikely that the fraud squad would be able to make charges stick, and he threatened to sue if there was any public discussion of the allegations.

Put in that light, the CEO's behaviour in no way deserved the interpretation that his critic had put upon it, however rational that interpretation might be. Yet that interpretation had come to do potentially fatal damage to his new company.

It is worth reflecting for a moment about what was going on here. First, there is the obvious point of the destructive potential of unsubstantiated gossip. But second, at a deeper level, there are issues of interpretation at stake. The original forced resignation was misread—and that misreading was accepted and used as a king-plank in the tactical thinking of two key departments of the company. There was, if you will, a serious issue of miscommunication or, as we shall come to recognize it, of distorted communication that disabled relationships to a damaging degree. The significant point is that no one was acting maliciously or capriciously or irresponsibly. The misreading that was at the bottom of the problem was entirely reasonable: some executives do terrorize their staff by firing those closest to them. Equally, it was a sensible precaution on behalf of the A & E folk to find out what they could about their new boss and structure their responses to him in the light of what they found out.

What is at issue then is how this particular text came to be written and then came to be read; and how it then had to be reread so that normal business could resume. Perhaps another illustration will help before we take a closer look at distorted communication and what lies behind it.

This is a story about the power of world view or ideology to warp not just the way people see their world, but also their possibility of working together. Charles was a senior figure in a major investment bank in the city of London. Unique among his peer group he was also an active member of the Labour Party, contributing to policy thinking at an exalted level. The bank was invited to work on the privatization of the railways, a policy with which Charles disagreed profoundly on two grounds: he thought it ethically and politically wrong (because it would lead to a less responsive system and therefore a lower quality of life); and he did not believe it would work efficiently, primarily because it would not attract the requisite level of investment, given the long paybacks typical of railway projects. Charles voiced his opposition to the bank being involved and was told that his political judgements were irrelevant: the only issues were whether the bank could demonstrate that it had a comparative advantage over its rivals; and, of course, whether it could make a significant profit from the fee income associated with the project.

Charles argued that those were indeed valid criteria, but they were not the only criteria. The bank needed to be able to show that it could look more widely than its own bottom line, and refuse potentially profitable business if it, corporately, considered that the project on offer was unlikely to be commercially and socially successful in the long run.

We need not follow the debate through its long and increasingly acrimonious course. It eventually became clear that Charles was being marginalized from any but the softest parts of the bank's work. When he complained, he was told that he had shown himself to be unreliable and that he should be grateful he was still with the bank at all. He left.

Here we are facing not the power of gossip, but the power of ideology—an ideology that says that the limit of discourse about a bank's role is the bottom line. The text of the bank is thus written within clearly defined parameters and has to be read within those parameters. If you want to read the text outside those parameters, you are entering a grey area: some will think you are misreading and may see you as a threat to the institution.

Let me offer a final illustration from the development arena. Official donors gave India a substantial number of high-performance water-drilling rigs for use in an arid area. A representative of the donor government visited the area and found that all the drills were being used to increase the irrigation potential of rich landowners. None was increasing the availability of clean water to the rural poor. To the donor government this read as a shocking misappropriation of funds for blatantly political purposes, which would lead inexorably to the suspension of the program. To the Indian civil servants involved, it was a perfectly natural use of free resources that enabled them to buy off one source of pressure and aggravation and use the drills in a way that would increase the food output of the region. When the aid was cut off, it became clear whose reading of the text was dominant, or if you prefer, who was writing the text. The legitimacy of the civil servants' reading could not be acknowledged by an aid bureaucracy with its own syntax.

With these three stories, all drawn from life, we are in touch with the four factors that play a key role in distorting communication between people.[23] They are fear of inequalities of power; excessive attachment to dogma; shrinking from critical self-reflection; and failure to generate a deep and real commitment to the process of communication in the expectation that it will have a genuinely illuminating outcome.[24]

Now if this is broadly right—that we discover the most important truths by aspiring to approach as near as we can to the principle of undistorted communicative action as defined by the four criteria above—then we can describe the best conditions under which we may read *and write* the text of our organizations or communities or villages. That is to say, with reference to the three examples above, the people in finance and strategy at A & E were not orienting themselves toward what Habermas calls an "ideal speech situation," vis-à-vis their new CEO, and therefore discovered falsehood rather than truth. By refusing or perhaps neglecting to address the issue seriously and openly, perhaps because they were frightened of inevitable inequalities of power, they ended up with a misreading of the text that nearly destroyed the organization. Similarly, in Charles's case, his colleagues failed to exercise their imagination beyond the determining role of ideology about what is right for a bank to do, and, therefore, good communicative action about a key issue simply could not happen. The organization was incapable of revising its text in the light of the metacritique that Charles was calling for. And in India, the aid agency had its own reading of the text that made it blind to the readings of others. It was simply not committed to a process of searching for a mutually illuminating reading that would leave both parties satisfied. So it used its (unequal) power.

5. The appreciative approach and ideal speech

It may seem that we have erred a long way from the appreciative approach. Not so. By exploring how people come to misread the text or fail to rewrite the text when some redrafting might be called for, we have specified the conditions that the appreciative approach will have to meet if it is to be successful. In other words, we need to be able to show that the appreciative approach makes possible a closer attention to "ideal speech" in all its characteristics—of the minimization of power asymmetries; a reduction in the intrusiveness of ideology; an increase in the level of commitment to the process; and the adoption of a critical self-reflection by all the parties as they seek to uncover the truth of the text. I shall say a word about each.

i. Power asymmetries

It is, of course, almost a truism of communications theory that inequalities in power make truthful communication difficult, and that is as true in the company board room as it is in the Indian village or the halls of the International Monetary Fund. What we need to add to that is a more subtle and far-ranging understanding of how manifold and multifaceted those inequalities might be—from differences in vocabulary to differences in accent to differences in life situation and in the power to hire and fire, the array of asymmetries is wide indeed.

What difference does the appreciative approach make to that? The whole point of the appreciative approach is to engage all the stakeholders of an organization in a series of one-on-one conversations in which the power discrepancies are minimized. This can be done by the careful matching of who converses with whom; by the setting in which those conversations take place (*not* across the CEO's rosewood table!); by the careful preparation of the agenda not to produce an over-rehearsed interview schedule that is then slavishly followed; but a well-briefed, carefully thought-through set of options of the directions in which the conversation might flow; and by ensuring that the data from the conversation will be weighed and probed by a working group that represents all interests and levels of the stakeholders.

It is, of course, true that the appreciative approach is not bully proof. The loud-mouthed, domineering lout *can* so terrorize his interlocutor that, however carefully planned the session, and however neutral and "safe" the environment, there is little prospect of "ideal speech" taking place. Real communication with such a personality is probably impossible under any circumstances short of a breakdown, but the appreciative approach will throw him (and I use the male gender deliberately, though some might argue unwisely) into territory with which he is not familiar. That is to say, the bully is usually a great deal readier to find fault than to judge an issue appreciatively. In my experience it sometimes happens that the bully is so disoriented by the appreciative protocol that his normal discursive reactions are short circuited and he finds himself, *almost in spite of himself,* entering a genuine conversation, perhaps a new experience for him.

But what of the manager who is very conscious of the need to manage—and is therefore reluctant to, as s/he would see it, let go of authority to the appreciative approach and those involved in it? There are two rather different points here and it is well to keep them apart from the start. There is first a personal or psychological problem, perhaps so familiar it needs no further elaboration here. We are all too well aware of the authority figure who cannot step out of role, just as we are of the reverse of that, the intimidated staffer who suffers from an excessive respect for authority.[25]

But second, as we shall see in a later chapter, there is the more important point that day-to-day management—which, however diurnal and routine it may seem, may still have major implications for the organization—has to go in parallel with any appreciative intervention. The wretched manager may thus find himself pulled in two directions at once. He may *want* to be participative and collaborative with the appreciative inquiry that is going on, but he may also be locked in tense negotiations about a policy decision that has major ramifications and which, as he judges, cannot be included in the appreciative inquiry—perhaps because it is highly confidential or because it demands an immediate decision. How do asymmetries of power look now?

There is no simple answer to that, and it does often happen—with virtually any intervention, not only the appreciative approach—that two processes of decision making become ensnarled or out of phase. The upshot can indeed be destructive. But it will be the more destructive the more withdrawn from the appreciative inquiry the managers involved are. The more the managers are demonstrating that they take the appreciative inquiry seriously, that they are trying to listen and communicate honestly and openly, that they are committed to making the process work, the easier it is for other people in the organization to accept that there are management issues that have to be faced outside the process of the appreciative inquiry.

Where that still becomes difficult is when the "management issue" actually overlaps (or even wholly constitutes) something that the appreciative inquiry is dealing with. For example a North American nongovernmental organization (NGO) had embarked on a very lengthy and detailed inquiry (roughly along the lines of an appreciative inquiry) into its relations with its donors. Less than half way through the process, management announced that it was changing the PR firm which handled 80 percent of such relations. Managers were surprised at the depth of resentment this caused among all the staff who were engaged in the inquiry about relations with the donors. "But we needed to make a decision," the CEO wailed. "We couldn't wait for every Tom, Dick and Harriet in the place to have their say. It's our job to manage these things. That's what we are paid for...."

This suggests a serious confusion in the mind of the leadership. True, such an overlap cannot always be avoided. And when it absolutely cannot, it needs handling with great skill, tact and care. Usually, however—and certainly here—management needs to come to terms with the fact that once a participative process is launched, then its turf has to be protected and respected with all the zeal of a devoted bodyguard. Invasions of forbidden territory are as unwelcome and as likely to result in a mess in the one case as the other.

ii. The intrusiveness of ideology

Communication does not happen when the communicants are blinded by their own ideology. They cannot see beyond it, or, to stick with the text metaphor, they can read the text in only one way. The current debate about the forgiving of Third-World debt by First-World bankers is a classic example.

Now the genius of the appreciative approach is that it draws people out of the pillboxes of their own heavily defended opinions, and encourages them to enter a no-man's land hitherto unexplored. For once they are not on the defensive. They do not have to dig themselves in ever deeper and cling doggedly to their position no matter what. They are being invited to look around, to see what gives them joy and satisfaction, to trace the sources of their deepest delight. It is surprising how even the most heavily defended ideologues are able to move when the environment is changed. More than once people have said, as the chair of a housing association remarked after a one-day introduction to the appreciative approach for her board, "I would not have believed how far people have been able to move. We simply could not have had the discussion we've just had before we did the day on the appreciative approach."

Just as it is true that the bully is not automatically delivered from his bullying by the appreciative approach—though in fact he often is—so the malign influence of heavy ideology, which ties people into one particular reading and closes their eyes to any alternative readings, may persist. Yet the record is that in reasonably skilful hands, the appreciative approach can—by probing behind the assumptions of a given ideology in a non-threatening way—enable people to raise their eyes beyond the limitations of their normal horizons.

We have seen this over and over again in gender and race issues. For example a colleague was invited to work on gender awareness and cross-gender collaboration with the predominantly male, not-very-highly educated workforce of a cosmetics multinational in Mexico, a country of much machismo. It looked a tough nut to crack: how were these macho Mexican men going to be persuaded that collaborating on equal terms with women workers was not only acceptable to themselves and their peers but also actually gave a much more rewarding experience of the workplace? When the men were enabled to hear what the women were saying—that is to listen with ears unblocked by cultural preconceptions— the change was surprisingly easy. And they were enabled to hear because they were enabled to converse with the women in a situation in which the patient exploration of prejudice, bias and conventional preconceptions was encouraged.

This should provide no surprise. Most ideologies are crude approximations to life, while the appreciative approach is designed to put people in touch with what gives them the fullness of life. To say that is not to impugn the significance and even importance of ideological construction. It is a necessary shorthand, a useful simplification of some of the complexities that beset us.[26] But for the very reason it simplifies, it also makes crude, and the point of the appreciative approach is to shift us away from stylized crudeness to the realities of our own *experiences*.

iii. Commitment to the process

It may seem obvious that you will not uncover truth if you do not commit yourself to a serious search. To put that in terms of our metaphor, we might say that you are unlikely to discover all the relevant readings of the text unless you take the trouble to hear carefully. As one of the case studies will bring out, we often notice a change in tempo as people move from a bored tolerance of an exercise which they frankly distrust—"Oh heck, one more management fad"—to a rising enthusiasm that here is a process that can actually help them function in a new way.

For what is involved here is not only a willed commitment to make the process work; rather, it is a matter of trust. We often find that people worry about getting it right, following the steps in the right order. Without denying that some expertise in the mechanics is helpful, we find we want to emphasize much more the need to trust the process and let the mechanics look after itself. As I shall emphasize again in the last pages of this book, if people lack trust, if they are suspicious, hostile, half-hearted or uncertain, it is most improbable that they will allow themselves to be caught up in the process and thereby be enabled to change. Most people have had the experience of a good conversation. Perhaps it started stiffly, formally, with polite exchanges about trivia. But then something happens. We find ourselves talking about something that fascinates us; more than that we find ourselves talking *to someone* who fascinates us. They have interesting parallels with our own experience. They put a new spin on things we thought we thoroughly understood. They challenge us, stretch us, make us laugh. We glance at our watch and find three hours have flown past in what felt like 30 minutes.

That is what I mean by being caught up in the process. When the appreciative approach is working at its best, all the participants should be caught up in it, almost despite themselves. Then they have surrendered their skepticism and cynicism and the process has taken over. They are discovering something of huge importance and significance, the precise delineaments of which may still be unclear to them. That does not matter. What has come through is the shift from a kind of intellectualized game to a deep wrestling with reality. They are, for once, being taken with ultimate seriousness as people.

Again we need to recognize that there are likely to be a number of people in any sizeable group who, for whatever reason, are incapable of making that shift. Perhaps it is too threatening for them. Perhaps they are scared of their own emotionality. Perhaps there is a history of deep hurt that makes it impossible for them to "let go" of their intellectual skepticism. Perhaps they are so insecure in themselves that they need the buttress of a lofty sneer at whatever is going on around them. Perhaps they are frightened, at the unconscious level, of accepting their need of others: they are then caught between the rhetoric of participation and collaboration on the one hand and their own inner terror on the other.[27] Perhaps they are over-impressed with their positions as managers.

The appreciative approach is not group therapy, and it is important that it is not abused by being subverted into that. The professional malcontents have to be tolerated and given the chance to become committed. If they are finally unable to make that leap, that is sad—for them and the organization. But that is all it is. They need to be heard, to be given the chance to speak—if necessary to be critical and even destructive—not least because their negativities may have within them the germ of something that the organization can learn from and work with, especially if it can be subsequently reframed in an appreciative way. Providing enough people are ready to move forward in appreciative mode, our experience is that the process will close over the disaffected and can still operate satisfactorily at the organizational level.

iv. Critical self-reflection

It may seem odd that the word *critical* should appear in a chapter on the background to the appreciative approach! By it, I should be taken to mean intensely self-aware rather than negative or judgmental. As I have already emphasized there is place within the appreciative approach for the negative and the down-side (though much less for the judgmental), but what I am concerned to highlight here is the sense in which the appreciative approach invites participants to read the text with their eyes wide open. The point of the appreciative protocol is not to wrap everyone up in a warm glow of self-satisfaction, but to put them in touch with sources of energy. That involves being aware of themselves and being no less aware of those with whom they work, whether fellow members of the community, customers, suppliers or colleagues. If the appreciative approach is going to work, it needs all the participants to be able to stand back from the press of daily business and reflect on their intellectual and emotional responses to their work environment.[28]

Let me make a rough analogy: the patient undergoing psychoanalysis (at least in most branches of that discipline) learns, among other things, to step back from his or her life and view it as a detached observer, noting responses, feelings, relationships, the emotional texture of everyday life, not as an outsider, but as an insider-*temporarily*-suspended-outside. This is sometimes called critical self-reflection not because she is invited to criticize herself, but because she is asked to become more alive to what is going on around her *and in her* than she would normally expect to be.

Many people find that difficult. They have been trained precisely *not* to look for emotional satisfaction in their work. It is as though part of the psychic contract with the employer is to surrender the prospect of happiness in exchange for a wage. (Here we are on the fringes of the whole alienation debate.) Perhaps unconsciously convinced, then, that work *means* "forget about questions of happiness; just grit your teeth and do the job," such people find it hard to step outside that mind-set and ask themselves or other people questions about the emotional fulfillment of their work. The first appreciative interview I ever did included a question along the lines of, "What is it that gives you greatest joy in your work?" I shall never forget the look on the face of my respondent as incredulity, mockery and delight chased each other across the line of his mouth. "Joy?" he eventually gasped. "Joy? Here? At work? Well...I've never even thought about it."[29] In the end, he recounted a rather moving story of how, as an apprentice, he had, after many disappointments and much ridicule from the foreman, mastered work on the biggest lathe in the factory and the *joy* (he did manage to get the word out) that his first perfectly machined part on that lathe had given him.

There is no need to dilate at length on the impoverishment this typical cut off from emotional truth imposes not only on the individual but also on the whole organization. (Nor on the unsurprising contrast we find in the *ease* with which many people in the Third World move into appreciative mode in contrast with the huffing and puffing that often marks the early stages of an appreciative inquiry in the rich world.) What is less obvious is the extent of the change of consciousness that is sometimes required to enable people to get in touch with their own emotionality in the context of work, and to accept that the health of the organization depends on how people *feel* just as much as what they *do*.[30] Without this change of consciousness—and the courage to talk about it in the course of the appreciative inquiry—the text of the organization will not only be misread, it will be nearly meaningless. It would be like reading *Hamlet* without the Prince of Denmark ever uttering a line.

As many of the case studies will bring out, the self-awareness of the core team of an appreciative inquiry is often crucial to its success. Again, to translate into the text metaphor, that group—and through them the whole organization—needs to be continually asking itself and each other: How are we reading this? Is this the only way? What would another reading look like? If we rearrange the data we have from the appreciative interviews, what other sense can we make of what we are hearing? It is only when the data are interrogated in this way—and when the data themselves have been generated from a no less searching, restless, delving process of conversation—that they will yield all of which they are capable in terms of both information and perspective.

Before leaving this subject, I need to acknowledge that critical self-reflection can reveal important gaps in the emotional life of an organization. For it can involve (and here is an example of the downside) being or becoming aware of where one might have expected to find energy—and actually find none. This can come as a moment of real revelation, and therefore of some distress. "I would like to be able to say," said one staffer of a Third World development NGO, "that I get a lot of oomph from our Awaydays, when the whole department goes off on retreat for 24 hours to think about the work. It's a good idea in theory. In fact it's a complete drag, dominated by the head of department and about as participative as a funeral. When I'm looking for sources of energy and delight in this job, I cannot honestly say that is where I shall find them." That may sound a very downbeat note on which to end this chapter. But it bears within it the promise of both honesty and the search for what *does* bring life. Before we tackle that central issue more thematically, we need to look more closely at how the text that is the organization comes to be written.

1   P. Sloterdijk, *Critique of cynical reason*, Minneapolis: University of Minnesota Press, 1987, p. 12.

2   That is not to deny that there may well be environmental and/or unconscious forces at work which predispose us to one construction rather then another. I shall have more to say about this later. See, too, Frank J. Barrett and David Cooperrider, "Generative metaphor intervention: A new approach for working systems divided by conflict and caught in defensive perception," in *The Journal of Applied Behavioural Science*, 26, 2, 1990, p. 221; and T. A. Williams, *Learning to manage our futures: The participative redesign of societies in turbulent transition*, New York: Wiley, 1982.

3   See David Matza, *Becoming deviant*, Englewood Cliffs, NJ: Prentice-Hall, 1969. Interestingly, Matza calls the second way of seeing the appreciative way. That does not imply in his work or in this a necessarily approbative stance, but it does imply empathy and a readiness to "see" from the "inside."

4   E. R. Shapiro and A. W. Carr, *Lost in a familiar place: Creating new connections between the individual and society*, New Haven, Conn.: Yale University Press, 1991.

5   The appreciative system of a culture "resides not in a particular set of images, but in a *readiness* to see and value and respond to its situation in a certain way." G. Vickers, *Value systems and social process*, London, 1968, p. 192.

6   Charles Hampden-Turner, *Corporate culture: From vicious to virtuous circles*, Piatkus, 1994, pp. 204-215.

7   For an individual and small-group example of this, see A. Isen and T. Shalker, "The influence of mood state on evaluation of positive, neutral and negative stimuli," in *Social Psychology Quarterly*, 45, 1982, pp. 58-63 and compare with Susan Long and John Newton, "Educating the gut: An application of psychoanalytic understanding to learning in organizations," paper presented to the *Annual Symposium of the International Society for the Psychoanalytic Study of Organizations*, London, July, 1995.

8   For a good discussion of the role of metaphor in organizational life, see the essays in Cliff Oswick and David Grant, *Organisation development: Metaphorical explorations*, London: Pitman, 1996.

9   See, for example, J. Davidson, *The secret of the creative vacuum*, Essex: Daniel, 1989.

10 Indeed, it is often deeply unconscious, reflecting unconscious processes that may manifest themselves in a whole array of behaviours. See, for example, E. Trist and H. Murray (eds.), *The social engagement of social science, Vol. 1, The socio-psychological perspective*, London: FAB, 1990.

11 *Global mind change*, Indianapolis: Knowledge Systems, 1988, p. 1.

12 For an early statement of this position, see, for example, L. R. Pondy and I. I. Mitroff, "Beyond open system models of organization," in *Research in organizational behaviour*, 1, 1979, pp. 3-39. Behind that lies the work of H. Gadamer, especially his *Truth and method*, 1975 and his *Philosophical hermeneutics*, 1976, both Berkeley: University of California Press.

13 This line of thought quickly elides into what has become known as the new institutional economics which makes the point, actually well known to both Adam Smith and Karl Marx, that any purposeful economic activity depends crucially upon a set of shared values, moral assumptions and interpersonal (and by extension inter-organizational) trust. See D. C. North, *Institutions, institutional change and economic performance*, Cambridge: Cambridge University Press, 1990.

14 I have been much helped in this section by a PhD thesis submitted to the Weatherhead School of Management at Case Western Reserve University, Cleveland, Ohio by Tojo Joseph Thachankary, *Hermeneutic processes in organizations: A study in relationships between observers and observed*, 1994.

15 This change in the relationship between observer and observed is not, of course, confined to the social sciences and literature. It is a major implication of quantum physics and has been applied directly to organizational life by Margaret Wheatley in her *Leadership and the new science: Learning about organization from an orderly universe*, San Francisco: Berrett-Koehler, 1992.

16 See Peter Vaill's important work on this theme, *Managing as a performing art: New ideas for a world of chaotic change*, San Francisco: Jossey Bass, 1989, esp. ch. 8.

17 The phrase is Martin Heidegger's, much echoed by Paul Ricoeur.

18 On this see S. R. Barley, "Semiotics and the study of occupational and organizational cultures," *Administrative Science Quarterly*, 28, 1983, pp. 393-413.

19 See M. Newman and R. J. Boland, "Hermeneutical exegesis and qualitative organizational studies," a working paper of the Weatherhead School of Management, Case Western Reserve University, Cleveland, Ohio, 1998. They helpfully review different traditions of literary criticism and thus put the argument in a wider and more academically sensible setting.

20 The literature in this area is huge and well known. Two obvious starting places would be R. M. Hodgetts, *Organizational behaviour: Theory and practice*, New York: Macmillan, 1991; and, very different in intellectual timbre, Tony Giddens, *Consequences of modernity*, Stanford University Press, 1992.

21 See D. M. Boje, "The story telling organization: A study of story performance in an office-supply firm," *Administrative Science Quarterly*, 36, 1991, pp. 106-126.

22 Karen Brison, *Just talk: Gossip, meetings and power in a Papua New Guinea village*, Berkeley, California: Berkeley University Press, 1992.

23 I am using a notion of "ideal speech" here which differs from that of Habermas. As I use the term—or the idea behind the term—undistorted communicative action is close to "best practice" in communication, not as (as in Habermas) a formal philosophical construct but as a goal which can be more or less achieved by members of any communicating community. To achieve this "best practice," the process of communication will be characterized by the four features in the main text. See J. Habermas, *The theory of communicative action. Vol. 1. Reason and the rationalisation of society*, Trans Thomas McCarthy, Cambridge and Oxford: Polity and Blackwell, 1991, especially pp. 286ff.

24 Interestingly and perhaps surprisingly, these are close to the criteria of David Bohm, much used by Peter Senge in his *Fifth discipline: The art and practice of the learning organization*, London: Century, 1990, pp. 239ff.

25 See for instance B. T. Mayes and R. W. Allen, "Toward a definition of organizational politics," *Academy of management review*, Oct., 1977 for an early recognition of this in the literature. Compare J. Pfeffer, *Managing with power*, Boston: Harvard Business School Press, 1992, and, for a more reflective view, see P. J. DiMaggio, "Interest and agency in institutional theory," in L. G. Zucker (ed.) *Institutional patterns and organizations: Culture and environment*, Cambridge, Mass: Ballinger, 1988.

26 On the whole issue of the role and structure of ideology, see John B. Thompson, *Studies in the theory of ideology*, Cambridge: Polity, 1984. I am not using ideology in the pejorative sense that the word often attracts.

27 See David Berg and Kenwyn Smith, "The clinical demands of research methods," in their edited *Exploring clinical methods for social research*, London and San Francisco: Sage, 1985.

28 By this I mean something more than traditional role analysis, as expounded, for example, by B. Reed in, "Organizational role analysis," in C. Cooper (ed.) *Developing social skills in managers: Advances in group training*, London: Macmillan, 1976.

29 Cf. E. Trist, "The cultural absence of the post industrial society," in F. Emery and E. Trist, *Towards a social ecology*, New York: Plenum, 1972.

30 This insistence is hardly new. See, for example, A. K. Rice, *The enterprise and its environment*, London: Tavistock, 1963. And of course you could trace it back to Vickers, whom I have already quoted above.

Chapter 2
The sources of appreciative inquiry

1. The resources behind the text

In the last chapter, I suggested that a metaphor that encourages an appreciative approach to organizational or community change is that of text or reading a text. But now we need to ask: from what material is that text derived? It does not, after all, exist in a vacuum. It is put together by the people who need to read the text of the organization in the course of their daily business lives. What resources do they call upon as they read the text of the organization?

I want to highlight two—memory and imagination. That is not to deny the importance of others, such as the whole raft of analytical skills that are brought to bear when we seek to analyze or describe our organizations or the group to which they belong. For example, one study of the Manhattan hotel industry has shown how many analytical variables managers take into account when identifying their competitive peer group. In their industry, this is a key process, for you can only hone your competitive edge when you know—or think you know—which other hotels your potential clients might be considering.[31] In ignoring these analytical skills here, I am in no way impugning their significance or the skill required to manipulate them successfully. Rather, I am seeking to concentrate on those resources within the organization that help it *to identify itself.*

Every organization, group or community has its own history, recalled or at least recollectable by people who have come into contact with it. The history does not, however, exist as an objective fact, a concrete block of remembered stuff that is as unproblematic as a piece of toast on your breakfast plate. Like all memory, the memory of the organization is created by each rememberer and is accordingly manipulated by the perceptions, associations, emotional responses and wishes of the rememberer.[32] There is even evidence that the circumstances under which we remember—for example whether we are alone or in the company of others who share the memory—affects the content of the memory. Many of the influences on our memory are quite unconscious, so we cannot compensate for them or correct the memory even if we wanted to.[33]

All this means that the history of the organization—its ups and downs; its traumas and triumphs; its successes and failures; its glory days and its gory days—is the artifact of those who do the remembering. And that in turn means that the history is not (as Weber, with his emphasis on history as official written record, seems to have thought) an unchanging constant, an indisputable fact that can be wheeled out and examined like an archaeologist examining the Rosetta Stone. It is rather an ever-changing kaleidoscope that will form a new pattern each time it is shaken by the act of remembering.[34] Reflect for a second on how the history of the community in which you live would be rendered by your neighbour, the local storekeeper and the head teacher of the local school.

There is, however, more to it than this. We do not, in the main, remember facts as cold, hard nuggets of the past. Rather we tend to put interpretations on to those facts. We gather them in strings of associations, often in causal chains with which we seek to explain our present reality. "The marketing department has never been the same since they switched the advertising account from Oddball and Willey to Tweexter and Stench. O&W were excellent. They used to come and talk to everyone—not just in marketing but in production and in finance too. They really understood the company while these new people…I don't remember ever seeing any of their people here. We are just another account to them…" Here a particular and perhaps particularly idealized set of memories of the past is being constructed as an explanation of the relative lack of success of the marketing department—a development that is almost certainly a great deal more complex and multifaceted than a change in advertising agents.

On a larger scale, we manufacture our understanding of the past of the organization or community *and change that understanding according to circumstances and needs of the moment.* An example: The staff of a small cottage hospital in Wales, threatened with closure, remembered the hospital as warm, friendly, intimately related to the community it served and still giving a good quality of care. Unexpectedly, the decision was made not only to keep the hospital open but also to expand and improve its facilities. As the work began and the staff became enthusiastic with the prospect of a much higher level of medical technology available under the new plans, the old hospital was remembered as limited, inefficient, lacking in facilities now seen as basic. The former memories of friendliness, informality and personal attention were not forgotten or denied; rather, they were much less emphasized and allowed to slide into the background so that they ceased to be part of the active self-memory of the hospital.

Two questions emerge from this story: who does the remembering? and how much choice do we have in what we remember? I want to unpack each of those questions because they are important in the context of the appreciative approach.

2. The making of memory

In the story of the Welsh hospital, precisely *whose* memories are we talking about? The doctors'? The patients'? The nurses'? People in the local community? Is there any reason for assuming that these groups would have the same set of memories and articulate them in the same way? Almost certainly, the memories of the patients and the memories of the doctors would be different in many respects. The doctors remember the frustration of working with inadequate diagnostic tools; the pain of having to decide whether to transfer seriously ill patients to the district hospital nearly 60 miles away; the long and sometimes life-threatening waits for lab reports. The patients remember the relaxed regime on the wards; the banter between patients and nurses whose families have known each other for three or four generations; the high morale of everyone that kept the place up and running.

Yet despite these differences, most organizations have a dominant myth, a group narrative to which most—but rarely all—participants will assent. It is the dominant myth of the hospital that I report above, as it switched from one interpretation of its ethos and history (friendly, warm and supportive) to another (technically under par).

How precisely the dominant myth is created and held in place is a matter of careful empirical research in each case. It is too easy to say that the organization's sense of its own history is created by the leadership and then forced down the throats of the other participants. That may happen but is in no sense usual. Rather, the dominant myth usually emerges from the organization's mythmakers, its storytellers, its narrative aces. Most organizations—and virtually every Third World village—have such people who may or may not be in positions of formal political power. They are what an earlier era called remembrancers, those who keep alive the story by telling it and retelling it to succeeding generations. They are the repositories and shapers of oral history, and as such play a key but neglected role in explaining the organization to itself.[35]

What makes them tell the story the way they do? How much conscious choice do they have over the type or timbre of history that they recall and pass on? Again there can be no glib, generalized answers to that. One thing does, however, seem fairly clear: there is an interaction between the current experience of the organization and its remembrancers' interpretation of its history. We construct history not just out of remembered facts but also in response to where we are now. We saw how this works in the Welsh hospital. An external change in the hospital's circumstances—the decision to upgrade it taken by a Health Authority many miles away—led almost immediately to a re-interpretation of the hospital's past.

Here is another example: A medium-sized engineering firm had a very easily identified remembrancer in the shape of the deputy manager of the finance department. He had been with the firm for over 30 years, was a cheerful extrovert—and known and liked by virtually everyone in the company. He was proud of the company's high-quality machine tools and his telling of the story of the company always emphasized the key roles played by the founder and his nephew in protecting that reputation for quality. A subtext of that history was that present management was in danger of forfeiting the firm's reputation. To his chagrin, the firm was taken over by an American concern whose engineers redesigned both product and manufacturing processes—and delivered a quality of machine that the firm had never approached in the past. Recorded downtimes of users provided incontrovertible evidence: the new machines were far better than anything the firm had ever produced before.

The deputy manager's reaction was interesting. He could no longer recall the glory days when quality was the firm's hallmark. He recast the history of the firm in terms of its Britishness. "In the old days, we didn't have all these Yanky notions of team work and just-in-time. We did it our way. And if we didn't know what to do, Mr. John would roll up his sleeves on the shop floor and find a way... We shipped machines to wherever the map was red. Those were the days...."

His interest was in idealizing the past to express reservations about the present. He was, in that sense, manipulating the story to make it serve a particular purpose. In many Third World settings, we find the same process at work, often structured and formalized in a particular role or office. The bearer of that office has the quasi-sacred task of remembering the past (*re-membering* the past) precisely to make the present comprehensible and to plan for the future. So important and solemn a task is this that it is often carried out within a particular ritual, which reminds the community of the value of its own memories.

It may seem that we have strayed a long way from the appreciative approach so let me gather up the threads before we have a look at imagination as another way we *construct* the world. What I have been suggesting is that we construct the past of our organizations—or we accept or perhaps challenge the constructions of our unofficial remembrancers. This construction is not isolated from the present, with its own array of images, expectations, stereotypes and projections, but is being continuously rephrased in the light of the present and perhaps even of the future. As this process goes on, we all have a choice of the kind of constructions we put on the past. We do not have to tell one specific story or collude with one particular interpretation of the past. We have some degrees of freedom—sometimes greater, sometimes less—that allow us to incorporate the joyful and life-giving memories that most organizations can find *once the remembrancers or the rest of us start to look for them*. So the Welsh hospital does not need to rewrite its self-history in terms of moving from a poorly equipped, low-quality institution to a hi-tech one; it can also remember, if it wishes to, that its earlier phase was one in which the quality of personal interaction went a long way to compensate for its admitted technical outdatedness. And the engineering firm can salute the fact that the founder's generation of engineers did their best, within contemporary technical limits, to build robust and long-lasting tools which found a market throughout the British Commonwealth, without denying that the firm had become something of a technical dinosaur before it was taken over and modernized.

It is this plasticity of memory and our freedom to remake the history of our organization that is essential for the appreciative approach. For what is at stake is the capacity to construct a narrative of the organization that highlights the worthwhile and life-enriching themes without denying the darker or more sombre tones that are also likely to be present. It is only when we can read the history from this perspective that we are likely to transcend the problematic present or the fearsome future. It is to that that I now turn.

3. Imagination

The construction or rather reconstruction of the past and therefore of the present is a prelude to the use of the imagination for the future. Clearly the imaginative construction of the future is less problematic, at the theoretical level, than the reconstruction of the past.[36] We can imagine what we like—the virtual office; the re-engineered company; the self-reviewing organization; the learning community; the sustainedly self-sufficient village. We have no difficulty exercising choice in how we imagine the future.

Or do we? Imagination is like many of our other faculties, from our memory to our muscles. If we do not use them, they wither.[37] And that withering has gone far to destroy people's organizational imagination because it is too infrequently exercised. In a culture, both corporate and social, that puts such emphasis on the analysis of the present, on understanding what is, there is little incentive—indeed there is frequently considerable disincentive—to dream of what might be.

A CEO of a major nongovernmental organization (NGO) assigned each sub-department the job of imagining their task and how it would optimally be discharged in five years' time. Nine of the 11 groups reported back with only marginal changes, most of which were already in the pipeline. And yet this NGO is known for the high intellectual and personal qualities of its staff. They are not stupid or lacking in imaginative resources; they are simply unused to engaging their imaginative powers in their work situation. Frightened of being considered utopian or unrealistic or far-fetched, they contract their imaginative horizon to their boot-caps and find that they are constantly being overtaken by events which demand that their work-style changes. Despite all the emphasis in the management literature of the last years on envisioning, the reality is that tiny is the proportion of the total number of stakeholders who believe that their imagination is a significant resource that they bring to their workplace.[38]

Further, the theoreticians of organizational change tend to use models of change that assume that organizations respond to external pressures like changes in technology, market structure or the availability of capital, rather than models that put emphasis on the capacity of stakeholders, whether as individuals or alliances, to respond creatively to external stimuli, *within an appreciative perspective of what the organization might become.* In other words the actors are seen as puppets, controlled by factors over which they have no control, rather than as responsible agents who can choose, certainly within limits, their own futures. It is exactly this neglect of the creativity of stakeholders that has been the origin of the protests against alienation.[39]

The skeptic will raise the objection that imagination is too easily detached from reality. "You can imagine a unicorn, but you'll never find one." That, I think, largely misses the point. The imagination we are talking about here is the imagination that is based on experience, that is, as it were, an extrapolation of the best experience of the organization so that it becomes the norm. That is why it is so closely tied, both in theory and practice, to memory: it is a chosen selectivity of memory projected into the universal.

That is not all, however. It is not *only* memory, central as that is. It is also the mobilization of our deepest longing for the work environment, a longing that arises not from idle dreaming (the unicorn symptom) but from our own most inward perceptions of what we and those around us could become. And if that sounds idealistic, in both popular and technical senses, that is a charge I will live with, for there is room for idealism in the appreciative approach.[40] It is not content to be determined by the past or by the politics of the present. It insists on pointing to what *could be*, not in a utopian or irresponsible way, but in a spirit disciplined by past, present and the most hopeful perceptions of the future. I shall give some examples below.

4. Using imagination

How then do we use our imagination, in association with our memories, to break open the mould of conventional thinking about our institutions or communities in a way that is not simply irresponsible?

The first point to make is that *nothing* is ruled out from the start. Just as creative teams in the media and the advertising industries have developed a no-thumbs-down brainstorming style in which any idea, however way-out and seemingly impractical, is accepted and held by the group, so in appreciative inquiry there are no limits in the first round of imaginings to what *might* be in the future. Here are some examples.

In a very heavily male-dominated city firm of lawyers, a young woman graduate dared to imagine the day when the genders would be equally represented at every level of the firm and she would be spared sexist innuendo as a matter of routine. That looked a very faint possibility 11 years ago. The firm is not yet quite there, but now that young woman is in a position to push it closer to her initial imagining.

Josiah, a black Jamaican immigrant, works in a local government office in South London. After the Brixton riots in 1982, the office officially adopted a "colour blind" recruitment policy. Josiah was delighted, but his delight turned to dismay as he saw how unconscious prejudices and details of procedure combined to ensure that the proportion of people of colour recruited into the office hardly increased at all. He dreamt of the day when his colleagues reflected the racial composition of the community the office served. To his fellow blacks, however, such an ambition merely revealed him as naive: they saw the whites hanging on to power and position and only paying lip service to a non-discriminatory policy. Josiah continues to hold up the vision. The whites continue to drag their feet. That does not render Josiah's dream absurd or unhelpful.

The leaders of the Chipko movement in the Indian Himalayas dreamed of a relationship with the Forest Department and the logging companies that encouraged all who live in and off the forest of the Uttarkand to respect the integrity of that fragile ecosystem, and thus make the living of each sustainable. In the early days of the movement, such a relationship seemed beyond the bounds of the possible. Twenty years later it has been achieved, and the forests are now protected to ensure sustainability for *both* the villagers *and* the logging companies.

In each of these examples, the "imaginings" were a subtle blend of experience (both good and bad), personal ethics, a rugged refusal to accept the conventional as setting the boundaries of the possible, and a rootedness in the present. It is in that interplay between the past and the potential future that imagination both needs the present and longs for its transformation. That is why some philosophical traditions see a connection between memory, imagination and *anticipation*, the hopeful waiting for a reality that is embryonically held in the present.[41] The process of appreciative inquiry, as we shall see, seeks to encourage people to give rein to their anticipatory imaginations, sometimes by challenging them in surprising or unconventional ways, sometimes by merely exposing them to the meta-metaphor of an organization like their own that represents (at least part of) best practice.[42] My own experience is that this is the hardest part of the appreciative process—to enable and encourage people in any organization to believe that their best anticipations are worth listening to, worth taking seriously. Perhaps because they have been mocked in the past, perhaps because they have, half unconsciously, lost hope of anything better, too many people are frightened of their own possibilities—and, for a still stronger reason, of the best possibilities of their organizations.

There is here, however, a deeper point. The use of the imagination can be very frightening, especially at the unconscious level. For it represents leaving, in wish if not yet in fact, the security of the known and tested and going out into the unknown and untested. At the primitive level, then, it is consonant with leaving mother and therefore, if one follows the Freudian tradition, with the whole separation trauma. If this is right, it is easy to see why people, already scared by the overt threat to their organizations, do not readily engage in imagining a future—even a better future. (For who guarantees that it will be *better*?) Yet such fears, wholly understandable as they may be, entail a great organizational impoverishment.

What, for example, would have happened if the people whose imaginings I reported above had been told that they were being absurdly ambitious when they first gave voice to what they wanted for their organization? Would it have made any difference? Or is there a relationship between what people long for—and the direction in which their organization actually moves?

There are four sets of reasons for believing that there is such a relationship, what David Cooperrider has called the heliotropic principle of organizational development. It is to that which we turn in the first part of the next chapter.

---

31 Theresa K. Lant and Joel A. C. Baum, "Cognitive sources of socially constructed competitive groups: Examples from the Manhattan hotel industry," in W. Richard Scott and Soren Christensen (eds.), *The Institutional construction of organizations*, London: Sage, 1995, pp. 15-38.

32 There is experimental evidence that *unconscious* wishes of the rememberer will effect what is remembered or how the memory is processed. See T. Hill, P. Lewicki, M. Czyzewska and A. Boss, "Self perpetuating development of encoding biases in person perception," in *Journal of Personality and Social Psychology*, 57, 1989, pp. 373-387.

33 There is a huge literature on these themes. For a recent review of some aspects see Gillian Cohen, *Memory in the real world*, Hove: Lawrence Erlbaum, 1989. In some ways more relevant to the main themes here is James Fentress and Chris Wickham, *Social memory: New perspectives on the past*, Oxford: Blackwell, 1992.

34 It is here that the observer/observed relationship becomes important and the readiness of organizational theorists to listen to "the new physics" significant. See Baum, Senge and Thachankary, all quoted above, and Margaret Wheatley, *Leadership and the new science: Learning about organization from an orderly universe*, San Francisco: Berrett-Koehler, 1992.

35 See Boje, *sup. cit.*

36 It may be helpful to distinguish between *foresight*—which rational-choice theorists of organizational life assume actors have in abundance (and indeed without it rational-choice theories will not work at all)—and *imagination* which I take to be a more creative and poetic faculty. The former leads to repetition or mimesis (which arguably rational-choice theoreticians too readily ignore anyway), the latter to innovation. Unsurprisingly, the management literature has a great deal more to say about the former than it does about the latter.

37 One is struck, for example, by the neglect of institutional imagination, despite all the literature on "envisioning" in many of the formal treatments of organizational change. To take just one example, the Danish theorists, Soren Christensen and Jan Molion, offer a very sophisticated model of organizational origin and transformation which seeks to synthesize classic and post-modern theories of organizational change. But they do so in terms of "opportunity structure," where the organization reacts to external stimuli, rather than *imagining* for itself a new set of opportunities or ways to respond to them. See their *Origin and transformation of organisations: Institutional analysis of the Danish Red Cross*, in Scott and Christensen, *op. cit.*

38 Which is why, of course, Senge, in his chapter on "Shared vision," writes mostly about securing commitment to the vision—i.e., *sharing* it—rather than actually *having* it. See Fifth discipline, *sup. cit.*, pp. 203-232.

39 There is, of course, a lot more to the concept of alienation than this, but historically, for both Marx and Hegel, the surrender of one's own responsibility in subjectivity was central. See Richard Schacht, "Social structure, social alienation and social change," *American Philosophical Quarterly*, 23, 1, 1986.

40 Following Polak, David Cooperrider has shown how essential to human development "utopian dreaming" has, pace Marx, actually proved. See his "Positive image, positive action in Suresh Srivasta," David Cooperrider and Associates, *Appreciative management and leadership: The power of positive thought and action in organizations*, San Francisco and Oxford: Jossey-Boss, 1990, pp. 111ff.

41 See, for example, Nicholas Lash, *A matter of hope*, London: DLT, 1981. But note, too, that in a search of 40 books and 200 journal articles on the concept of hope, James Ludema found that none had been contributed by the management or organizational sciences. James Ludema, *Narrative inquiry: Collective storytelling as a source of hope, knowledge and action in organizational life*, PhD Dissertation, Case Western Reserve, May, 1996. Compare Sean O'Riordan, "The psychology of hope," *Studia Moralia*, 7, 1969, pp. 33-55. O'Riordan is equally impressed by the neglect of hope in the philosophical and even theological literature.

42 This was the technique used by Cooperrider and associates in the now-famous "Medic Inn" intervention, one of the first applications of appreciative inquiry. See Barrett and Cooperrider, *sup. cit.*

Chapter 3
Making appreciative inquiry work

1. The heliotropic principle

The heliotropic principle states that organizations operate like plants: they move toward what gives them life and energy.[43] What reasons can we adduce for making such a claim?

The first arises directly from the text metaphor for organizations. Actors act the text as they read it; they are incapable, if they have any integrity as actors, of responding to the text in any other way. The fulcrum point of Shakespeare's *Coriolanus* comes when Coriolanus, a successful general, has been voted out of office by his own people. In an agony of rejected pride, he murmurs the line: "There is a world elsewhere…." Scholarly opinion is divided as to the real meaning of this line. Is this the first hint of his eventual betrayal of his own country, or is it a general reflection on the relative insignificance of all our human loyalties? How you read it crucially determines how you play that scene—and indeed how you play the whole part.

Now the analogy should be clear. If we (corporately) read the text of our organization with a particular set of anticipations, then the organization will inevitably move in the direction of those anticipations, just as a dramatic production will move in the direction of the reading of the main actors. And if that seems far-fetched, recall how the reading of the Manhattan hotel industry shaped the way managers responded to each other's competition. If that reading had been anticipatory as well as purely classificatory, the effect on action and therefore system behaviour would have been even stronger. Or consider Chipko. It was the longing for a sustainable relationship with the forests of Uttarkand that kept the movement in being when there was little sign of major changes in the acts and attitudes of government and loggers. Yet the *anticipations* of the Chipko participants moved all the actors to a new place.

The second reason for taking the heliotropic principle seriously refers to the conversation, negotiation and conceptual construction that goes on at very many levels within any organization. By injecting the view that a city law firm should be much more open in its recruitment and promotion policies to the talents of women, one does not necessarily bring that development about. But one prepares the way for it by obliging people to confront their prejudices, to reinterpret their memories, to look afresh at the long-term wisdom of excluding able people from employment. That some will resist and others be indifferent is not denied. At issue here is not change at the political level but rather change at the level of consciousness. And it is at this level that discourse, the ways people speak about a proposition, and the consequent subtle shifts in assumptions, logic and judgements, make their impact. Without the impact of changed discourse that comes from articulated imagining, there is unlikely to be change.

The third reason why the heliotropic principle is significant is that at the unconscious level of the organization people usually tend to move toward what offers life.[44] We shall have more to say about this later, but for the moment it may be helpful to think in terms of the classic Kleinian schema of good and bad breast as fantasies common to individuals and by aggregation to organizations.[45] Except for people who have quite severe problems in their own psychic development, the tendency is to seek to hold on to the good breast and minimize the scary influence of the bad breast that is experienced, at the unconscious level, as frightening and threatening. How this plays out in detail obviously differs from organization to organization, as the abundant literature on this theme demonstrates.[46] The key point for our present purpose is to note that processes that make it easier for organizations to move toward, at the unconscious level, the good breast enable such organizations to discover a life and energy that is otherwise denied them. And sharing a positive imagined scenario, or stating a deeply held wish for the way the organization might work are examples of just such a process. That is not to claim that such a move is unambiguous or psychically painless, a point much underplayed by the current literature on appreciative inquiry. It is to claim that the anxiety and psychic trauma of making the shift usually proves well worthwhile.

The fourth reason for taking the heliotropic principle seriously is that there is some evidence that it has been at work in history. Fred Polak, for example, has argued that what explains the rise and fall of cultures is the anticipatory image a culture has of itself. "As long as a society's image is positive and flourishing, the flower of the culture is in full bloom. Once the image begins to decay and lose its vitality, however, the culture does not long survive."[47] More concretely, consider the historical impact of the anticipatory images of their countries projected by, for example, Hitler, de Gaulle, de Valera, Churchill, Peron and David Ben Gurion. Propaganda, rhetoric, manipulation—perhaps each would have to plead guilty to such charges. But for our purposes, that is irrelevant. The success each had in persuading his countrymen to become more than they imagined they could become lay in his capacity to show them the future possibilities that already lay in embryo in the womb of the present. As their people were persuaded of the reality of that embryonic form, so they moved reality toward it.

What I am suggesting, then, is that in memory and imagination we have resources that enable us to shape the way we read the text of the organization or community, and that that choice of reading will affect the way in which the organization changes. If the chosen readings offer more positive outcomes, more hopefulness, meaningfulness and enjoyment, then organizations will follow the path of least resistance and move in the direction of that reading.[48] Is there any experimental evidence for that hypothesis?

2. Evidence for the heliotropic principle

The evidence comes from the behavioural sciences that have shown how expectations form performance. The most abundant source of case study material in this area comes from the teaching profession in which the so-called Pygmalion effect has been exhaustively researched. Study after study has shown that students' performance is critically—and in some cases overwhelmingly—shaped by the teachers' expectations. Poor expectations, poor performance; great expectations, great performance—and that irrespective of the innate ability of the students.[49] That is an astonishing finding: expectation is actually more determinative of academic performance than any supposedly objectively tested real mental ability.[50]

What is striking about that is that the tests of academic performance carried out on students toward the end of their school careers are actually testing a very narrow range of competence, just as the IQ tests carried out earlier on the same students did. Students with relatively modest IQs, who have been taught appreciatively perform well not because their IQ has risen much, but because they are highly motivated, value their own performance and are confident of their ability. To put it in a nutshell, this strongly suggests that it is the emotional environment in which the students are set that influences and perhaps even determines the quality of their work rather than their innate abilities.

Now if that is true in the schoolroom, where, to repeat, experimenters are concerned with a narrow band of abilities and performances (essentially cognitive and intellectual), how much more is it likely to be true that competencies over a much wider area—inter-personal, analytical, intuitive, judgmental, decision-making—are affected by the climate of expectations that surrounds their expression? The celebrated Hawthorne effect—which showed that workers responded positively to *any* demonstration of well-intentioned interest in their environment—long ago gave grounds for expecting that a more carefully structured and communicated message of interest would have profound positive effects. This is a line of thought that has been pursued by those with a particular interest in worker performance in general and the ethnic origins of observed differences in work performance in particular. Perhaps nowhere do self-fulfilling prophecies have more damaging effects than in situations in which white supervisors oversee a small number of black employees.[51] Yet even that can be stood on its head. When supervisors expect the best of their workforce, they are the more likely to get it. If, in a word, an appreciative approach works in the classroom, it is more than likely to work in the workplace. And that is true whether the workplace is a hi-tech factory, a left-over 19th-century industrial slum, a credit union in the rural areas of a poor country, a hospital, a city law practice or a virtual office composed of a network of employees who interact mainly through electronic media.

There is some confirmatory evidence from a different quarter that is worth a moment's digression. The Pygmalion effect, remember, points out the fact that we behave in response to the mental attitudes of those in authority over us. But there is increasing volumes of evidence that we respond performatively but unconsciously to *our own* mental attitudes. Consider the medical evidence. This runs from research on the placebo effect to studies of people in trauma, from those trying to survive on a mountain side in a blizzard to those recovering from major surgery. In nearly every study, the conclusion is that mental attitudes—or to use the language of the last paragraph, peoples' expectations of themselves—affect outcomes. The hopeful, determined, positively oriented do better. Those who expect improvement (as in the placebo studies) are much more likely to achieve it than those who do not.[52] Nothing succeeds, it seems, like the expectation of success; and nothing fails like the expectation of failure

It would be false to claim that the *relationship* between the healing processes of the body and the belief systems of the mind are yet perfectly understood. Although this has become a major new area of research that is generating evidence very rapidly, the variance between different individuals and between different disease patterns is too marked for the easy formulation of general laws. That is a necessary caveat. Nonetheless, there is now sufficient evidence that there *is* some kind of causal relationship for some people in some disease patterns[53] for us to see here an analogue of the more general organizational point: that anticipatory belief can affect outcomes. Further and in some ways more surprising, there is some evidence that the beliefs that have this causal effect are wider than those of the patient alone. The beliefs and anticipations of the doctor, the family and the carers seem also to play a significant role.[54] Just as the company in which we remember effects *what* we remember, so it seems the company in which we hope effects the realization of those hopes.

It is thus no surprise to find that when expectations are raised on the shopfloor, results are achieved *irrespective of the nature of the intervention raising those expectations*. The experimental evidence for this was produced by A.S. King as long ago as 1974. In a carefully designed and controlled experiment, he showed that what raised productivity was not the *form* of the intervention—he used job rotation (the placebo equivalent) and job enlargement (the real pill)—but what managers were expecting to happen. When managers believed that job rotation would raise productivity, it did just that—even though in a control group it was shown to be wholly ineffective.[55] The reading of the intervention determined its outcome.

Dov Eden and his collaborators have taken this line of thinking a step further, designing experiments in the Israeli Defence Force that looked both for the classic Pygmalion effect—so that instructors were fed a pattern of expectations that were then realized in their recruits—and for what one might call the reverse Pygmalion effect—where recruits who were labelled as above average ranked their instructors' leadership skills more highly than did those labelled as average or unclassified. Clearly what was going on was that the instructors were reacting more positively, energetically and creatively to their good recruits—or to those they read as good—than to the also-rans. As Eden concludes, *managers get the subordinates they expect.*[56]

A final piece of confirmatory evidence comes from a less likely source. A study of battle-traumatized soldiers in the Israeli army showed that the expectations laid upon the traumatized soldiers by their superior officers—expectation that is of a quick recovery and return to active duty—was the most effective intervention. Where all other conditions were held constant—regime, drug therapy, level of accommodation and care—it was the expectations of those in authority that explained differences in recovery rates. (And, for the skeptical, recovery is measured by a range of mental and mechanical competencies.)

Putting all this together, we do not have knock-down proof that the appreciative approach works automatically. This book will nowhere make that claim, not least because, as we shall see, there are clearly circumstances in which it will not work and in which it would be foolish or worse to try to make it work. What we do have, though, is some evidence for the basic claim on which the whole edifice of the appreciative approach is erected; that is to say, the belief that the way we construct the world, the way we read the text of ourselves, others and our whole environment has an impact on the way we all function.

To summarize the argument so far, I have suggested that the appreciative approach starts from the assumption that we can choose how to read the text of our organization, or, for that matter, of other organizations, whether competitors or suppliers. There is not one real concrete thing that exists independently of the way we read it, understand it, appreciate it, but rather that we make it as we choose in the process of conceptualizing it, talking about it, living with it and in it. I have assumed, for the moment, that such choices are consciously made, and have argued that they do not need to be made from a negative, critical or problem-focused stance. I looked more carefully at two dimensions within which we choose our constructions—memory and imagination. I argued that these two dimensions provide the architecture within which we do our constructing and I showed that we have a substantial area of choice within them. Finally, I have adduced some evidence that suggests that the way we read our organizations actually affects the way they operate and how we operate within them. I shall argue later in this book that we can *learn* to improve our reading, that is, we can become more attuned to what readings are available; we can become more intentional about what readings we select; and we can become more inventive in creating new readings that reinforce the life-giving forces in the organization.

3. The approach at work

Much of this material has inevitably been presented in these introductory chapters in a preliminary and fairly crude way. Some of it will be spelt out in greater detail in later chapters. At this point, it may be helpful if I sketch out the operational processes of the appreciative approach to make the next chapters easier to follow. In the final section of this chapter, I suggest some criteria for judging whether appreciative inquiry is the most appropriate intervention to introduce. After a review in chapter 4 of some of the *unconscious* processes that the appreciative approach needs to tackle, I shall, in chapters 5 to 9, be following one application of the appreciative approach in considerable detail and, lest the reader get lost in the minutiae, I offer now a quick and dirty sketch of the process. I hope this will act as a set of sign posts in the next chapters.

Once we see that we are free to read the text of the organization in new and more life-enriching ways without anxieties about what is really there, we need a participative process that will allow such a reconstruction to take place. That is, I know, an important assumption: it is one I do not intend to defend at any length in this book. Suffice it to say that the basic stance of the appreciative approach is that organizations are more effective in the long run if change is essentially negotiated from the bottom up, rather than imposed from the top down, not least because of the evidence indicated above that memory, imagination and healing are *essentially* group activities. That does not impugn the function of management, nor does it contribute to a sloppy populism (as some, especially in the NGO sector, too readily assume.) Rather, consistent with the reading-the-text metaphor, it accepts that everyone is obliged to read the text; that some have more enriching readings than others; that readings are interdependent rather than independent; and that it therefore makes sense to collect as many of the readings as possible and examine them for what may give life to the organization as a whole.

There is no *one* right way to bring that about, and different situations will indicate different processes. The appreciative approach, however, starts with three principles: the *participative* process at its heart turns on appreciation of the good and life-giving rather than the destructive or tawdry; it should be *collaborative* across as broad a spectrum of the stakeholders as possible, rather than confined to one dominant group; and it should issue in *provocative* or challenging propositions that stretch the mind of everyone in the organization to new vistas of the possible, rather than being a rehash of group-think. How these principles are worked out in practice will be discussed more extensively in the following chapters and illustrated in detail in the case studies, but here is a thumb-nail sketch that shows all three principles in action.

A group representing all the stakeholders—perhaps no more than 10 or 12—is instructed in appreciative questioning; that is, in putting questions into an appreciative format. They learn to ask not: "What problems do you experience in your work?", but rather: "Under what circumstances does your work give you the greatest satisfaction?"; not "What is lacking in company personnel policy?," but: "What aspects of company policy on personnel are particularly important to you and why?"

Or, in the context of an appreciative inquiry in a community, the questions will not be: "What are the problems faced by this village?", "What are your priority needs?", but rather: "What resources do you have?", "What have you already achieved by using those resources?", "What are you most proud of in this village?"

The central thrust of the reframing is to shift from deficits and deficiencies to accomplishments and achievements. As we shall show in one of the case studies in part 3, even in a very hostile environment like a Saharan village, one can reframe the questions from traditional problem mode—"What are the problems the villagers face?"—to questions about what the villagers have achieved: "Tell me about the things you have done in the village in the last 10 years that give you the most satisfaction." And if that sounds as if one is collecting very different data from an operational point of view, we shall show that although the data may have a different *slant*, the substance is the same. The big difference is that the villagers are not trapped in dependency thinking, but have been affirmed in what they can achieve for themselves in the future.

To take another example (which is not included in the case studies), the current interest in development circles in sustainability tends to lead investigators to focus on what is *not* sustainable. Questions tend to be framed in ways that highlight the breakdowns in sustainability; e.g., "Why has no one maintained this pump?", "Why do you allow your goats free access to common land when you can see they destroy the browse beyond recovery?" These are, of course, crucial questions that need to be answered. But they are the more likely to get satisfactory and meaningful answers if they are reframed in ways that cast sustainability in appreciative mode; e.g. "What are the advantages to the village when the pump is working?", "How do people feel when they have plenty of good water readily available?" Such questions can lead on to a conversation that shifts the central locus of sustainability issues from the immediate causes of *un*sustained processes to a much broader set of criteria—criteria that together define the community's conception of its priorities in terms of investing in sustainable strategies.

As we shall see, this reframing is not easy or trivial. It takes time to learn and even very experienced practitioners sometimes catch themselves slipping back into problem-dominated language. With a little coaching, however, the initial group of stakeholders will be able, with some judicious help, to draw up a protocol of appreciative questions around the topic under review: personnel practices; intra-organizational relationships; marketing; production; the merging of different entities into a new organization; the search for sustainable development strategies at the micro-level or whatever it might be. This protocol is then used in a series of conversations (interviews is a word that usually gives exactly the wrong signals) between members of the initial group and everyone else in the organization. (If the organization is too big for that to be practicable, a cascade can be arranged as discussed further in chapter 6.) It is these conversations, based on the appreciative approach, that generate the data—and the psychic energy—for new ideas, new visions, new possibilities to emerge. Processing that data can be a laborious business, and, as we shall see, there is room for ingenuity and creativity in reducing that to manageable proportions. Out of those data, duly weighed and considered by the whole group, will come what are often called provocative propositions—statements of intent that determine a new set of possibilities and ways forward for the whole organization. If the work has been done with integrity and thoroughness, those possibilities will be both stretching *and* congruent with the values and actual context of the organization. Once a consensus has been built around the provocative propositions, action planning can begin.

There is one more part of the cycle that is important to emphasize at this stage. After the action planning has been finished and the implementation stage has been carried out—both in an appreciative mode as we shall see—the organization is likely to move to an evaluation phase. Typically, evaluations are seen as criticisms levelled by external agents who have ransacked the organization in search of more or less objective data with which to buttress their arguments. They are resented by the actors under criticism, who react defensively (and sometimes destructively). Further, it often happens that by the time the evaluation has been commissioned from external consultants, by the time the consultants have learned enough of the detail of the organization to ask the hard questions and then written their report, by the time management has read that report, called for debate on it and listened to counter-views, and by the time all that has taken place, the organization has moved to a place quite different from that which the evaluators were originally commissioned to study. Some key people may have left. The external context may well have changed. Major assumptions about that context and the way the organization can relate to it may well have been found to be unsound.[57]

There are two interrelated but distinct features here that are worth spelling out a little more clearly. First there is the issue of psychological resistance to evaluation. Perfectly natural as it is, it can lead to a whole raft of difficulties, from the evaluators being seriously mis- or underinformed, to unacceptable levels of stress among those being evaluated. Second, there is the issue of delay. Because we have come to see evaluation as part of the project cycle, it tends to be—perhaps is inevitably—carried out at the end of the project cycle, *after* the mistakes have been made and their full effects have begun to become all too apparent.

By contrast, the appreciative approach seeks to build evaluation into the normal life of the organization, not as an externally imposed, end-of-cycle judgement, but as a process of continuous self-learning and self-challenging that expects to pick up difficulties, tensions, denials of energy and creativity long before they emerge as problems.

This is not achieved by magic or alchemy. It is achieved by conscious choice of what we look at, of how we define the reality that is our organization or community. We can choose to read the text of the organization for the faults, the failures, the glitches and glums and emphasize those in an improvement plan. Or we can choose to read the sources of satisfaction, joy, fulfillment and delight and seek to enlarge their area of operation. The choice is ours to make. In the same way, to pick up the sustainability issue again, we can focus on the things that have proved unsustainable and identify them as problems, or we can identify *what is being successfully sustained* and move from that.

The skeptic will respond: Why set it up in this polarized way? Surely any evaluator worth his or her salt will seek to do both? To praise the good and expose the bad? Well, yes and no. As we shall see in many chapters in this book, the appreciative approach does not pretend that the bad is not there, that everything is for the best in the best of all possible worlds. On the contrary it can and does expose remorselessly whatever is at work in the organization that is denying it the opportunity to move toward its best embodiment of its stakeholders' vision. But it does so not in a spirit of fault finding, harsh judgement or culpability, but rather in the exploration of what *might be* if changes were made. Our experience is that this is a vastly more enriching, enabling and energizing way of looking at the same data. It is to see the potential within the actual, rather than to criticize the damage inflicted by the actual. In one sense, this is the difference between affirmation and appreciation. Affirmation is positive, rigorous, unambiguous, masculine. It owes much to super-ego, and therefore it is quick to condemn what does not reach its high standards. Appreciation is more poetic, feminine, intuitive, owing much to libido. It is therefore slow to condemn or judge, preferring to highlight the life-ful rather than pass judgement on the deathly.

Neither affirmation nor appreciation, however, can escape two of the harsh realities of the world. The first is that *any* change can be painful; even its contemplation can generate great resistance and anxiety. I shall argue that, while that is true at both the conscious and unconscious levels, the negative reactions to change are minimized by the appreciative approach. The second is that no organization can survive for long if it ignores its primary task. To put it crudely, even in the midst of an appreciative inquiry, the production of widgets has to be maintained if the wage bill is to be paid at the end of the month. Again I shall argue that, while no intervention is costless (just as no suspension of a necessary intervention is costless), one of the virtues of appreciative inquiry is that by focusing on best practice in its largest sense, primary task is highlighted rather than obscured.

It is now time to look more closely at the circumstances in which appreciative inquiry may be the best type of intervention to propose. This will conclude this prefatory material, leaving us to look at unconscious processes that impact upon appreciative inquiry in the last chapter of this part. Then we can walk, at a leisurely pace, through a detailed account of appreciative inquiry in practice.

4. When to use the appreciative approach?

Under what circumstances would it be clear that appreciative inquiry would be the intervention of first choice? I want to highlight some criteria that may help answer that.

First, it is essential that the organization concerned be open to a genuinely participative process that includes, at least conceptually, all the stakeholders, including *all the staff.* Boardroom appreciative inquiry is a contradiction in terms. And I italicize the staff because one often hears surprise expressed at the idea that low-skilled, hourly paid workers be included in the inquiry. It is worth saying now, then, that illumination can—and sometimes does—come from unexpected quarters. Many of us have been surprised and delighted by the wisdom that has come from people who have never before in the course of a whole working life been asked their opinion about anything in the workplace.

In the same way, in a community appreciative inquiry, it is important that the community as a whole be open to a participative process. In a rigidly hierarchical village, for example, it is tempting to get the chief or headman to agree and then leave him to tell his people what is going to happen. In extreme cases, that may perhaps be literally inevitable, but the ideal is for the whole village to understand at least a little about their own role, and for the existing power-holders to see that they will not be able to control the development of the process.

Second, it is essential that the organization is clear about what it wants the subject of the inquiry to be, and, ideally, that determination should have been made by a widely consultative process already. Just as no boardroom appreciative inquiry, so no boardroom agenda for the appreciative inquiry. Of course the agenda may have—almost certainly will have—been considered by the board and it might well have originated there. But the kiss of death to any appreciative inquiry process is if it can be represented as an attempt by the board to sell to the employees a particular policy, or even this particular process. Sometimes it happens that the board approaches the facilitator about doing an appreciative inquiry on X without having tested that initiative out on a wider swathe of opinion in the organization.

Responses naturally vary to that situation among different consultants. My preferred response is to say, "Fine. That is one possible approach. I will help you explain it to your employees and compare it with other possible interventions; e.g. Open Space or SWOT or team-building. Then I hope as wide a representation of your company as possible can decide which way they would like to go." If that is resisted—"Well, actually the board has decided that we want an appreciative inquiry"—I tend to be extremely circumspect, suspecting that the reason why the board wants an appreciative inquiry is that they imagine that it will gloss over the real sore places in the organization and convince everyone that the *status quo* is much to be appreciated just as it is. Of course, no set of expectations could more guarantee its own disappointment or do more damage to the people in the organization. If the board cannot be moved on from that fairly early on in the conversation, I would be reluctant to continue.

Third, everyone in the organization must be prepared to put in the time and work to give the process a fair chance. In a large organization, appreciative inquiry can be a painstaking and iterative process. It is seldom a quick fix, even in small organizations with a well-defined and limited agenda. Because, as we have already seen, the number of steps is small and the process easy to understand in its basic architecture, some people make the mistake of believing that it will not take much staff time and that the results will be quickly to hand. That is seldom the case.

And that raises a fourth criterion. Appreciative inquiry is not a crisis-management tool. An appreciative inquiry intervention can, it is true, sometimes turn a crisis round by providing a different and unexpected perspective on the facts of organizational life. In general, however, appreciative inquiry takes a longer time, a deeper trust and a more reflective mental posture than can be offered by an organization in crisis—one, for example, suddenly threatened with a takeover, or with all the key executives resigning simultaneously. [58]

That suggests a fifth criterion, a readiness to trust the process and its outcomes. As has already been implied many times and as will certainly appear extensively in the case studies of part 3, appreciative inquiry demands the trust of the participants. It cannot be planned out in great detail like a military campaign, with every development and contingency foreseen and countered, nor, by definition, can the outcomes. Indeed, it is usually the case that the participants themselves are surprised by the outcomes, sometimes almost shocked: "Did we really come to *that* conclusion? Why, that's great...."

Sometimes, however, we find that organizations want—or more often certain key people in the organization want—to be able to predict where it will all end. A large organization in Canada, for example, was having difficulties adapting to the changed circumstances in which it found itself. Some of the key executives start ed wondering whether an appreciative approach to their realities would represent a creative response. In the course of conversations with them and the CEO, however, it became clear that the latter was only prepared to countenance a process in which he could remain finally in control. As he put it: "There are some things I know about which no one else here does—or not to the same degree. Frankly, I'm not open to some populist process that gives the same authority to the typist or the telephonist as it does to me. I have the responsibility of this organization—and so I have to have the power that goes with that responsibility. And that power includes the power to say, 'No. That is not the way this organization is going', no matter what head of steam there is behind it."

In part the CEO had missed the point of appreciative inquiry. In part, however, he had a valid point. Appreciative inquiry *is* a participative process and that does involve the whole organization—including the CEO—having the courage to trust each other and the collaboration that the process seeks to induce. That does *not* involve the abdication of responsibility by the CEO—and one case study will make clear that such abdication can be quite destructive—but it does mean that the CEO's basic orientation has to work with the flow of the appreciative inquiry, rather than maintain mental reservations that will allow him or her to walk away from it if unacceptable results begin to emerge. We are back to multiple readings of the text of the organization and learning to live with that plurality. And if that is true of the CEO, it is no less true for everyone else in the organization.

And that "everyone else" includes people on the margins who would normally consider themselves—and be considered by others—to be voiceless. In formal organizations, it extends to trade unions, works councils or other fora of employee representation and opinion formation. Sometimes such groups feel threatened by any process that departs from what they see as their hard-won right to represent workers. This is likely to be particularly troublesome where there is already competition—overt or covert—between two or more such bodies (including, of course, two or more unions that may well be jostling for wider representative powers). I know of at least one example in the UK, where rivalry between a union, seeking but not yet accorded recognition by management, and a works council, widely distrusted as Uncle Tomish by the employees, destroyed any hope of mounting a genuinely participative process because there was insufficient trust between management, the union and the council to allow even joint sponsorship of the inquiry to generate commitment among all the employees. (Interestingly both the organization in Canada and the one in the UK, separated though they are by many years, fell back into appointing a management guru to come in and tell them what to do. Both had subsequently stormy histories, because a proportion of the employees could not or would not own the guru's findings. For the guru was offering one definitive reading: he was not able to or even interested in respecting the multiplicity of readings that were held in the organization.)

From this it should not be concluded that *any* conflict within the organization renders appreciative inquiry inappropriate in that organization. (If that were true, appreciative inquiry would never be used: the only conflictless organization is a dead one.) Again, as the case studies will bring out, appreciative inquiry is usually mobilized when organizations are beginning to suffer from unresolved issues—and the very fact of irresolution is itself both the origin and the expression of deep conflicts. Most of these conflicts, however, stem from the *substance* of the organization's work rather than fights over power within the organization. For example, they may be over future directions the organization should take, rather than over who gets to decide that.

It is important to get the nuance right here. I am not suggesting that serious internal power conflicts always make it impossible to use appreciative inquiry.[59] What I am saying is that, where such conflicts exist, it is well to take extra care to ensure that there is a full and genuine commitment to the process by all the warring factions, that each will take the time and trouble to read the text of the other. One part of that commitment—and one that is difficult to judge in advance—is that none of the factions will seek to use or even hijack the process to advance their own sectional interests in terms of power allocation. As we shall see more extensively below, there are design features that one can build in to reduce the likelihood of that happening. Indeed, the whole thrust of the appreciative approach, with its emphasis on group work, is designed to be adaptive in Lewin's sense.[60] Clarity on the issue of trust from the start may, however, help reduce the strain on the design.

A subset of the criterion of trust is that of hopefulness. It is worth a few lines of its own. Part of what it means to trust the process is to be hopeful that the exercise of the appreciative approach will radically change things for the better. Every organization, of course, has its cynics and its skeptics. They have their own jaundiced reading of the organization's text. They may, however, *for that very reason*, be necessary to its survival. The danger arises when their style of thinking becomes so dominant that it deprives everyone in the organization of the energy of hope. As we shall see in the case studies, the fundamental psychological dynamic of the appreciative approach is hope that the best can be universalized. Now if that possibility is denied by the whole ideology of the organization—so that it is literally and tragically hopeless and deeply mired in an infectious cynicism—it is likely to prove a Sisyphean task to generate the style of thinking on which the appreciative approach depends: that the best is good; that it can be approached more often; that the pay-offs to doing so are huge and widely distributed. I am reluctant to say that the appreciative approach is not suitable in these hopeless organizations. I believe that would be too sweeping, not least because it is our experience that just asking appreciative questions can change the dynamic in surprising ways, as I shall demonstrate in the final chapter.[61] Yet we need to acknowledge that the facilitator who sets out on the road of the appreciative approach in an organization that has systematically killed hope may find he or she has a longer and more difficult journey than he or she had ever imagined.

Finally, a word about size. Are there limits to how big or small an organization can be? In theory yes, in practice probably not. On the downward side, groups of professionals as small as four or five use appreciative inquiry routinely as part of their approach to management discourse. For example, the staff of a small consulting firm have come to frame the agenda of their staff meetings within an appreciative approach. Thus the agenda would not be set up in the way with which we are all familiar: "What are the problems we are having with client X?" Rather, it would be: "What have been our best experiences with client X since our last meeting? How can we build on that?"

On the upside, the major constraint to using appreciative inquiry in ultra-large organizations are the problems of ensuring genuine participation on the one hand, and sufficiently sensitive data analysis on the other. Although we shall see that there are ways of handling the latter that allow for very large numbers of appreciative interviews to be processed in a way that forms the basic input into the provocative propositions, there comes a point where issues of unwieldiness, a possible loss of detail, delay and alienation become pressing.

At this point, it may be preferable to break the organization down into component pieces and do a separate appreciative inquiry with each unit. I am aware that that is not a perfect solution and that it can point in the wrong direction in two senses. It can reinforce structural divisions rather than transcend them. And it can lead to the need to integrate the separate studies later in a way that may feel quite false to the participants of the original inquiry. "We worked hard to produce provocative proposition X and now they've gone and elided it with the other group's proposition Y—which may be dealing with the same issues but which has far less teeth than ours." Nonetheless, the history is that appreciative inquiry has been used with a whole inner city (in "Vision Chicago") and is being discussed for a whole continent ("Imagine Africa"). It is being intensively used in the United Religions Initiative, with people from many cultures from all over the world. One should not be too hasty, then, to draw the limits narrow.

A more appreciative way of ending this discussion would be to identify the size of groups with which appreciative inquiry works best. Different practitioners will have different responses to that depending to some degree on the style with which they work most comfortably. With suitable tentativeness, then, I would argue that for a short, intensive, face-to-face type of inquiry, groups of up to 70 work well. With a longer, more formal, more bureaucratic style, organizations of up to 2,000 are quite normal.

So much for the positive criteria; what of the negative? Appreciative inquiry is a tool of *organizational and community development*; it is not a substitute for management. It is crucial to keep these two dimensions separate. Community development is about enabling groups to articulate and move toward their own objectives. Organizational development is about nurturing the health and effectiveness of the work group. Management, on the other hand, is about the conceptually more limited task of maximizing outputs for a range of inputs. Now the picture is made more complicated by the overlap between these functions. For example, strategy setting—even the definition of primary task—and some aspects of organizing to fulfil the primary task are indeed both matters of organizational development and of management. When Tony Eccles, a visiting professor at Cranfield School of Management, echoing a well-established reaction,[62] seeks to re-establish the priority of management against empowerment of the workforce by emphasizing the hardness of many key decisions and the speed with which they have to be made, he concludes, "Voluntarism has its limits and not every dilemma can be transformed into productive consensus."[63] Precisely. And the key to excellence in management—an issue he largely dodges—is knowing precisely where the limits are. Twenty, even 10 years ago, they were drawn far too narrowly in the interest of hierarchical management. It *may* be true that in some environments the pendulum has swung too far toward what Eccles derides as "the invisible hand of natural co-ordination." But from that it does not follow that "orchestrating consensus is no longer a credible policy for success." Rather it follows that success is achieved by those organizations whose managers have the wisdom to differentiate between issues and situations in which "tough action" (sic) is indeed the only way forward, and the far more common issues and situations in which the participative processes represented by appreciative inquiry are likely to be more creative.

And that raises my last point. As I hinted above, the appreciative approach cannot be and should not be reduced to some set of procedures, applied in a more or less mechanical way. It is art as much as science, poetry as much as prose. As some of the case studies will demonstrate, the approach is likely to fail as soon as it is reduced to a rule of thumb or a collection of routine interviews followed by dumb, numbed data analysis. As with reading any worthwhile work of literature, unless the *reader* always retains a spark of creativity, of humour and humanity, of the capacity to surprise and be surprised, the cutting edge will be lost and the blunted instrument will, like an edgeless scalpel, do more harm than good.

For in the end, the appreciative approach is not just a technique for managing community or organizational change. It is a way of being, a way of looking at and living in the world around us—a way, if you like Peter Vaill's metaphor, of giving a performance. It demands a shift in perspective that goes far wider than our professional, business or community lives. It comes to involve not just our intellectual and even emotional processes. It commands the assent of our very spirituality, of what makes us who we are and how we are. But that is to anticipate.

---

43 Cf. Fritz, *sup. cit.*, and M. Sinetar, *Do what you love: The money will follow*, New York: Dell, 1988.

44 By saying that I do not preclude the possibility of a corporate death-wish, which may result in irrational aggressiveness in a way analogous to Freud's now much criticized *Todestrieb*. See Ernest Becker, *The denial of death*, New York: Free Press, 1973.

45 See, for example, C. Fred Alford, *Melanie Klein and critical social theory*, New Haven: Yale University Press, 1989.

46 Anton Obholzer and Vega Zagier Roberts, *The unconscious at work: Individual and organizational stress in the human services*, London: Routledge, 1994.

47 F. Polak, *The image of the future*, New York: Elsevier, 1973, p. 19. Quoted in Cooperrider, *op. cit.*, p. 111.

48 The idea of organizations moving along the path of least resistance has its most forceful statement in R. Fritz. *The path of least resistance*, Salem, Mass: DMA, 1984.

49 One of the most complete, though now rather dated, reviews of this literature is to be found in C. Jussim, "Self-fulfilling prophecies: A theoretical and integrative review," in *Psychological Review*, 1986, 93, (4), pp. 429ff#. This is an important contribution because it tries, unusually, to integrate educational and cognitive social-psychological perspectives. A more up to date and methodologically probing summary is Elisha Babad, "Pygmalion—25 years after: Interpersonal expectations in the classroom," in Peter Blanck, *Interpersonal expectations: Theory, research and applications,* Cambridge: Cambridge University Press, 1993. His bibliography will be very useful to anyone who wants to follow this debate more thoroughly. For more specific data on the comparative influence of measured IQ and teacher expectations, see Cooperrider *op. cit.* and the numerous references there cited.

50 It is also, of course, heavily determinative of the teacher's own performance vis-a-vis a given pupil, which is why the mediation of expectations has attracted so much interest. See Blanck, *op. cit.*

51 See Marylee C. Taylor, "Expectancies and the perpetuation of racial inequality," in Blanck, *op. cit.*

52 L. White, B. Tursky and G. Scwartz, (eds.) *Placebos: Theory, research and mechanisms*, New York: Guilford, 1985. Compare that with Russell A. Jones, *Self-fulfilling prophecies: Social, psychological and physiological effects of expectancy*, Hillsdale, New Jersey: Lawrence Erlbaum, 1977, pp. 204-238.

53 For example, Kirsch reports that placebos are effective in one-third of patients presenting such symptoms as headaches, rheumatoid arthritis, hay fever, warts and bleeding ulcers. I. Kirsch, *Changing expectations: A key to effective psychotherapy*, Pacific Grove, California: Brooks, 1990.

54 B. O'Regan, "Psychoneuroimmunology: The birth of a new field," in *Investigations: A bulletin of the institute of noetic sciences*, 1, pp. 1-11, 1983.

55 A. S. King, "Expectation effects in organizational change," *Administrative Science Quarterly*, 19, 1974. Compare with Dov Eden, *Pygmalion in management: Productivity as a self-fulfilling prophecy*, Lexington, MA: Lexington Books, 1990.

56 Dov Eden and A. B. Shani: "Pygmalion goes to boot camp: Expectancy, leadership and trainee performance," *Journal of Applied Psychology*, 72, 1982. The study is neatly summarized and compared with other work with the IDF along the same lines in Dov Eden, "Interpersonal expectations in organizations," in Blanck, *op. cit.*

57 The tangency of this approach to that of Senge's "learning organization" is apparent.

58 But see the interview with Joep de Jong in chapter 10 below. He gives a good example of the opposite case, where an appreciative inquiry intervention worked well despite simultaneous organizational mayhem.

59 As the celebrated "Medic Inn" case study (see note 40) so clearly demonstrated in the very early years of the development of appreciative inquiry. See Barrett and Cooperrider, *sup. cit.*

60 K. Lewin, "Group decision and social change," in E. E. Maccoby, T. M. Newcombe and R. L. Hartley (eds.) *Readings in Social Psychology*, New York: Holt, 1958.

61 For example, just the telling of stories can engender hope in what had seemed a *hopeless* organization. "The significance of collective storytelling is that it is a means by which groups of people can create new knowledge—grounded, practical, "realistic" yet moral knowledge—that offers them fresh possibilities for collective being—and this is the essence of hope." Ludema, *op. cit.*, p. 192.

62 See, for instance and in some ways, given the nature of his earlier work, rather surprisingly, Elliott Jaques, "In praise of hierarchy," *Harvard Business Review*, Jan/Feb, 1990, pp. 127-133.

63 Financial Times, July 12, 1996, *"Management power and strategic change."*

Chapter 4
The role of unconscious processes in appreciative inquiry

1. The unconscious and the appreciative approach

In the previous chapters, I have assumed that the way we read the text of the organization is determined entirely by conscious processes—intellectual, rational or emotional. I have so far said rather little about *unconscious* influences on our readings, even though there are some instances where the unconscious may have a major effect on the way we construct the world around us and therefore on the way we behave. Certainly that was the view of one of the first people to write about the appreciative process. Geoffrey Vickers wrote in 1968: "It may well be that the conscious operations of the mind, though essential, are the least central to the process of appreciation. Such at least is the impression left on my mind by some experience of highly skilled 'appreciators'."[64] In this chapter, I want to go some way toward correcting this omission and explore the ways in which the appreciative approach can aid a more constructive response to the unconscious processes often at work in organizations, groups and communities.

It is important to emphasize from the outset, however, that I am not suggesting—and should not be taken to be suggesting—that the appreciative approach is a substitute for either individual or group psychoanalytical work where that is required. Nor am I advocating a kind of corporate amateur "psych-in." Nothing could be more potentially dangerous. What I am suggesting is that, by contrast with traditional methods of organizational inquiry, the appreciative approach can play a part in helping the whole organization to reflect on its conscious *and unconscious* emotional life as well as on its performance of its task. For it can help illuminate the ambiguity of experience, which, mediated through memory as it is, has been worked upon by both conscious and unconscious processes, and which can therefore both "delude us and... inform us in unique ways."[65] If people in the organization can be helped to understand something of the richness of this ambiguity, then they can give themselves over to the primary task as something more approaching whole persons, rather than as ciphers or pawns in someone else's game, where that someone else may also include their own unconscious.

The evidence for a connection between the two—the emotional and the task-oriented—is now overwhelming. Daniel Goleman's best-selling book *Emotional Intelligence* has argued the point at length, but in a wider sense, the rise of information-based industries, the collapse of hierarchies, the processes of delayering and the rise of networking as a normal mode of production have all served to put emphasis on the task-centredness of quality relationships. In the management literature this has had a wide variety of expression, from managing with heart; to trust; to management spirituality, but the core concern is the same; namely, that what gets the job done best is a quality of trust, interaction and personal fulfillment in the emotional life of the worker that cannot be taken for granted or simply assumed to happen. Even less can it be assumed to happen without pain, conflict or resistance. As with any deep learning at the individual or group level, an organization that takes its own emotionality seriously may find it comes with a price attached—the price exacted by any process that challenges both structural conventions *and* their accompanying psychic equilibria. At the very least, like technology, finance and marketing, emotional learning has to be nurtured, conserved and incorporated with the other elements of the business if it is to be as effective as its promise. I shall argue below that the appreciative approach has a major role to play in allowing that to happen, and at minimal psychic cost.

I shall divide the discussion into three sections. In the first I will look at the role of anxiety in the emotional life of individuals and organizations, and then consider what help the appreciative approach can be in enabling people to manage it better. That will lead to a consideration of projection. Finally, in some ways a special case of projection, I shall discuss stereotyping. In each case I shall bring back the discussion to the appreciative approach and the contribution it can make to handling these unconscious processes.

2. Anxiety

It is almost a truism that this is an anxious age. From fears of job loss and subsequent prolonged unemployment to fears about death (still one of the great taboos of our culture) and failure (another great taboo in the culture of success), the generalized anxieties that beset us tend to get focused in two key areas: our families and our work. It is not coincidental that divorce and workaholism are both so common and often so connected. Both frequently point to an addictive pattern of behaviour—and addiction is one of the commonest forms of the unconscious expression of anxiety. Bulimia and anorexia are classic—and tragic—examples.

I am less concerned here with pathological patterns of individual anxiety, of which workaholism would be the most immediately relevant, than with the line of thinking that starts with Melanie Klein, runs through Menzies-Lyth and Eliot Jacques to Hirschhorn and then to Obholzer and his colleagues at the Tavistock Institute. Common to all these writers is the observation that organizations can often be read as having structured themselves in a way that enables major actors in them to defend themselves against anxiety. So far as I am aware that insight has not been applied scientifically to Third World communities, but a reading of developmental ethnography from this perspective suggests that many features of village life in poor communities that so puzzle aid workers can well be interpreted as defences against community anxiety. Think, for instance, of the elaborate precautions taken to protect the village from evil spirits or the malign impact of the ancestors. Indeed, one interpretation of sacrifice, so central to some ethnic groups, is that it focuses and relieves the anxieties of the tribe, perhaps made conscious in the dream of a tribal notable.[66]

The classic study, in a Western context, is Menzies-Lyth's work on the organization of nursing in a London hospital.[67] Noticing how much of a nurse's work is anxiety-provoking—fear, pain, death, dread, grief, anger, suppressed sexuality, resentment are common enough emotions on the average ward—Menzies argued that the nursing profession has evolved in a way that helps nurses, often young women with little experience outside their hospital training, cope with the emotional demands of the job. Further, drawing on the work of Klein, Menzies emphasizes that these emotional demands make contact with *unconscious* fears in the nurses' own psyches—of death, destruction and dismemberment. All of us have such fears. Most of the time they are inactive, buried in the unconscious. Every now and then, however, we come across a set of experiences that plug into these unconscious fears, and that makes us both psychically vulnerable *and* less able to do the overt job of dealing with sick, distressed or grieving people.

How exactly can a hospital be read as having been organized to help the nurses cope? Menzies points to a number of strategies. For example, too close a familiarity with patients is discouraged. Uniforms emphasize the distinctiveness of roles. Nurses are moved quite frequently from ward to ward. They tend to know little of the background of their patients and are discouraged from divulging anything about their own wider circumstances. "The kidney in bed number 8" may be a caricature of nurse-patient relationships, but it is sufficiently near the actuality for the National Audit Office of the UK to comment unfavourably on nurses' failure to relate to patients as *people* as recently as 1992.

Second, Menzies notices how the tasks assigned to nurses, especially younger ones, tend to be monotonous, routine and standardized. It is as though the medical profession as a whole is saying, "These young women cannot be trusted to be sufficiently in control of their emotions that they will be able to think logically and coherently in a difficult situation. So standardize the procedures until they can do them in their sleep." The result is well known—a high turnover of bored, disenchanted nurses, especially the better educated, more intelligent ones; a huge overload of work for senior nurses to whom any non-standard issues have to be referred; and an almost complete failure so far to adopt the Canadian model of nurse-practitioners who are not only encouraged to develop their own skill-range, but, even more important, take some of the weight off the also exploited sector of medical personnel, the junior hospital doctors.

Let me provide a final example. Menzies points out that young nurses, like the rest of us, want and need to be carefree and irresponsible from time to time, to let their hair down. They may be able to do that off the job, but that need continues at the unconscious level even when they are on the job. So how do they cope? They split themselves (a notion to which we shall return below) and project their serious, responsible selves onto the doctors and senior nurses, investing them with almost superhuman powers of control, of discipline and gravitas, while simultaneously they project their irresponsible selves, of which they are both frightened and ashamed, on to their juniors who are despised as giggly, stupid, immature, and, of course, irresponsible. And because we all unconsciously *tend* toward the roles that are projected on to us by others, sure enough the senior nurses become starchy authoritarians who take a pride in running a military dictatorship, and the juniors sometimes behave irresponsibly, especially when they are out of uniform.

I recount Menzies work at length because, despite being somewhat dated, it is still a classic statement of the way in which organizations come to structure themselves as defences against anxiety—both at the conscious and the unconscious level. In most of the corporate sector, the presence of pain and death and grief are not, at first sight, so obvious as in the hospital ward. But look again. In a period of down-sizing, re-engineering, outsourcing and outplacing, the fear, even terror, of losing one's job, of being unable to maintain the mortgage or service the credit-card debt and of having to compete in an over-supplied labour market with younger, brighter, more highly computer-literate jobseekers is so striking as to bear comparison with the emotional climate of the hospital ward.

And if that is true in the industrialized world, it is often no less true in poor countries, where the social and economic—and ultimately psychic—costs to be paid for the loss of a job in the formal sector, or the loss of a place at school or university, or the loss of a close relationship with a big man are horrendous indeed. We tend to think of insecurity as a Northern malaise; it has its Southern manifestations that are no less damaging for being less copiously researched.

The management literature is, of course, full of accounts of what insecurity does to the way people organize their work lives and how it affects their performance. Stress and anxiety exact a terrible toll in terms of performance, from loss of memory to an inability to think logically, from incipient paranoia to reduced attention span, the effects of anxiety on the way the individual performs the daily task are not only unpleasant for the individual but potentially lethal for the organization once such effects become widespread.[68] For, among other things, too much anxiety can panic people into unwise decisions, into actions that, in an unstressed state, they would regard as premature, disproportionate or inappropriate and, sometimes, into confrontational relationships that damage their effectiveness and marginalize them in their work group. Functioning less effectively intellectually and relationally, they are, as we so often say, "their own worst enemies." They make more likely to occur the outcome they most dread—their loss of the job.

What is missing from this account is the connection between the fear of job loss and the *inner* fear of the annihilation of the self. It is this which forges the connection between overt and quite rational anxiety about the security of employment and the unconscious fear of the moral equivalent of death. From Freud onward, successive waves of psychoanalytic thinkers have stressed the fear of death, both literally and metaphorically, as a powerful unconscious process at work in us all—at least in the West.[69] Now given our tendency to over-invest, psychically, in our jobs, the fear of job loss goes a lot deeper than fear of the economic and social consequences of a loss of income. What is at stake, at the unconscious level, is not just the mortgage or the American Express Gold Card; what is at stake is *our very selves*. We do not just identify with the job or role; we have internalized so that it has become part of our very selves.[70] *We* are on the line. If we do not meet this quarter's sales target, or if the head office review committee decides that our plant's product could be made more cheaply in the Far East, it is not just our jobs that will go. *We* will cease to exist. *We* shall be wiped out. No wonder suicide rates rise dramatically in the wake of large-scale closures, or that bankrupt farmers, threatened with the rupture of the strong emotional link with their land and their stock, have among the highest suicide rates of all.

Now put into this mixture a traditional organizational intervention. In comes a consultant to work with a group of executives to help them find ways of reducing the cost of production. Everyone knows that costs have to be reduced by 10 percent to keep the plant open. No one knows where that 10 percent is going to come from—the gobbledygook of efficiency savings fools no one. Immediately everyone is out to protect his or her patch, and if possible make it more secure against the next round of cost-cuts that everyone knows, but no one says, is on the horizon. The consultant sees through a lot of the defensive posturing: that is what he is paid for. The executives quickly realize that he sees through it, and that makes them more frightened, more defensive and less able to concentrate on the real task which is to cut costs (and not to protect their jobs).

This sad scenario has many ends, none of them either healthy or efficient.[71] Those who can, bail out. That tends to be the brightest and the best. Holes are left in critical parts of the company, which no one will fill because a job gone is a little money saved. Working relationships sour as turf is protected ever more vigorously. One department enjoys showing another in a bad light to encourage forced savings there. It is by no means unknown for one department to sabotage deliberately the work of another—so that production is deliberately late with deliveries to embarrass the sales people—because the staff have so lost a grip on reality that they can no longer see the obvious interdependencies. Most tragically of all, the job losses required to force costs down are bigger than they need to have been because productivity gains are much smaller than they could have been in a less psychically traumatized environment.

Notice what has happened, almost (perhaps entirely) unconsciously. The text of the organization has shifted from being about the primary task—building the business by providing high quality and good value to satisfied customers—to being about each micro-unit, and ultimately each individual, defending his or her livelihood, *at no matter what cost to the organization as a whole*. No one now reads the organization in terms of the primary task; the task is to defend the job. Conscious anxiety has fed unconscious anxiety, and between them they have subverted the text.

What difference would the appreciative approach make? In a period of an organization's life which is necessarily anxiety-raising, does it make sense even to speak of the appreciative approach? Is not this a contradiction in terms? We need to go a little deeper into unconscious processes at work in a situation like this before we can begin to answer that.

The fear of job loss is, as I have explained, related to the fear of death and dissolution of the self. This is such a primitive fear that it quickly become destructive, both of creative ways of behaving (and reacting to crisis or emergency) and of the psychic health of the individual and the group (so that classically various kinds of paranoia take over and a sense of reality becomes, at best, blurred). The psychoanalytic tradition of Klein and Bion see one way of helping people cope with that primitive fear as a close analogy to the way a mother helps her baby or small child cope with extreme emotion—she contains it for the child. That is to say, she accepts the projections the child is putting on her—she is the wicked witch who is causing all the child's pain—and then slowly, as the child is able to cope, feeds it back to him in, as it were, bite-size pieces. Eventually the child begins to see that mother is not the wicked witch, just as she is not the fairy godmother either. She is the usual human mix of good, bad and run-of-the-mill, and it is the child himself who splits the experience of the one person into two.

Now this containing of raw emotion is a crucial function in any group that is going through a crisis that may have a very physical side to it—cutting costs by 10 percent—but which also delivers a huge emotional kick. The question is whether an appreciative approach is more likely to enable a group to contain, in this sense, its own anxiety than other approaches.[72]

There are a number of reasons for thinking so. First, the appreciative approach encourages all members of an organization to be honest about their emotional condition. Feelings are important data, as important as the more physical data traditional approaches tend to emphasize. Second, if the approach is well planned, people are encouraged to be honest about a deeper level of feelings than are customarily discussed in a work setting. That is not to say that the appreciative approach becomes a psychoanalytic or counselling session; but it is to insist that it can create a holding environment in which people can admit to feelings of loss, anxiety, dread, fear, anger and envy—because they know that they are not going to be judged for having such feelings nor are they alone in admitting them. Naturally, the facilitator has a key role to play in this regard. If he or she can contain the feelings of the work group, there is a good chance that the work group will be able to contain the feelings of the wider community. As we shall see in part 2, this sometimes requires a very intentional effort by the facilitator. Most of the time it is a more or less unconscious or normal part of the facilitator's relationship with the work group.

Third, at its best the appreciative approach lets everyone in the organization know that there are deep feelings—some of them perhaps functioning at the unconscious level—which are both common throughout the organization and which shape the way the organization is functioning. For example, a large architectural practice was suffering from a very high rate of turnover of staff in the late 20s and early 30s age group, exactly the kind of people who ought to have been generating the new ideas and challenging the conventional wisdom enshrined in the senior partners. In the course of an appreciative approach it became clear that many people in the firm, and not exclusively in this age group, experienced the five senior partners as paternalistic and over protective. The senior partners themselves saw this pattern of behaviour, instilled in them by the founder of the firm, now retired, as kind, sympathetic, and which created a caring environment in which people could maximize their creative skills.

In fact younger people saw it as an emotional fire blanket which smothered them, making them anxious about expressing any strong views about their work, or anything else in the context of the office. Frustrated by the conflict between their intellectual and creative need to be independent of—and even critical of—the senior partners on the one hand, and their emotional need to continue to relate to them as pseudo-parents on the other, many younger architects left. For they could not face the trauma of establishing their independence from their pseudo-parents—and yet if they were to develop professionally that is exactly what they needed. As one leaver put it, "I am sorry to be going professionally, but the sweet scent of freedom...!" An appreciative inquiry in the practice revealed to the senior partners that what the younger architects most enjoyed was not, as they had assumed, the family atmosphere of the practice, but the cut and thrust of real professional debate, where they were treated as professional peers, with their ideas tested rigorously along with those of the seniors—no quarter given or sought.

It might be objected that this example has little to say about the containment of anxiety as such. The sense of suffocation reported by the younger architects is however a classic symptom of anxiety and the way the senior partners had conceived of the organization as a family might well be interpreted as a denial of their own mortality and therefore as a way of dealing with their own anxiety about this. They wanted the practice to serve as a continuation of their own lives. If that seems too analytical, take the case of the accountancy firm that was combining two of its major functions in one, brand new, purpose-built complex. As the two existing units moved into the new building, managers noticed a sharp rise in absenteeism, then a significant increase in resignations. They persuaded themselves—and they had some evidence from comparable moves to support their view—that this was just a blip, following the move. But they also began to notice that the extensive consultative network throughout the organization seemed to be getting increasingly mired in petty disputes that ground on and on, absorbing totally disproportionate amounts of everyone's time. From car-parking arrangements to planning the Christmas party, trivial issues became major mountains.[73] When the first round of rationalizations was announced, the anger and bitterness in the building were almost palpable. A rash of computer viruses, admittedly in peripheral programs, raised the question of whether a campaign of sabotage was beginning.

An appreciative inquiry found that the managers were half right. The move had been very disruptive, but not, as the managers had assumed, at the physical or administrative levels of the way people organized getting to and from work, or relating to their new physical environment. What was going on at a deeper level was a process of mourning for the old days, the cozy, smaller-scaled, tightly task-oriented world of work that the old divisions had made possible and seemed to protect. In the new super-division, people did not know how they fitted in. They craved for the old certainties, the old sense of knowing who they were and where they were. Perhaps inevitably, this deep sense of anxiety about their own identity in the new workplace was focused on the redundancies that were expected to follow the move and the integration of the two operations. Here, the organization could not organize to defend against anxiety; the only form of defence was to erect into mega-issues trivia that in a healthy, non-anxious organization would have been dealt with as such.

By allowing the employees to recognize, acknowledge and honour the mourning of the old days, to share their sense of not knowing who they were in the new integrated organization, and to find ways of importing into the new situation some of the best of the old, the staff were able to achieve two remarkable pieces of emotional learning. First, they could, in time, leave the past behind and face the future—so that making the new arrangement work happily became a genuine pleasure. The former obstructiveness and bloody-mindedness disappeared.

But second, and even more remarkable, the staff as a whole was able to think creatively about the issue of rationalization. They came to recognize that the integration had indeed thrown up areas of overlap that needed to be eliminated. But rather than assume that the people in the overlap should be laid off, the organization as a whole set about expanding the range of services that the firm could offer clients with a view to minimizing and if possible eliminating any forced redundancies. As one of the participants in the appreciative inquiry put it to me later, "The key moment was when we came to think about the provocative propositions. It was clear to us all in my group. The only proposition that was going to be provocative enough was to say, 'This firm does not make people involuntarily redundant.' That did it. It made the action planning more demanding, but you could feel the change in the atmosphere. People switched from being defensive and frightened to being creative. And that was true right through the group. A silly example: we found we had too many catering staff. We could have—would have—laid off about four of them. But one of them who was in our group pointed out that we could save a fortune if, instead of buying in ready-made foods for the canteen and the trolley service, we made our own. Bingo. We saved money. We kept the jobs, and we eat a whole lot better."

At the process level, what had been achieved can be put like this: The intensive interviewing procedure that lies at the heart of the appreciative approach had allowed people to acknowledge to themselves and then express to someone else in the organization the reality of their own feelings—of loss, grief, anger, anxiety. They had found that they were not alone in these feelings, that they were natural, widely shared and perhaps inevitable. That very fact was part of the containment of those feelings, making them easier to bear and less disruptive. But they had been prevented from locking a large number of people into a gloomy despondency that life was intolerable because, by focusing on the best of the past and its reincarnation in the present, participants were helped to move emotionally from grief to hope—or, in Kleinian terms, from the paranoid-schizoid position, where they felt persecuted (by the management and/or the move) to what she would see as an improvement—to the depressive position, where they were able to think more creatively about the future. That is emphatically not to cheapen or diminish the reality of the grief, but it is to refuse to be locked into it, to give it the last existential word.

Further, as the report of the executive quoted above brings out, the process does not allow the hope, normally expressed in the provocative propositions, to remain at the abstract or conceptual level. By moving on to action planning, based on the provocative propositions, it demands that the participants determine how the hope may be substantiated.[74]

This emotional shift from grief to hopeful planning for the future is akin to—though not identical with—the classic shift in positions first detected by Melanie Klein.[75] She writes of the shift from what she calls the paranoid-schizoid position to the depressive position. The former describes an emotional state in which we feel we are being got at, that life is so hard that we have to split ourselves into two or more bits as a way of surviving. The shift is to a state in which we can actually empathize with how others feel and make gestures of reparation to them for the harm we may have done them. Klein sees this shift (and its reverse, back from the depressive to the paranoid-schizoid) as constituting the most funda-

69

mental structure of emotional life, and, for that matter, of emotional learning. The success of the shift, in the Kleinian scheme, is largely determined by the *containing* offered by the emotional environment, especially during the paranoid-schizoid position.

Now what I am suggesting is that appreciative approaches offer a form of containment through the interviewing procedure that allows people to shift from the equivalent of the paranoid-schizoid position to the equivalent of the depressive. That is to say, people may well be feeling persecuted, misunderstood, undervalued, patronized, not taken seriously and therefore, often, torn apart. All these feelings, give or take variations in terminology, were reported by both the junior architects and the staff of the accountancy firm. But, by being challenged to reread their own script and that of the organization and, in the process, by being *empathetically listened to within an appreciative environment*—i.e., one that takes them seriously as people in their own subjectivity—the people concerned are able to acknowledge those feelings as real *but not as determinative*. Without manipulation or conscious discussion, they are enabled to experience the emotional space and capacity to move into the future. True, this is not exactly the same as Klein's acts of reparation, since those are motivated at least in part by guilt. But the emotional quality of hopeful action that presages a more tolerable future is very similar in the two cases.

Whereas Klein was primarily concerned with the individual, we are concerned with the group.[76] To us what is important is not only that the individual be allowed to develop emotionally in relation to the workplace, but that that development be generalized to a degree that ensures that the organization itself becomes an emotionally healthy and therefore potentially effective unit. That is why the classic structure of an appreciative inquiry moves from intense one-on-one conversations to group work. In the group the data from the conversations are considered within disciplines of confidentiality and anonymity that protect the integrity of the one-on-one conversations but allow the full emotional—as well as substantive—force of those conversations to be appropriated by the whole group.[77]

3. Projections

I want in this section to look at the way in which the appreciative approach can help manage the common but potentially very destructive unconscious process of projection. I shall discuss three variants of this process. In the first, I shall be considering the case where one group of workers projects its own negative feelings on to another group, thereby making hostility toward and lack of effective cooperation with that group almost inevitable. In the second I shall be addressing the more difficult area of individuals or, more rarely groups, coming to be the *incarnation* of organizational problems that remain unaddressed, buried in the unconscious of the organization as a whole. The potentially damaging effect this can have on the individuals is only exceeded by the long-run harm it can do the organization. And in the third—in some ways an amalgam of the first two—I shall be considering the case where a work group projects its negative emotionality on to the facilitator.

The simplest form of projection is when the individual sees in others what he or she does not want to—or is frightened to—see in him- or herself. The unacceptable side of the self is projected—thrown forward—on to someone else who can carry the projection and whom it then becomes permissible to dislike or even hate. One of the side effects of this process is that the person who carries the projection never becomes known for who they actually are. Indeed, knowledge of the real person behind the projection would require the projector to withdraw the projection (and most probably dump it on someone else!).

I am less concerned here with this individualized form of projection. It goes on in every workplace and is part of the stuff of human relationships which many people learn to recognize and cope with as best they can—both as projectors and projectees. Rather, I want to focus on the way it works, usually unconsciously, at the group level, for there it can both do much harm and be much harder to treat. Vega Zagier Roberts provides a helpful example.[78] At a residential care home, the severely incapacitated patients, for whom there was no hope of significant improvement, were separated from the less severely afflicted. The former were cared for by a group of nurses who became demoralized and ground down by both the pressures of looking after people who were, in effect, waiting to die and by the sense that they were marginalized and ignored by the rest of the staff in the institution. The latter, less ill group of patients was the focus of the attention of the paramedic professionals and therapists, who argued that the patients derived more benefit from their services than would the seriously incapacitated. Unconsciously, however, the paramedics felt guilty about abandoning the severely ill, for they suspected that though the work would be much less rewarding, it was not wholly true that the severely ill would derive *no* benefit from, for example, speech therapy. And who is to weigh benefits in these cases anyway?

At the unconscious level, the paramedics handled their guilty feelings by blaming the nurses for their lack of co-operation, their defeatism, their lack of creativity in their care of the severely incapacitated. What the paramedics disliked in themselves—their failure to care for the most needy people in the institution—they projected on to the nurses. Working relationships between the two groups were so bad that they began to endanger the effective working of the whole institution—and had a particularly negative effect, of course, on the quality of life of the most needy group of all.

In this particular case, it was only when, quite accidentally, failures in some aspects of care by the paramedics were brought to light that they were forced to shift out of blame-the-nurses mode and look much more critically at their own work patterns, albeit with the less severely disadvantaged patients. Once they had withdrawn the projections from the nurses, they were enabled to read them as compassionate and competent professionals with whom they could and should cooperate to secure a higher standard of care for the whole patient body.

Now it might be thought that there is something special about the caring professions that makes this process of projection more likely in that environment than in the normal commercial business. I do not believe that to be true. At the individual level, one often sees, for example, the exploitive, authoritative manager[79] who, oblivious to his own insensitivities toward his own subordinates, complains endlessly about the arrogance and bossiness of his superiors. Unconsciously ashamed of his own ways of relating to his staff, he projects that guilt on to the only people who can carry the projection, those who mirror the authority he cannot handle properly.

But if it is easy to spot at the individual level, what of the group level in the commercial environment? One of the most common examples, in my experience, is the stuff that gets projected onto the other in the case of mergers, acquisitions and takeovers. Much of it is the outward expression of what gives particular form to this anxiety; i.e., how much of this really belongs to the group itself?

A building materials firm took over a smaller rival and proceeded to integrate its operations into its own structures to maximize the cost savings that had inspired the takeover. In the process of integration, the sales staff of the rival were surprised to find that the new owners were insistent upon going through all the detailed documentation relating to past sales of a certain product. What was especially surprising was that it was a product that the larger firm was known to supply very competitively, so much so that the sales of the smaller rival had dwindled rapidly. Why, then, choose *that* product as the subject of this intensive inquiry, with the implication that the sales force of the smaller company had not been doing its job, or had, in some way, been acting improperly. It was only much later that it emerged that the larger company had been cheating on the specifications, and had thus been able to cut the price and scoop the market. The inquiry had been motivated—at least in part—by a fear that the smaller company had known of this deceit—or *had been involved in the same malpractice*. Once it became clear that neither supposition was correct, the inquiry was dropped. "They made us feel like criminals," reported one of the senior sales managers of the smaller company. "It never occurred to us that it was they who had been acting dishonestly. It was as if they could not believe that we hadn't been up to the same game."

How far the surveillance of the smaller company was motivated by all too conscious fear and how far by less conscious guilt need not detain us here. What is important in this context is that the imputation of criminality to the smaller company was not only unjust and inappropriate, but also made the bedding-down process much more difficult and conflictual than it need have been.

It is not hard to find parallels to this projection in the development field. One quick example will suffice. In Transkei a development worker managed, against great odds, to link his village to a mountain stream and thus supply the village, four miles distant, with an inexhaustible supply of clean water. Hugely pleased with the outcome, he was dismayed by the hostility of the villagers, and even more so by the repeated cutting of the pipe. It eventually came out that the villagers felt guilty that *they* had good water, but that their cousins in the next village did not. They projected their guilt feelings on to the aid worker, accusing him of bad magic, and ultimately destroyed his handiwork as a punishment of his magic.

I want to hold over a discussion of the important role projection plays in organizations and the need to be aware of this in our consideration of the appreciative approach until I have introduced the second and more difficult dimension of this topic. Again Vega Zagier Roberts, this time in association with Anton Obholzer, provides a classic example.[80] They give a case history of Thorne House, a progressive therapeutic community for the treatment of disturbed adolescents. The functioning of the community was jeopardized by continuous sharp disagreements between two members of staff, one very anti-authoritarian, laid-back and permissive in his attitudes to the behaviour of the inmates, the other more disciplinarian, controlling and demanding in his attitudes.[81] The disagreements between these two surfaced at every staff meeting and quickly dominated discussion to the point where the rest of the staff were either bored or irritated. In either case the real need of the inmates and the community as a whole went unaddressed—with the predictable negative consequences.

Now Roberts and Obholzer argue, in my view persuasively, that what was going on was that these two were carrying the projections of the community as a whole. The *community* could not make up its mind what it, as a whole, thought about the role of discipline in such an environment and therefore projected on to the two people most able to carry them the extremes of the two sides of the argument—permissiveness and authoritarianism. It would only be when the whole community could grasp the nettle, decide an agreed line and implement it coherently, that the projections would be withdrawn and these two unfortunate men be allowed to become reasonable, rational beings who could cooperate in implementing whatever policy had been decided. For on this account they were more victims than perpetrators. Certainly both were accepting the projections laid on them and playing into them, lacking the capacity to stand back and see what their endless wrangling was doing to the institution. But that is to ask a lot of them: Roberts and Obholzer see them as, at least in part, being unconsciously manipulated by the rest of the community into playing roles that everyone in the community needed to accept for themselves—instead of dumping on to these wretched men.

A Third World example from my own experience is sited in Zambia. There a tobacco producers' cooperative was falling apart through ceaseless internal wrangling between the treasurer and the chairman. One reading of this would be to see it as a power struggle between two ambitious men. But a more interesting reading is to see the treasurer carrying the great, but largely unexpressed, anxieties of the community about their inability to pay back the large loan they had received from the Ministry of Co-operatives, and the chairman carrying the community's projected desire to make large amounts of money from successfully growing tobacco. Because neither the community as a whole nor its constituent individuals felt able consciously to work through these anxieties—e.g., by talking about them openly—they obliged the co-op officials to carry them for them. And because they were, at least at one level, the antithesis of each other—if they repaid the loan, they would not be able to build proper curing sheds—the bearers of their projections were locked in perpetual conflict. The co-op eventually went out of business.

I submit that this kind of projective process is a common phenomenon in work groups of all kinds, whether in the caring services, the voluntary sector or the corporate sector. That is to say, I believe that work groups tend to project onto a few of its members—or sometimes those outside it—particular roles that are at once the incarnation of unresolved problems within the group and the embodiment of destructive processes that, left unchecked, will corrode the linkages of the group. This is to stand on its head the observation that is common currency in facilitators' circles: that groups always reflect the issues that are present in the leadership. While not denying that, it recognizes that some elements of leadership may become the repositories of unresolved conflicts or confusions within the group. As long as that projective process endures, so long will resolution likely be delayed.

Let me give another generic example. In many companies there is a reluctance to establish a time frame. People speak loosely of short term and long term, never specifying what they mean or what objectives pertain to what time frame. In an international trading company this time vagueness came to be incarnated in two directors. One was constantly demanding that decisions be made in terms of the profit and loss account this year or next, while another took the view that international trading is, by its very nature, dependent upon a network of trusting relationships which take a long time to develop. The former became increasingly impatient with the latter whom he saw as irresponsible, uncommercial and sloppy. The latter maintained that short-termism was ineffective, counter-productive, undesirable and, as he put it, "a bit sharp." One of the oddities of this situation was that these two men were old and close friends. Outside the boardroom— indeed even inside it on matters that did not trigger these issues—they related well, not necessarily always agreeing but respecting their differences and acknowledging in each other the highest integrity and sincerity. When the short-term/long-term issues raised their head, however, the atmosphere changed like a thundercloud passing before the sun. "It's as if they don't know what they are saying, or even own the tone of voice in which they are saying it," the chairman told me. "They seem to be literally out of control on this issue."

This, I think, is crucial. Of course there are major policy disagreements in many a forum that owe nothing to the unconscious projections of others. But when people begin to act, not exactly irrationally—for in this case each of the warring directors could put his case with great forensic skill and lucidity—but in ways that cease to regard the wider context, the well-being of the entity for which they are responsible, it becomes clear that they have lost a sense of perspective. That may possibly be because they are unconsciously carrying the projections of the unresolved material in the whole organization.

Certainly in the case of the international trading company, inquiry revealed that there were two views in the organization, sometimes held by the same person, and that there was near chaos at the operational level as executives were confused about the way in which they were to relate to clients and potential clients. Did they want immediate profitable business? Or did they want a long-term relationship which might mean a less profitable deal this year but the long-term prospect of building a greater volume of business? Lack of clarity on this was endangering the business—and forfeiting the trust and respect of potential clients—with the result that there was a great deal of latent anxiety around this issue. (In this particular case it was made a great deal worse by the fact that most executives were paid a low set salary but a very high profits-related bonus. The unresolved tension in the business at large was therefore also an unresolved tension in the personal finances of the executives.)

What has the appreciative approach to offer to organizations suffering from the various manifestations of projection that we have been reviewing? It might be helpful to note how the projective processes break down into a number of elements. There are, first, the unconscious fears, anxieties, guilts and envies in the individuals or units that are doing the projecting. Second, there is the search, almost always unconscious, for someone or some group to carry these projections. Third there are the carriers themselves, who, again largely unconsciously, act out the role they have been assigned—or appear to do so. Fourth, there is the emotional response of the projector to the projectee. This is not at all unconscious; indeed it is usually, at least in its presenting symptoms, all too conscious! And fifth, there is the reciprocal of that; namely the way the projectee reacts to the projector and his or her emotional response. Last and in many ways most important of all, is the effect all this has on the organization's capacity to discharge its primary task.

As I have emphasized above, I do not believe the appreciative approach can or should be subverted into a kind of amateur dabbling with the individual or corporate unconscious. From that it does not follow, however, that actions, assumptions and modes of relating that have been formed by unconscious processes cannot be first illuminated and then changed through the appreciative approach. Indeed, the intensity of non-blaming, non-judgmental self-reflection that is enabled and encouraged by the appreciative conversations makes possible a bringing to consciousness of assumptions and attitudes that may well be heavily influenced, even determined, by unconscious processes. Furthermore because the emotional tone of those conversations is set by the appreciative mode—so that one is looking for the best experience—the recognition of negative unconscious material is rendered less traumatic and potentially destructive.

It may be thought odd to juxtapose *best experience* and *negative unconscious material*. The oddity lies, I think, in the expression rather than in the fact. For, when one is conducting an appreciative conversation, one is often struck by an *aha* factor when the respondent mentally juxtaposes the best with the actual or normal. Thus it is not in the least unusual to have respondents say, "That was the best. But it isn't usually like that. Usually, we spend too much time arguing or hating the other department, distrusting them, seeing what is bad about them. It is then perfectly natural, unintrusive and within the proper bounds of the nature of the conversation (that is, not straying into amateur psychology) to encourage the respondent to reflect on the nature of the difference between the best and the worst. "What is special about the good times? What do you think you and your colleagues need to do or to be in order to be able to maximize the chances of the good times becoming the norm?"

The danger is, of course, that the projective process has gone so deep that the answer will be another form of projection, a kind of dumping all the responsibility on to them. For example, the answer to the last question might come in the form, "It's not up to us. The good times will become the norm when they grow up and start behaving like adults." And of course there may well be truth in that. In the case studies I have sketched above, all the projectors could have answered in those terms. The paramedics could have said, "Don't look to us to change. It's only when the nurses stop being so uncooperative and stick-in-the-mud that things will change for the better." Or the directors of the international trading firm could have said, "It's only when he realizes the error of his position that we can give the executives a clearer idea of how they are to run the business."

The appreciative approach challenges people to look afresh at these projections precisely because it has at its heart the belief that all apprehensions of reality are socially (and we may now add psychologically) constructed. That is to say, the approach takes for granted that what I see as truth is actually my construction and needs to be held against other peoples' constructions in the search for a less partial knowledge of the wider truth. Once I start from there, it is not difficult to see that my constructions may well be distorted by the kind of projective processes I have been describing; or, to revert to the metaphor of the text, my reading is distorted by my own projective processes. I therefore *need* your reading and his and hers to show me the distortions I am putting on the text as a result of my own subjectivity.

That is why the framing of the appreciative protocol is so critically important. One cannot, of course, foresee from the start of the process every example of projection that is likely to be revealed in the course of the data collection. One can, however, ensure that the interviewers, even in a large and much-cascaded inquiry, check that the questions call back the respondents to their own experiences and their own responsibility for their own readings. For example, the response to the paramedics' attempt to dump on to the nurses would be to ask, "Tell me about an occasion when the nurses have seemed to be more cooperative." Or, "If you look back over the years, when were the nurses more cooperative? What do you think was operating then that is not operating now?" With the co-op officers, one might ask, "What has been the greatest achievement of the co-op since it was founded? How can we build on that achievement?" And with the directors, "You clearly have great difficulty with your colleague on this issue. Tell me how it is when you enjoy a sensible argument and can come to a solution that both of you can respect. What makes that an enjoyable and satisfying exchange of views? Why is the short-/long-term issue so different?"

My impression is that the first type of projection we examined is a great deal easier to deal with through the appreciative approach than is the second. In other words, the appreciative conversations are likely to alert people to the projective process whereby they are giving or receiving the personal negativities of either individuals or groups. But where individuals or groups are the *locus* of the pathologies of the organization as a whole, it requires a much greater effort of imagination and hopefulness at the stage of forming the provocative propositions to transcend what has become an important defence mechanism for the organization. (Which is no doubt one reason why framing provocative propositions is always the most testing part of the process, and why it is generally true that the more toxic the organization, the harder it finds the framing of *provocative* propositions.) It is easier to allow the projective process to deliver the organization from the need to make major and possibly disruptive decisions than to face them head on. And the temptation is for all the participants in the appreciative inquiry to collude with this, even at the cost of continued organizational malfunction.

No one can *guarantee* that the appreciative approach can break through this collusive carapace. Two variables are key: the strength of the best memories, and the courageousness of the vision that lies behind the provocative propositions. (And of course the two are linked: the better the memories, the more courageous people are likely to be in an attempt to use them to generate vision.) Where a skilled facilitator can help is to challenge the group to extend the visionary range of their provocative propositions. It is often a sign of a sick organization that its propositions will be safe, unthreatening, not only rooted in but also limited by current practice. Sometimes they will be no more than restatements of current policy, perhaps in slightly more flowery language. In that case, the facilitator, whose general stance should, I believe, be one of minimal interference, may need to draw to the group's attention what they have done—which is usually to ignore the data![82]

In these instances the data are most likely to have within them the seeds of propositions that do not accept the *status quo*, whether it is mutual bitching between nurses and paramedics, or pointless inquisitions and implied charges of dishonesty or incompetence, or failure to resolve a key strategic issue (to mention only three of the symptoms we have discussed above). The data, to repeat, will almost certainly have experiences that transcend these present ills, and the work groups may need to be recalled to those data and encouraged to take them seriously. In my experience, there are people in the work group(s) preparing the provocative propositions who are disenchanted with the *status quo*—or, perhaps more usually, are inwardly split. Half of their inner selves accepts it, the other half hates it, rebels against it, longs for something different, but, perhaps, is terrified of change. When the provocative proposition part of the process is working at its best, it is to that disenchanted half that it appeals, giving it encouragement to take risks, to move beyond the known, to share a vision of how the workplace might be.

This brings me to the third type of projection, one with which any reader who has acted as a facilitator will already be familiar. As the case studies will bring out, the facilitator works very closely with the work group, and is therefore open to the normal range of transference and countertransference transactions that are common in such relationships. I want to focus on two specific examples of transference, partly because they are likely to surface in an inquiry and partly because they will act as exemplars of a wider range of phenomena which facilitators may well meet.

Work groups naturally find the work associated with an appreciative inquiry strange and taxing. They quickly become aware of its significance for the life of their organization and therefore of the gravity of the responsibility which they have assumed. Even if everything goes smoothly, without complications or conflicts, they are still likely to feel that they are on the edge of their individual and corporate competence. The question then arises: how do they cope with those feelings?

One obvious way is to project their feelings of insecurity and incompetence on to the facilitator. They may do that in one—or more confusingly in both—of two ways. They may see the facilitator as parent, especially as a demanding parent and relate to him/her in ways that they have learned, in their childhood, to cope with that aspect of their own parents.[83] Or, they may see the facilitator as child, as someone who wants them to play, to be irresponsible (e.g., in framing *provocative* propositions), to challenge accepted norms, conventions and authority structures. (Indeed, one of the classic defences against the threat that the appreciative approach may represent, especially in the early days of its application, is to dismiss it as just a game, as not serious, or unprofessional.)

Typically, these projections will generate emotional reactions, sometimes much stronger reactions than seem appropriate to the issue in hand, to the facilitator. They may take the form of personal attacks, of carping criticism, of withdrawal of cooperation, of deliberate failures to do the work on the one hand, or of condescending, patronizing behaviour, or mockery on the other. These reactions are not, of course, unique to the appreciative approach, but they do represent a particular threat to the approach as they make it the harder to hold the group in the appreciative mode—without which the inquiry will degenerate into a traditional bit of half-baked research on best practice.

It is therefore important that the facilitator understands what is going on and, first and most important, does not intimate either consciously or even unconsciously that s/he is prepared to accept these projections. As John Heron has pointed out, for example, one might do so quite unconsciously by something as simple as the tone and timbre of one's voice.[84] An authoritative, let-me-tell-you voice immediately plays into the parental projections, and a pleading or defiant voice immediately plays into the child projections. In either case, the group is unlikely to be able to relate satisfactorily to the facilitator or maximize its own chances of deep learning. The need, then, is to let the group see that just as they, like everyone else, read the text of the organization in their own way, so they read the facilitator in their own way—in ways shaped by their own past, with its conscious and unconscious memories of, amongst other things, their own childhood.

I am emphatically not suggesting that it is the facilitator's role to offer the work group some kind of psychotherapeutic counselling. That is not his or her task and to go down that road is both dangerous and anti-task. What I am suggesting, however, is that it is part of the facilitator's role to be aware of the unconscious processes at work and, when the occasion demands it, to point out to the group what they are doing and why it is not acceptable.

Indeed this can itself become an occasion for *demonstrating* the appreciative approach. Rather than saying, "You are making me into a demanding father figure and are relating to me as you probably related to such figures in your own childhood. Please stop it…," a way of dealing with the same situation that is more congruent with the appreciative approach is to say something along these lines.

"I quite understand how you are feeling… (angry or anxious or fearful or envious)…We all have these feelings in the kind of work situation we are all in at the moment. The question is, how can we best deal with them? You *can* of course dump them all on me. That is the easiest thing to do, and in some ways the most natural. But I am not at all sure it is the most creative or productive, not least because it makes it difficult for us to work together effectively. Maybe you need to acknowledge the strength of your feelings to yourself, and so far as you feel comfortable doing so, to each other. Once you have owned your feelings and come to accept them as natural reactions to your position, maybe we can get back to a healthy relationship of mutual trust and regard, and address our task with all the vigour and creativity that this work group shows at its best."

There are three important messages here. First, it is normal to feel as they do. Second, they need to own those feelings; in a counselling situation, one would talk about "working through them." That may not be appropriate here, but to take the first step of that "working through"—i.e., recognizing that that is in fact how they feel—is necessary if they are to withdraw the projections from the facilitator. Third, the work group is normally healthy and effective. They need to hear that, and although there is a risk that this will play into their fantasy of the facilitator as a demanding parent who has been placated, it is worth reminding them of their own experience of the best of the work group so that they can consciously move toward it.

There is one other form of projection that is worth brief mention in this connection. It sometimes happens that when things go "wrong" in the course of an appreciative inquiry—and the inverted commas remind us of the *in*congruency of that kind of language with the main thrust of the appreciative approach—some members, perhaps even all the members, of the work group will project their feelings of guilt and inadequacy on to the facilitator and blame him or her for what has gone wrong. It is psychically a great deal easier to dump the blame on the facilitator—"He's in charge after all"—than to come to terms with their own feelings, especially if those feelings resonate with difficult material from earlier in life.

Again, the most constructive response is to play back to the group the way they are feeling—and the way those feelings are being allowed to determine the way they read the text. Why is the present situation being interpreted as having gone wrong? Whose reading is that? Is it the only reading? And why is the situation constructed as one where blame is a helpful category? Who does it help to read the text that way and why? A great deal of sensitivity and skill is required to enable a group that is caught in blaming mode to shift back to the appreciative mode. That takes us into the wider skills of facilitation which I do not intend to pursue here.[85]

4. Stereotypes

Stereotypes are, at one level, a special case of projection. That is to say, one way in which stereotypes come to be developed is by my splitting off parts of my own unconscious emotions and dumping them on groups of roughly similar people out there. Thus my split-off meanness gets dumped on Scotsmen or my split-off aggression gets dumped on football hooligans. Or, for that matter, Joe's zest for life may be projected on to his teenage sons and his love of music on to his gifted nephew.

In the workplace the process may be identical. The laziness I fear in myself gets split off and identified with the catering department, or the greed I am so ashamed of and refuse to acknowledge is dumped on the directors whom I glibly—and stereotypically—label "fat cats."

That, however, is to give too individualized an account of the process of stereotyping. For it begs the question: Why *Scotsmen?* Why *the catering department?* Why not Canadians or the post room? It also leaves unanswered the question of why everyone else in our culture associates Scotsmen with a certain tightness, and why everyone else in this firm associates the catering department with a certain allergy to hard effort. In other words, stereotyping is both a *social* process and an individual one.

One way of looking at this would be to think of the need any group has to distinguish itself from other groups. And that need operates both for the group as a group and for the individual within the group. That is to say, the individual needs the group of which she is a member to be distinct, because she needs to build her own identity in terms of membership of the group. If her group is amorphous, boundless and excessively open, it gives her no sense of belonging to it, and therefore no reference for her own understanding of who she is. Tribes are strong; nations are weak.

At the same time the group as a whole needs to differentiate itself from other groups, partly to advance a sense of group belonging but also as a way of making sense of any large organization. Groups cannot function effectively in relation to other groups if the boundaries are not in place, for it ceases to be clear who is in the group and who is not. (So that, at the simplest administrative level, it is not clear who is to receive which bits of paper or be called to which meeting.)

One of the most basic psychological mechanisms that functions for the individual and for the group to make this boundary drawing possible—even mandatory—is the simple mental process of differentiating between the in-group and the out-group. There is some evidence that this separation into "in" and "out" is very primitive developmentally. It is clearly critical evolutionarily, since in primitive conditions knowing who belongs to your in-group and who does not could make the difference between life and death.[86]

The social ramifications of this process are far-reaching; indeed, some social psychologists see in it the roots of war.[87] Organizationally, the results seem not very different! For when the out-group also has dumped on it negative projections from the in-group, harmonious cooperation is already made difficult.[88] And, as plenty of experimental evidence has shown, once stereotyping of the outgroup has taken place, the outgroup is inevitably perceived through the lens of the stereotype—*and counter-evidence is dismissed as faulty or unreliable.*[89] Even the most generous Scot is therefore seen as close-fisted. Stereotypes thus become self-justifying and indeed self-reinforcing, for the evidence that is consistent with the stereotype—the genuinely shirking worker from the catering department—is seized upon and remembered, while the counter evidence is ignored.

At a time when there is a much wider recognition of the damage done to corporate health and effectiveness by racism and sexism, and to developmental progress by tribalism and ethnic intolerance, it is hardly necessary to give case examples of the negative impact of this process of stereotyping; but here are two slightly unusual ones. In one famous British hospital, known for its research record, the orthopaedic department had become stereotyped as a low-tech, unexciting plumbers' haven. It was therefore starved of funds and staff by the fashionable departments that could boast of hi-tech innovations that attracted international interest. The paradox was, however, that there was much greater demand from patients for the services of the orthopaedic department than there was for some of the hi-tech departments that were creaming off scarce resources. Even when a national auditing body demanded a reallocation of resources in favour of the over-stretched orthopaedics department, the majority of consultants in the hospital still spoke disparagingly of the department and regarded the reallocation as a waste of money. In this example, the stereotyping of one discipline as low-tech had contributed to a pattern of resource use that diverted the hospital from its primary task, the relief of human sickness.

My second example has been chosen because it illustrates another organizational effect of stereotyping, the tendency of stereotyped groups and individuals to *act into the stereotype*, and thus reinforce the stereotype. At a major British steelworks, the relationship between management and trades unions were not good, with many of the predictable results. Conducting an inquiry into the causes of the friction, it became clear to me that management had stereotyped the union leaders as bolshie, shrill, thick, unrealistic and time-wasting. (They had also stereotyped their own role in a catchphrase I heard all over the plant: Managers must be allowed to manage.) One of the results of having stereotyped the union leaders in this way was that managers, convinced of their right to manage, tended to give little attention to what the union leaders were saying. By that I do not mean that there were not meetings between the two sides. There were. But at those meetings the managers did not *listen* to what the union men were saying. They had made it impossible for themselves to do so, because they had already, at the unconscious level, decided that the union people had nothing to say worth listening to. Frustrated by what they (rightly) perceived to be arrogant and demeaning behaviour by the managers who were, as it appeared, merely going through the motions without any intention of paying heed to what they heard, the union leaders became bolshie and shrill. The whole dreary cycle started all over again.

Before turning to the role of the appreciative approach in countering negative stereotyping, I want to make three short observations which put a slightly different spin on the story so far. First, there is nothing intrinsically wrong with stereotyping *per se*: it is almost certainly a necessary mental short cut. It functions like a crude filing system, waiting for the space for finer classification of data. And that is the point. As long as it seen as a holding device, a temporary stage waiting for more data, it can be perfectly healthy. That waiting, however, demands mental energy and discipline, and that is where we often fall short.

Second, I have written above of negative stereotypes. Many of our stereotypes are positive. They tend to get discussed less, but from that we should not assume that they cannot be a menace in organizational life. For they, too, invite us to read one text as definitive, rather than see it as one possible reading among many.

Third, it might be thought that the increasing use of networks and virtual organizations makes the boundedness of groups, which lies behind much stereotyping, less of an issue. On this account, the less structured an organization, the less construction of out-groups goes on and therefore the less largely negative stereotyping. That is an empirical question that has still to be tested. My own view, however, is that the more unstructured an organization becomes *formally*, the more energy people put into creating *informal* in-groups—and therefore out-groups. The reason is simple: we all need group loyalties and the association we derive from them. If they are not ready made in the workplace, we make them ourselves, perhaps along work-functional lines, perhaps not. But make them we do. And as soon as we do, the temptation to dump split-off emotions on the out-groups and then read the text of the outgroups accordingly becomes almost irresistible.

Given then that stereotyping is inevitable, what role can the appreciative approach play in liberating us, our stereotyped victims and our organizations from the baneful effects of this process? How can the appreciative approach allow us to read other texts than those dictated by stereotypes?

The answer is not quite as simple as may at first sight appear. For there is no obvious reason to assume that we do not take our stereotypes—and the blinkers they impose—with us into the appreciative inquiry. If we find ourselves interviewing someone who is carrying our projected, split-off emotions, we will not automatically withdraw that projection and the stereotype it supports just because we are supposed to be in appreciative mode.

As with the discussion of projection, then, we are back to the importance of the appreciative protocol. The significance of the appreciative protocol is central whether the inquiry we are concerned with is overtly about stereotypes or, valuing differences—or not. In the most obvious case, where the inquiry might, for instance, be about men and women working together, the appreciative protocol will itself challenge both the interviewer and the interviewee to look beyond the stereotype and try to isolate examples of when the stereotype was contradicted by experience. If the stereotype is that men are dominating and insensitive supervisors, one set of questions in the appreciative protocol may well be about the best experiences women have had of men as supervisors. The question expects the answer that sometimes men are *not* in fact dominating and insensitive, but can be the reverse. The protocol might go on to explore the conditions under which this reverse pattern of behaviour is generated and thus give both interviewer and interviewee a chance to look again at the expectation that "men are always _____ ."

The more difficult issue is when the inquiry is not overtly about questions that refer directly to stereotyping at all. It might, for example, be about determining future strategy for the company or about bedding down after a merger. In this case the appreciative protocol will be primarily concerned with quite different questions and the dangers of contamination by stereotyping are therefore all the more real. In one Third World development agency for which I acted as facilitator during an appreciative inquiry, it became evident that there was among many of the North American executives an attenuated racism that assumed that all African executives were if not incompetent then certainly hard pushed to do their jobs even moderately well. As one of the strategic issues before the group was whether to devolve more power to the Africa-based executives (the majority of whom were African) it was crucially important to establish a text beyond the stereotypes and uncover (discover) the facts that lay, as it were, on the other side of the stereotypes.

Part of the appreciative protocol therefore had to include questions about best experience of working with Africa-based personnel. Sure enough there came out a set of stories of African executives exerting themselves to the utmost and showing great determination and resourcefulness in meeting tough challenges in emergency situations. *Of course* this is not the whole story. Of course there are in that organization, as in any other, Africans who do not pull their weight, just as there are Americans, Britishers and Asians who do not. That is not the point. The real point is that we were able to use the stories of best experience to challenge the largely subliminal prejudices that had built up in the organization and send all the executives, of whatever nationality, back to the specifics of the case. Some are good in some situations, others in others. And it is only when the text you are reading defines the specific situation in which a specified person is going to work, that you can form a judgement of his likely response. In this particular organization it was interesting to watch the dynamics of the discussions around the provocative propositions change as this simple challenge to prevailing prejudices took root. It would be foolish to suggest that all racial prejudice had been extinguished. But it would be equally foolish to deny that the organization was able to make much better strategic use of its African personnel once this group of stereotypes had been revealed for what they were.

5. The appreciative approach, the unconscious and risk

In this chapter I have sought to show how the appreciative approach relates to some of the more common unconscious and emotional processes that influence the effectiveness of people at work. I want to emphasize in conclusion that I am not suggesting that the appreciative approach is some kind of panacea that can offer a quick fix to all the maladies that unconscious material can inflict on organizations. There is no such universal panacea. There are occasions when the power of unconscious pathologies is such that they need to be confronted by a professional with the relevant skills and worked through over a long period. The attraction of appreciative inquiry, by contrast, is that it is a highly participative process, with the role of the facilitator deliberately circumscribed and semi-submerged. It is in stimulating honest, open and accepting conversations across the company or work group that the strength of the appreciative approach lies. I have argued above that, handled well, that very process, without recourse to professional organizational psychologists and psychiatrists, can bring a greater awareness of the forces at work. And out of that awareness, organizational health can be increased and work effectiveness enhanced.

But that should not be taken to deny the possibility that the surfacing of unconscious material and the need to confront it both in the work group and in the organization at large can be a painful and distressing business. Those who imagine that appreciative inquiry is by definition a pain-free, contented chewing of the organizational cud of recalled best practice need to bear in mind that any attempt at depth learning within an organizational setting is likely to exact its own psychic price. There is no such thing as a free crunch.[90]

For that reason, embarking on appreciative inquiry is a risk. That will become familiar as a theme throughout this book. *Any* organizational or community intervention is a risk, and the more participative it is, the greater risk because the less the control that can be exerted. That risk is raised to a higher power if the group as a whole is dealing with emotions and unconscious material that may be deeply unsettling, even when raised within an appreciative mode of operation. The risk, however, has to be put into a context in two senses. First, I believe the risk is not that things get out of control or that raw emotion and unconscious fears, anxieties and projections take over and destabilize the organization in a potentially lethal way. The real risk, as I have hinted above, is that the participants in the process play safe and do not touch the kind of material that is actually playing havoc with the organization's health and effectiveness.

Second, any organization contemplating going down this route has to ask itself this question, Which is the greatest risk: (1) going on as we are?; (2) initiating a problem-focused process?; (3) initiating an appreciative inquiry, knowing that it obliges us to face stuff we would rather avoid? It is usually when organizations have rejected the first option—because they know that in the long run it will be self-defeating—that they consider the second. It may still require a degree of organizational courage to begin the process. In the next chapter we will begin to see some of the dimensions of that courage.

For in the next five chapters, I take the reader through a "factional" account of an appreciative approach. It is factual in the sense that all the issues are real, all have happened, all are drawn from life. It is fictional in the sense that the study is a pastiche of many actual interventions, with some liberties taken in order, in content and in setting.[91] I have chosen to demonstrate the appreciative approach in action rather than give a more extended theoretical introduction because there is a danger of over-theorizing what is essentially a praxis.

---

64 G. Vickers, *op. cit.*, p. 153.

65 Long and Newton, *op. cit.*, p. 6.

66 See for instance Anthony Joseph Barrett, *Sacrifice and prophecy in Turkana cosmology*, Paulines, Nairobi, 1998. Barrett does not make the link to the stream of thinking in Western psychoanalytic circles that I mention in the text, but he does show how specific events, including dreams, focus the anxieties of the Turkana.

67 The original article was I. Menzies Lyth, "A case study in the functioning of social systems as a defence against anxiety: A report of the nursing service of a general hospital," *Human Relations*, 13, 1960, pp. 90-121. But see too her later book, which has other examples of the same idea: *Containing anxieties in institutions: Selected essays*, Vol. 1, London: Free Association, 1988.

68 See M. Horowitz, *Psychological responses to serious life events: The denial of stress*, New York: International Universities Press, 1983.

69 See Jacques Choron, *Death and Western thought*, New York: Collier, 1963; and Ernest Becker, *The denial of death*, New York: Free Press, 1973.

70   For this distinction, see H. C. Kelman, "Three processes of social influence," in *Public Opinion Quarterly*, 25, 1961, pp. 57-78.

71   See C. Argyris, *Strategy, change and defensive routines*, Boston: Pitnam, 1985.

72   Some writers see this containment as the role of management. For example, Jon Stokes, "Institutional chaos and personal stress," in Obholzer and Roberts, *op. cit.*, p. 128, but compare Obholzer's own more judicious summary in his *Afterword*, p. 206.

73   This is of course a famous pathology, well analyzed early in the history of the discipline by Elliott Jacques in his famous study of Glacier Metal. See his 'Social systems as defence against persecutory and depressive anxiety' in M. Klein, P. Heimann and R. E. Money-Kyrle, *New directions in psycho-analysis*, London: Tavistock, 1955.

74   It thus gives substance to the emotional possibilities of the depressive position which otherwise remains abstract and unrooted—and therefore vulnerable to transition back into the paranoid-schizoid position.

75   For a good and relevant review of Klein's work, albeit with major adaptations of some of Klein's ideas, see C. Fred Alford, *Melanie Klein and critical social theory*, New Haven: Yale, 1989.

76   It is significant that in the most thoroughgoing attempt to apply Kleinian ideas to group or social environments, Fred Alford readily admits that he has had to distort or elaborate some of Klein's own ideas. See his *Melanie Klein and critical social theory*, *sup. cit.* Historically, it was Wilfred Bion and David Winnicott who applied the Kleinian approach to groups.

77   That is why some practitioners seek to avoid the notion of the *analysis of data*, and prefer to stay in storytelling/story-listening mode at this "syneralysis" stage. See G. R. Bushe, "Advances in appreciative inquiry as an organization development intervention," *Organization Development Journal*, Fall, 1995.

78   "Till death us do part: Caring and uncaring in work with the elderly," Obholzer and Roberts, *sup. cit.* pp. 75-83.

79   The phrase, indicating one end of a spectrum which runs from authoritarian to participative, is that of R. Lickert, *The human organization*, New York: McGraw Hill, 1967.

80   *op. cit.*, pp. 129-138.

81   Notice that these two sit at the opposite ends of Lickert's spectrum above.

82   For a further comment on the facilitator's role when the work group is being unadventurous in its presentation of provocative propositions, see sections 4 and 5 of chapter 10.

83　They may also idealize the facilitator, especially as a way of improving the bond between the members of the work group itself. I do not pursue that possibility here. For a Kleinian treatment of this, see Otto Kernberg, *Internal world and external reality: Object relations theory applied*, Northvale NJ: Jason Aronson, 1985.

84　John Heron, *Group facilitation: Theories and models for practice*, London: Kogan Page, 1993, pp. 52-53.

85　The interested reader is referred to John Heron, *The facilitator's handbook*, London: Kogan Page, 1989; and J. Mulligan and C. Griffin (eds.) *Empowerment through experiential learning*, London: Kogan Page, 1992. This may sound as if the facilitator's role is to avoid all blame because he or she never makes a mistake. As part 2 will make abundantly clear, facilitators do make mistakes and need to own them publicly to minimize the damage. But that is quite different from accepting the improper projections of the work group.

86　In a post-evolutionary sense, this was of course the point of the famous experiments by Sherif. See his *In common predicament: Social psychology of intergroup conflict and cooperation*, Boston: Houghton-Mifflin, 1966.

87　See Anthony Stevens, *The roots of war: A Jungian perspective*, New York: Paragon House, 1989.

88　Indeed, this can be the starting place of the "vicious cycles" Senge writes about in *The fifth discipline, sup. cit.*, pp. 82f.

89　See C. S. O'Sullivan and F. T. Durso, "Effect of schema-incongruent information on memory for stereotypical attributes," in *Journal of Personality and Social Psychology*, 47, 1984, pp. 55-70.

90　I am well aware that many practitioners will disagree and that this aspect—the psychic vulnerability implied by appreciative inquiry—has not been acknowledged in the modest literature currently available. That I think is because those who have contributed to it have tended to neglect the role of the unconscious in group life, an oversight I have tried to correct, in however a preliminary a way, in this chapter.

91　By this kind of collation of factual material into one extended case study the main story line of which is fictional, I have felt able to use direct speech and report on affective shifts which would otherwise be bound by the normal conventions and courtesies of confidentiality.

Part 2
Anatomy of an appreciative inquiry

Chapter 5
Making a start

1. Getting underway

In this part, I will take the reader through a step-by-step account of an appreciative inquiry from a severely practical perspective. Some of the theoretical issues we have been looking at in the last three chapters will naturally re-emerge, but the object of these chapters is not to pursue them, but to show how an appreciative inquiry is designed and implemented.

Immediately we are up against one particular problem in that an appreciative inquiry does not exist in a vacuum. It is a response to a particular situation, usually but by no means exclusively, concerned with an organizational or community issue and within that broad frame, covering anything from fostering collaboration to finding a new marketing strategy. It might be concerned with envisioning a new form of work or evaluating a past program. Now, clearly, the *design* of the appreciative inquiry will be affected, perhaps even determined, by its context. Indeed it is in fitting the design most appropriately to the context that the facilitator makes his or her biggest contribution. And to that extent these chapters have to be read with a good deal of caution, and they have to be read against the detailed descriptions of actual appreciative inquiries in part 3 of this book. For it is most important that the reader does not get the idea that there is one correct formula which can be slapped willy nilly on any situation and expected to work. Appreciative inquiry is not a mechanistic procedure, like double-entry bookkeeping or finding the square root of a prime number, in which, providing you follow the requisite steps, you will emerge with the right answer. It is a deeply human process, seeking to tap into the memories and imaginations of a large number of people, all of whom are different, many of whom are bruised, most of whom are, at some level, anxious and confused. It is about enabling people to read many texts in the same organization, and to learn to respect each other's preferred text. The beginning of appreciative inquiry wisdom, then, is the acknowledgement of the situational specificity of any particular design.

That having been emphasized, it is, of course, true that there are likely to be common features of anything that is recognizably appreciative inquiry. And, more than those procedural features, there is likely to be a continuity of feel, of approach, of world view. And that is true whether we are dealing with a large corporation in New York or London, or a tiny co-op or credit union in rural Africa. The process will have the same feel. For as I shall repeat many times, the core of appreciative inquiry is not actually the doing of it, but the being of it.

Having thus shared my predicament in planning these chapters, I shall proceed thus: I shall introduce the reader to a stock corporate situation (in fact a fictionalized amalgam of actual cases) and then explain how the appreciative inquiry developed, looking carefully at the main features and explaining why it was designed as it was; how it might otherwise have been designed; what happened and what might have happened. In this way I hope to catch some of the openness of the process and challenge the reader to be on his or her toes as we follow the inquiry through. From time to time, however, I shall be obliged to depart from the narrative and explore substantive issues at some length. This will inevitably give a slightly jumpy feel to the exposition but I shall try to minimize that with suitable summaries and recapitulations as we go along.

There is one more important prefatory comment. I have chosen to relate the narrative from the point of view of the facilitator, primarily because that is the perspective I know best. There are, however, other readings of each of the events recounted in the following chapters. Many of the key developments would have looked very different to each of the main actors: members of the board, employees, customers and other stakeholders. In other words, the narrative that follows could be written in many, many versions and the gaps between those versions might prove to be surprisingly large. I have sometimes indicated such gaps where I was very conscious of them or where they were especially relevant to the process of the inquiry itself. I am all too aware, however, that there are many that I have ignored and more that I was not at the time, and am still not now, even conscious of. The reader should therefore always bear in mind that this is one person's story; it is by no means the only story that could be written.

2. The context

The company that was the subject of the appreciative inquiry was a fast-growing, relatively young private health care provider in the UK. Healthco, as I shall call it, had begun in 1985 when a failing conglomerate span off its private nursing homes as a separate entity through a highly leveraged management buy-out. Four managers had assumed control and had, by the time of the appreciative inquiry, nearly finished repaying the £10 million loan they had taken to finance the deal. They were thus, at least in a financial sense, about to become their own masters. This was, therefore, a good moment to look at the future direction of the company.

So far Healthco had offered generalized nursing home accommodation, mainly for short stay, physically affected patients. Some of the nursing homes had quite well-equipped operating theatres, capable of handling routine surgery for all the major surgical disciplines. All had developed paramedical therapies, such as physiotherapy, speech therapy, occupational therapy and nutritional counselling.

The bread and butter of the business, however, was recuperative treatment—patients coming in for three to six weeks after major surgery, strokes, bad falls, accidents or serious illness. Occupancy levels for this type of patient were in the 90-plus percent area and the profit per bed from this class of patient was substantially higher than the more expensive surgical cases.

The joker in the pack was two newer units catering for elderly patients with moderate to severe senile dementia, known in the trade as elderly mentally infirm patients or, more colloquially, as EMIs. Demand for places in such units far exceeded supply, prices were therefore high, costs were moderate. Profit margins, therefore, were extremely attractive. Furthermore, two insurance companies, selling total-care policies, were anxious to enter into arrangements with the company whereby they would make available cheap capital to finance this type of accommodation and guarantee specified usage rates. The business arguments for expansion in this area looked overwhelming.

However, some of the caring professionals, from the senior nurse-managers to the paramedics to the most junior auxiliaries were less than enthusiastic about this development. Few of these critics were trained in mental nursing, fewer still wanted to be so trained in the future, and all of them feared that the centre of focus of the company would follow the money to life-long care for EMIs, thus leaving them increasingly marginalized. There were rumours, indeed, that the long-run plan was to dispose of the short-term care units and concentrate exclusively on long-term care. Resignations had doubled in the last nine months, staff morale was low and sinking, and relationships between the directors and the staff at all levels, hitherto unusually close and harmonious, were approaching total breakdown.

So how did appreciative inquiry enter the picture? As often (too often?) happens, the connection was accidental. Two of the directors of the company had been to a conference in Atlanta, Georgia, where they had met some senior practitioners from the Cleveland Clinic in Ohio. That clinic, one of the biggest and most complex medical facilities in the US, was famously the scene of one of the first applications of appreciative inquiry, carried out by a team under the leadership of David Cooperrider of Case Western Reserve University in Cleveland.[92] The Cleveland Clinic people were enthusiastic about the experience and about the continuing benefits they thought the Clinic was deriving from the appreciative inquiry. That enthusiasm inspired the two Healthco directors to explore the possibility that the approach could help them through what was beginning to look like a very stormy patch in their company's development.

I recount this at length because it frequently happens that clients come having vaguely heard about appreciative inquiry and determined to give it a try. Like most practitioners, I always wince when I detect this over-pragmatic approach.

For it is by no means clear that appreciative inquiry *is* the most appropriate intervention and I hope for a more open-minded discussion with all the parties about what that intervention might turn out to be. Here, as so often, the two directors with whom I had initial contact were at least in theory open to other methods; in reality the Cleveland Clinic people had done *too* good a job and the minds of the directors were virtually made up. What was good enough for the Cleveland Clinic would be good enough for them.

3. The design of the process

Reflecting on the criteria we examined at the end of chapter 2 in the light of what I was beginning to learn of Healthco, I was at least reassured on the question of size. With less than 300 in all on its payroll, it was not so large an organization that one would have to think immediately of complicated cascaded interviews and computer-driven data analysis. Some of the other criteria we looked at in chapter 2, however, looked more uncertain. The directors seemed to have taken a position on appreciative inquiry (thanks to the propaganda from Cleveland); and, more significantly, relationships between them and the staff, especially the senior nursing staff, were now so fragile that the latter had not been consulted and would likely resist anything that they saw as a device or ploy by management to win them round to a course of action to which a significant and vocal number of them were increasingly opposed. Participation, trust and openness, all essential ingredients of the process and all therefore highly desirable as *prior conditions* were seriously compromised. How to proceed?[93]

With some difficulty I persuaded the board to allow me to talk to as many of the staff as I could manage with an entirely open agenda. There was to be no expectation that I was to sell anything; I was merely to gather impressionistic data on how the staff was feeling about the way the company was going and the ways in which it might develop in the future. It was with even greater difficulty that I persuaded the board to let me approach, in the same spirit, other stakeholders— patients, their carers or relatives, medical consultants, suppliers and the major insurance companies whose cover financed much of the care. This was to be a quick and dirty operation, in which I wanted to assess whether the key criteria outlined above could in fact, with the necessary care and sensitivity, be met to a degree that would give appreciative inquiry a good chance of being accepted.

What came out of this pre-appreciative inquiry phase of the work? In some ways less than I had hoped and expected, but there were four nuggets of information that would affect the design of the inquiry in major ways. First it became clear that the staff felt patronized and demeaned by the directors. "There's a lot of stroking but not much listening," was how one senior physiotherapist put it. Even the consultants were aware of this, though they tended to put it in more professional terms—that is in terms of the conflict between commercial criteria, which they tended to think were given too much weight, and professional and medical criteria. This suggested two things: the directors were reading their relationship with their staff wrong; and there was indeed a great plurality of readings within the company of the relationship between profit and the provision of care.[94]

The second finding of this pre-inquiry was that patients were aware of a chasm between the professionally trained nurses and paramedics on one hand and the auxiliary staff on the other. And, surprisingly, it was the auxiliary staff who were most appreciated for their compassion, readiness to take extra trouble and sensitivity to the patients' needs and moods. This class divide was less commented upon by the staff themselves though it was clear to me that the professional staff regarded it as a waste of my time talking, sometimes at length, to the auxiliary staff. I began to wonder if there not some unconscious process going on. Maybe the nurses felt guilty that they were not able to give the time to individual patients that they would like to, and were unconsciously resentful of the fact that that the auxiliaries were better able to do so. Whatever the truth of that, it was already clear that nurses and auxiliaries were reading the organizational text in subtly different ways.

Third and most surprising, there was a good deal of reluctance to talk about the future of Healthco at all. It was as though it had become a no-go area. Even appreciatively framed questions—e.g., what values that Healthco has established over the last five years do you think it should hold on to in the future?—generated much less of a response than I am accustomed to. The future was too frightening or distasteful to contemplate. Not so much a plurality of readings, then, as a possibly pathological refusal to read that bit of the script at all. I wondered what would happen when we came to try to draft provocative propositions. Some significant changes would have had to have taken place in the collective consciousness if that part of the process was going to yield anything. A mental note to myself: trust the process.

Finally and much less surprising, I noticed a strong idealization of the past, the good old days phenomenon.[95] The good days when relationships were much closer and more harmonious; when everyone, from the finance director to the ward orderly, turned up for the 90th birthday of a patient; when staff worked overtime without thinking about it if they could make a difference to a patient's health and comfort. The phenomenon is, of course, very common in any organization in difficulty, but here there seemed an especial poignancy and wistfulness, and I was struck by the contrast between the readiness to reminisce about the past and the fear—or so it seemed—to think aloud about the future. Here, then, was one bit of the text that everyone—or nearly so—seemed to be reading in the same way.

What I had not picked up from this pre-survey was a clear sense that appreciative inquiry would *not* be appropriate. It would need extremely careful presentation and the inclusion of a wide group of patients, ex-patients and home-based carers—but it would, I was confident, be supported by the staff. More substantively, I had to find a way of shifting the mental effort of the company as a whole from the past to the future, in a way that would not be resented as an attempt to force the board's plans down unwilling throats.

With some trepidation, then, I presented to the board a plan for an appreciative inquiry which would focus on the future role of Healthco. To be called *Whither Healthco?*, it would be based on the different units of the company and would involve *all* employees, consultants, carers and as many patients as possible. Based on the earlier conversations, I decided not to include insurance companies or suppliers, neither of whom had had much to contribute. (Some members of the board pressed for the inclusion of the insurance companies, but their motivation in doing so was so transparent, they did not get overwhelming support and I was able to resist it.)

Like most boards, Healthco's wanted to know how long it would all take, how much staff time it would gobble up, as the least enthusiastic member put it, how soon they would get a report on which action planning could be based. The whole tone of this set of discussions left me deeply uneasy. Too many members of the board—though mercifully not all—were still thinking in terms of forcing through their own plans on an unwilling staff. They were seeing me—and what I represented in terms of the appreciative inquiry—as an accomplice in carrying out their will, not as an independent consultant with his own integrity whose commitment was as much to the patients and the ward auxiliaries as it was to the board. To use another vocabulary, they were stuck in the old paradigm and they were trying to get me to collude with that. Or, to use a third language, they were reading the text of the organization in a very hierarchical way, and had not yet learned to read it as a participative process.

What worried me about that was not only what it said about the board and the way in which it would react to the results of the appreciative inquiry, but the ease with which this old-paradigm thinking would communicate itself, perhaps unconsciously, to the rest of the company. And I knew that if it did so, the appreciative inquiry process would, however carefully I designed the process, become an empty charade; indeed, one that would have within it the seeds of great destructiveness.

4. Getting the board on board

I was so exercised about this that I decided, unusually, to make it a condition of my continuing to work for Healthco that the board spend a whole day in retreat working on issues of participative inquiry, the social construction of meaning and its implications for decision-making. They needed to learn to read the organization in new ways. In presenting this condition to the board, I knew that two members (who needed such time most acutely) would resist it strongly, two would support it, and two would be uncertain. I was, however, confident of my ground. Unless the board could be educated out of old-paradigm thinking before the appreciative inquiry started, there was a real danger, given the dynamics already in play, of their attitudes contaminating the process. Such contamination would serve well neither them nor me.

After two hours of debate, the board voted four to two to go ahead on my conditions.

It is worth reflecting for a moment on the basic issue this story presents. It is, of course, by no means unique, but it raises the fundamental procedural point: do you need to convert the board (or its equivalent) before you begin to work with the organization at large? In general, most consultants would say no, but at Healthco there were a number of factors operating that are common individually but less so in combination; specifically

- The directors were all personally involved in the company and known—sometimes quite well known—to most of the staff.

- Everyone seemed aware of a marked deterioration in the quality of relationships between staff and board.

- It was widely known that the board had a development plan in embryo of which most staff were suspicious and to which many were opposed.

- And, taken as a whole, the board itself was in transition. The two directors who had been to the Atlanta conference were beginning to realize that what was at stake was not just selling a board decision to the employees, and then obliging them to implement that decision, but a fundamental shift in the way decisions were made and reviewed throughout the company. Their more conservative colleagues, however, were just about ready to think of selling a board decision, rather than communicating it. There was no way, however, that they were going, as they put it, "to be told by a lot of women in white uniforms how to run this company." With such an ideological rift in the (small) board, I judged it essential to gain time to explain at length the nature of the issues before embarking on a process that the conservatives might otherwise disown, subvert or wreck.

As I have implied above, Healthco was unusual in having all these features in one smallish company. In cases where there is a selection of them but not the totality, it is harder to know whether it is necessary or desirable to take the board through a pre-immersion process before beginning the appreciative inquiry. The case of the Canadian organization mentioned in chapter 2 is a good example. There the CEO was firmly, almost pathologically, locked into the old paradigm and single-handedly made it impossible to proceed with an appreciative inquiry. It is highly arguable, however, that had I been more skilful in persuading him and his board to reread the text of the organization, he could have learned that his fears needed to be put into a much wider perspective. He might then have been prepared to go ahead, and he and his organization could have been saved much later annoyance.

5. The board retreat

Of what did the Healthco retreat consist? There were three components. After a fairly detailed account of the intellectual background of appreciative inquiry, we moved into a session of sharing hopes and fears for the application of appreciative inquiry. This proved illuminating and liberating for the conservatives who could now express their anger at what they saw as their colleagues' abdication of their authority and responsibility. It was the two uncommitted directors who handled this set of emotional reactions; I needed to say very little. By emphasizing the unusually important role played by the commitment and enthusiasm of the staff in delivering the highest quality of care, they could show that it was counterproductive to treat the staff like machines. As one of them put it, "Healthco stands or falls, commercially, by the reputation we have for caring professionals delivering top-quality care to all our patients. That is as true for the EMIs as it is in the surgical areas. Commercially it's got to make sense to do anything—and I mean anything—that keeps our staff on board. That is where we know we are now slipping. We've got to get back to pole position on that one or else we shall see occupancy levels fall. And that is the way to bankruptcy for a business like this."

Typically, it was this common-sense linking of commercial prudence with personnel management that began to shift the prejudices of the conservatives.

The second component was a review of modes of leadership. This was led, at his suggestion, by the chairman who described, in a low-key, non-threatening way the shifts in mainline understanding of leadership in service-oriented industries during his (long) commercial life—"from tyrant to enabler" was the way he characterized it.[96] That led to a frank discussion of the meaning of responsibility in today's boardroom, where consultation and participation are taken seriously. To my surprise it was the finance director, hitherto in the uncommitted camp, who made the strongest pitch. He drew a parallel with the auditing function: "Just as auditing used to mean matching every voucher with every cheque, and now has come to mean testing *systems* for their robustness and accuracy, so responsibility has shifted from every buck stopping on the desk of the CEO to allowing a corporate system to evolve where there are no—or at any rate a helluva lot less—bucks being passed back and forth."

The notion of appreciative inquiry as the introduction of a new *systemic* element into the company seemed to help all the directors, and not just the conservatives, see it in a much wider perspective. To some degree this was a conservative introduction to the appreciative approach—but one which worked well with this conservative group. They were beginning to think less of getting their way with the commercial development of the company and more in terms of generating a self-renewing organism that moved, as it were under its own power, in search of its own long-run commercial advantage. The rereading had begun.

That gave me the right of admission to a final session on the heliotropic principle, but rather than lecture them about it, I asked each of them to write down, in telegramatic format, what they thought gave life, energy and enthusiasm to (a) the employees of Healthco, broken down into broad functional groups; (b) themselves; and (c) patients in a Healthco facility. I then asked them to pool their results, produce a common list of not more than six factors and then ask themselves as a group what difference it would make to the company as a whole if these six were substantially increased over the next 12 months. There was a tendency in the group to express skepticism—even ridicule—at that suggestion, but they had no difficulty in seeing how a greater sense of commitment to the patients, a greater sense of doing good well, an increase in expressed appreciation and gratitude, and an increased sense of meaningfulness in their work would revolutionize the company. Although there was a subtext of "chance would be a fine thing…" even the conservative directors could sense a shift in the board's energy level as they contemplated the possibility of such a change in the emotional-learning environment. I had the impression that new texts were being glimpsed at last.

It would be false to conclude, however, that at the end of the day the board as a whole was enthusiastically committed to new paradigm thinking. That was never likely. There *had* been the beginnings of a shift. The conservatives were much less dismissive, and although one of them continued to be grudging and ungenerous in his opinions of the staff and excessively concerned with short-run profitability, as though that existed in a vacuum, the overall *geist* of the board was more open, more constructively curious and more hopeful.

It no longer seemed a foolish risk to go ahead to plan the appreciative inquiry for the whole company.

6. The wider testing of the approach

The first issue was testing out the idea on the staff and patients in general, keeping in mind the real possibility that there would be such strong resistance that the plan would have to be dropped. It was here that my earlier, pre-inquiry research proved of immense value, far more than I suspect the board ever realized. For I had built up networks of people who had had the experience of genuinely being asked for their opinions, for their impressions of working in Healthco and for their aspirations, both for themselves and for the company. It was therefore relatively easy to go back to most of these contacts, explain the nature of an appreciative inquiry and ask them to talk to their friends about it to check out if people would be prepared to give the time and energy to it. I knew better than they did at this stage how demanding that might prove. I was therefore clear that I needed some kind of legitimization before I could move ahead.

Only a tiny proportion of the staff expressed reluctance but it was clear that there remained a small core of staff, mostly older nurses, who were deeply suspicious of what they saw as an attempt to get them to agree to something that was in the interest of neither them nor the patients. Interestingly, I had spoken to none of them directly, and I began to wonder how far their hostility was an unconscious sense of pique at not having been personally consulted. If that was the situation, I was confident that the appreciative inquiry process itself would pour oil on those particular waters.

The trick, I suspected, lay in involving as many of the other stakeholders as possible. Here that seemed to boil down to the patients, both post and present and those who cared for them at home. When I approached them, I discovered them to be intrigued but puzzled. "But I know nothing about business," said one elderly lady who had been in one of the nursing homes nearly six months. "Of course, I'd be glad to help in any way, but my husband always handled our affairs." She was not alone in reacting to the suggestion that the inquiry include data from the consumers by emphasizing her ignorance. It would take time and effort to switch these people from a disabling sense of their non-competence to an appreciation of the significance of their best experiences of Healthco. That would, we eventually learned, be the turning point of the whole process. For only they could finally tell us what constituted best practice.

Broadly speaking, then, all the pieces were now in place and although some of them were suboptimally positioned, I judged that we were ready to begin planning the process in detail. Two issues stood out: who was to be on the work group that would run the inquiry? and how were the interviews to be organized? Each of these need some unpacking.

7. Constituting the work group

As in any appreciative inquiry, the work group needed to be as representative as possible, without becoming either too large or packed by people who saw their job as defending a particular sectional interest. So far as possible the key figures on the work group should be people from the company who were widely known and trusted throughout the organization. They did not need to be the "remembrancers"—they could be plugged into the process later—but they did need to have been around for long enough to have developed a sense of the tight places in the company, a sense of the history and a sense of the future possibilities. And, so far as one could tell at this stage, it would be helpful if we could avoid those who were especially anxious about the future and those who were carrying the projections of the company's unresolved difficulties.[97]

No less important than the *who* questions were the *how* questions; that is, how were names going to emerge? Given the rising levels of mutual mistrust between the board and some of the employees, this was going to be a key issue if all the factions in Healthco were going to end up owning the process, rather than seeing it as an objectionable imposition. Some kind of democratic nomination was therefore indicated. I had to trust the good sense of the bulk of the staff that we would not end up with the loud-mouthed or the hopelessly partisan.

Now it may well be the case that one can often skip the rather laborious process described in the next paragraph—*if* you can be sure that everyone will have confidence in the work group that is nominated in less participative ways. Our experience, however, is that when the going gets tough—e.g., with the appearance of ultra-provocative propositions—it is easy for those who feel threatened or otherwise uncomfortable to use the argument that the work group is somehow unrepresentative as a way of insulating themselves from its findings.

After consultation with some of the people I had met in the pre-inquiry, we came up with the following process, which may sound extravagantly baroque, but which worked well in practice. I took responsibility for forming a steering group of four whose terms of reference were limited to selecting the work group. The steering group's existence was formally notified, over my name, to every employee and to current patients, those discharged within the last six months and, where appropriate, their carers. The same letter called for direct nominations to the work group and explained that we would be seeking a balance of genders, ages, length of service with the company and functions within it. We were not settling on a size at this stage, but had in mind a group of somewhere between eight and 12. It also explained a complementary procedure by which functional groups in the company, cutting across the different units, would each be asked to draw up a list of between three and five names for forwarding to the steering group.

This somewhat convoluted process therefore gave every staff member two chances to put names forward, directly or through their cross-unit functional groups. Other stakeholders, patients and their carers, had only the one opportunity.

The cross-unit functional groups themselves constituted something of an organizational innovation. My view was that if the appreciative inquiry was going to challenge the whole company and its consumers to think afresh about its future, we needed to transcend the unit-centred thinking that was a hallmark of Healthco and ensure that participants stepped empathetically outside the safe, known world of their own immediate environment. The appreciative inquiry was a chance to ensure that people from different backgrounds and skill groups listened to each other across the frontiers of their own units, and listened to what was working, what was energizing, what brought fulfillment into lives that often felt depleted by the pain, anguish and sorrow of their clientele.

8. Drawing breath

But that is to anticipate. In the next chapter, we shall resume the story from the selection of the work group. I finish this one by highlighting some of the central practitioner-related issues that have surfaced in this chapter.

1. A request for an appreciative inquiry is not, by itself, evidence that an appreciative inquiry is the most appropriate intervention.

2. Appreciative inquiry is by its very essence a participatory process. Care therefore has to be taken to ensure that the organization as a whole is consulted and feels comfortable with the inquiry.

3. When there are serious conflicts within an organization, whether overt or covert, care needs to be taken to ensure that neither side hijacks—or is thought to have hijacked or can be represented as having hijacked—the process.

4. Old-paradigm thinking in any significant power centre of the organization is worth trying to defuse before the inquiry begins. That will usually, as in Healthco, be at board level, but it could also be at union or, just possibly, at works council level. If it cannot be defused or at least partially disarmed, the possibility of abandoning or at least postponing the appreciative inquiry has to be taken seriously. (That does not exclude the decision to carry on, but it does alert us to the higher risks involved.)

5. Pre-inquiry construction of networks within the organization can pay off handsomely, but care needs to be exercised to guard against the criticism of cronyism or nepotism.

6. The facilitator's only card is the trust people in the organization have in him or her. That is true of any intervention. It is especially true of appreciative inquiry.

7. The mirror image of that is the trust that the facilitator has, first, in the process itself and, second, in the people who are participating in it. The more experience we have of appreciative inquiry, the more this double trust seems central.

8. Choosing a work group can be the most significant intervention of all. It is the first opportunity publicly to walk the talk of collaborative inquiry. The process must be open, honest and acceptable to all parties.

9. Empirically there may well be a link between the way the work group emerges and the way the actual inquiry is structured. In terms of perception, there will almost certainly be such a link. Careful strategizing round these issues is therefore worth the effort.

10. It all takes time. Do not allow yourself to be stampeded.

11. People find learning to reread the text demanding and sometimes upsetting, another reason for giving the process time and patience.

---

92 Frank J. Barrett and David Cooperrider, "Generative metaphor intervention: A new approach for working with systems divided by conflict and caught in defensive perception," in *Journal of Applied Behavioural Science*, 26, 2, 1990.

93 A friendly critic raises the question of what would have happened if the board had approached the staff directly with the idea of an appreciative inquiry—and couched their advance in appreciative mode: e.g., "We want to find out about best practice—and what you enjoy about working here." What response would this have elicited? It is hard to be sure. It might have gone some way toward reassuring some of the more discontented, but the level of trust between the senior nurses and the top management had fallen to a position where *any* initiative would have been met with much resistance.

94 See, for example, A. Donabedian, J. C. Wheeler and L. Wyszewianski, "Quality, cost and health: An integrative model," *Medical Care*, 20, 1982.

95 See M. Beer, R. A. Eisenstat and B. Spector, "Why change programs don't produce change," *Harvard Business Review*, Nov-Dec, 1990.

96 I do not know whether he had read it, but I was much reminded of Jeffrey Pfeffer, *Competitive advantage through people: Unleashing the power of the work force*, Boston: Harvard Business School Press, 1994.

97 On this see the discussion in chapter 3.

Chapter 6
The spade work

1. Selecting the work group

In the last chapter, we saw how Healthco moved slowly through the preliminary stages of the appreciative inquiry. The board had been given exposure to some of the basic principles in an attempt to counter an authoritarian tendency that would endanger the process. The facilitator had built up informal networks among some of the key stakeholders. A steering group had organized a process for selecting the working group that would actually run the appreciative inquiry. And a start had been made in engaging people in cross-unit dialogue, which was already emerging as likely to be the most creative way to handle the appreciative interviews. I shall pick up the story with the selection of the working group.

Somewhat disappointingly, there were few direct nominations to the work group. Those that did come in were predictable. Thus the board nominated one of their number—the personnel director, one of the Atlanta pair. The administrative staff at the unit where most of the central administrative functions were concentrated nominated a young accountant, Derek, who had achieved national celebrity in ballroom dancing. The cross-unit functional groups took longer to organize than even I had expected and, because people tended not to know each other, they were slow to nominate people for the work group.

Within six weeks of the letter of invitation going out, however, we had had nominations in from each of the six cross-unit functional teams. While the members of the steering group were enthusiastic about the people thus nominated, we quickly realized we lacked representatives of the least-skilled, least-formally educated hourly paid workers. By contrast it emerged that we had a surplus of younger people with less than three years service, of people from the main administrative unit, and of women. We were short of people from the normal recuperative care units, and from the most distant regions.

What I found interesting was that in the attempt to secure a reasonable balance, considerations of effectiveness, of relevant experience, even of likely availability were forgotten. That I regarded as a healthy sign.[98] There was no attempt to pack the work group with safe workhorses or to weed out people whose style might be considered abrasive or views radical. I would be able to reassure anyone who asked that the selection process had been as objective as possible.

On the patient side, the steering group had received six nominations, five of them from former patients. Of these three were of carers and two were of former patients themselves. The sixth was of a present, long-stay patient. It was easy to decide to choose one carer and one patient, much harder to choose between them or even to decide any meaningful criteria. In the end we chose one male ex-patient, who happened to be a recently retired investment banker, and one female carer, who, until the care of her ailing mother had become overly demanding, had worked as a social worker in Islington. Some of the staff remembered her as "a bit of a tough cookie."

The steering group decided to submit a detailed report to the employees and to patients and carers who had responded in any way to our initial letter. The report would include a description of our categories and an analysis of how the nominees fitted them. It would also include photographs and brief biographies of the selected nominees, and a glowing tribute to the unnamed non-selected. With the report issued, the steering group declared itself abolished. No member of the steering group was selected for the work group, though two had been nominated (despite it having been made clear from the start that none would in fact be selected).

2. The work group forms

Personally, I felt that we had now taken a decisive step. There could be no going back and no attempt by management or anyone else to pre-empt the process. It was important now to brief the work group and encourage it to start its work as soon as possible. I was confident that once the appreciative interviews began, the sense of participation and excitement would begin to displace the nervous wariness that I could sense below the surface.

The initiation of the work group, its forming phase, is critical, and that in a number of senses.[99] The members need to understand appreciative inquiry as deeply as possible, but as none has done it before, that depth will often feel very superficial. A process of initial briefing which gives them the knowledge base without pre-determining the shape of the inquiry has therefore to be handled with some subtlety. In another sense of initiation, the group has to learn to work together and that, so far as possible, within the spirit of appreciative inquiry. And in a final sense, the group has to be briefed about the nature of and background to the inquiry. One cannot assume that everyone knows in detail the history of the company or the ways in which it is faced with tough strategic decisions.

In an ideal world one may be able to meld these three processes of initiation so that the work group begins both to build a sense of solidarity and mutual accountability as they learn the history, and to acquire a familiarity with the logic of appreciative inquiry as they get to know each other. Whether that ideal can be perfectly approached, it is clearly unsatisfactory to, for example, tell the history of the company in problem mode, and then brightly seek to introduce the group to the theory and practice of appreciative inquiry.

Team building, on the other hand, is a natural application of the appreciative approach and for Healthco, that is where we started. After the briefest scene setting which laid out, in very preliminary fashion, the object of the inquiry, I, as facilitator, suggested that we should spend the first two of our weekly two-hour sessions getting to know each other and learning to trust our common wisdom. We began with standard ice-breakers and then moved into exercises that were explicitly in appreciative mode. One such was an invitation to describe to two other people in the group a number of our peak experiences—our most exciting, our most frightening, our most mysterious, our most memorable, our most significant-for-the-rest-of-our-lives.[100] Another was to talk to someone we did not know for 30 minutes and then write a 15-line obituary on them, as for the local paper.

By the end of the second session, the feel of the group was remarkably good, with the usual in-jokes, the nicknames, the stock responses that show that a group is beginning to feel comfortable with itself. They were beginning, however, to show signs of impatience: when was the real work going to begin?

I therefore spent some time at the beginning of the third session explaining the nature of appreciative inquiry in broad outline. I emphasized especially the role of memory and of imagination, commenting that the former is easier to tap into than the latter, especially in a work setting, but that it takes a little skill to learn to tap into the best experiences-type memories, even with the former. And I went through the heliotropic principle with them, asking them to recall how they had felt in the last session when asked to recall some of their own peak experiences. By suggesting that the same principle operates at the organizational level—i.e., that an organization that is in touch with its own best practice tends to move in that direction—I persuaded them that this extended foreplay was not just fun but a significant part of learning to run the appreciative inquiry. Interestingly, the text metaphor communicated much better than I had dared hope. "So it's all about learning to read the text of the company from a new perspective," concluded the physiotherapist in the group. "Like reading the *Telegraph* as though you were reading the *Mirror*?"

There was, encouragingly, some skepticism that you can draw too close an analogy from the experience of the individual—who is admittedly energized by drawing on peak experience—to the expectation of corporate behaviour. "Won't it just heighten the general level of frustration and therefore of demoralization?" was the question from a younger nurse from one of the recuperative units. It was tempting to get into a long discussion of the relation between individual and group behaviour, from Bion to Hampden Turner, and there were times later when I wished I had done that. But I was anxious to keep the learning as experiential as possible and precisely to avoid indoctrinating this work group with theoretical ideas that I feared might contaminate the doing of the work itself. I therefore suggested that one way of constructing the idea of an organization is to conceive it as a network of individual interactions. The way the organization operates may be more than the sum of those interactions, but it cannot operate—nor even exist—apart from them. The questioner was at least half satisfied, but I was hearing that it was time to start the appreciative inquiry proper.

3. Identifying the themes of the inquiry

I therefore asked them to break into three groups and brainstorm what they thought the inquiry was all about. I knew there had been a good deal of speculation and gossip, both within the work group and within the company at large on this, and so I was a little taken aback by the shocked horror that my request evoked. After a silence, the accountant, Derek, said, "But surely you know that. Or what are we here for? Aren't you going to explain it to *us*?" There were murmurs of support.

This represented a watershed in my relations with the work group. Despite all the emphasis that I had sought to put on the notion of participative inquiry, here they were behaving like dependent children, waiting to be told what to do. In retrospect I suspected I had fostered such dependence in the early stages of the process. I had been the centre of the process, meeting people, talking about the inquiry, sitting on the steering group, writing to every one about the selection procedures and their outcomes.

Perhaps it was inevitable that in their minds I had become identified so closely with the inquiry, which after all was the only reason I had for being on company premises or in touch with any of the staff. And at a deeper level, in their anxiety, they were looking for an authority figure whom they could idealize and on whom they could dump their fears. (Two of them, I was beginning to suspect, were also dumping their aggression, but I took that to be another anxiety-response.[101])

I was going to have to deal with this carefully. Too abrupt a challenge to their dependency and its associated projections would make it hard for them to move forward, too gentle a challenge may not be taken seriously.

I pointed out therefore that the most *general* area of the inquiry was well known: how was the company going to develop over the next years, given that it was now virtually debt free, profitable and, in an expanding market, had fresh capital readily available. But that was only a very general formulation of the issue; there were many strategic and even more tactical questions implied in that overall question, and it was up to the work group to begin to tease them out so that they might form the backdrop to the questions they would be putting to the staff.

I could feel the tension in the group as they heard me out in silence. Body language was telling me that some were angry, some feeling defeated, some suspicious.

"So to help you," the body language changed immediately, "I suggest you structure your conversations within your small teams like this: Tell each other when you have been proudest to be associated with this company, when you have felt most truly yourself, when you have felt this is the right place to be and the right work to be doing, and when you have found yourself saying to yourself, 'Yes. If only it were like this all the time….' And finally tell each other your wildest dream for the future of Healthco and your part in it. Notice that only you can answer those questions. I cannot, because I have never worked here. That's why it's got to be down to you."

It is worth reflecting on this moment a little longer. What I was trying to do was to take their projections on to me—essentially as the daddy-expert—and use them as a lever to shift them into appreciative mode as they began to work (though they did not know it yet) on the appreciative protocols. By inviting them to ask each other what are known technically as generative questions about their peak experiences at Healthco, I was making it clear that they were going to have to draw on experience that I did not have. I would be around to help them and facilitate their working together but there was no way I could do their work for them.

The change in the mood of the work group was little short of astonishing. They were rearranging the chairs as soon as I had stopped speaking. They did not even wait to be told how long they were to take, and the intensity of the discussions ensured that the session lasted much longer than the scheduled span. Nor did it take long in the next session to recapture that sense of involvement in the process. The danger was that the feedback and the discussion of it would take too long, and further delay our launching the inquiry in the company as a whole. Indeed, some members of the work group told me that they felt themselves caught: on one hand they wanted to go on with their discussions both in the small teams and in the work group as a whole, on the other they were picking up from their colleagues a gathering sense of bemusement that "nothing is happening with this inquiry thing."

As a holding measure, I asked permission of the work group to draft a letter to all the employees and current patients explaining that we were working hard but that it would be a little time before we could be ready to launch the inquiry throughout the company. The letter would be signed by all the work group. This bought us a little more time, but I was conscious of the need to move now as fast as the work group was able, *subject to the condition that they went on building their ownership of the process.*

4. The appreciative protocols

It was that condition that lay behind my determination to use the exercise they had just done as the feedstock for framing the appreciative protocols. Before we could move directly into that, however, I had to establish that the work group could now answer its own question: What is the inquiry all about?

Perhaps surprisingly, all the *angst* and uncertainty of the last session had evaporated in the wake of the conversations in the small teams. In Tuckman's terminology, we had moved relatively quickly, through storming to norming. "What we have to discover," was how the Vietnamese cleaner, a surprising but as it turned out inspired nomination to the work group, put it, "is what makes this company tick and how it can tick better in the future." The accountant was naturally anxious to ensure that financial ticking was also included, but in general the work group was not then nor later hung-up on the issue of profitability. Everyone accepted that capital had to earn a good return; the real questions were seen to be much deeper than that. They were about the subtle relationships between staff, patients and society on the one hand and the role of private medicine on the other. How could the peculiar blend of resources represented by Healthco make its best contribution to medical and long-term care? Or, to put it another way, how could Healthco meet the real needs of its client group and simultaneously reward its stakeholders properly?

These statements of the central thrust of the inquiry needed the minimal of facilitation by me; my only significant contribution was to formulate the ideas of the work group in as succinct and pointed a way as I could. Its members seemed to share a sense of liberation that these issues could be talked about openly, that no questions were ruled off limits, that the accountant and the personnel director were as much a part of the group as anyone else and were ready to admit their own sense of bewilderment, uncertainty, questingness in the face of the big questions.

The group was, too, keen to stay with the big questions, to avoid trivializing the inquiry by zeroing in on less problematic issues which were more likely to produce real answers. The role of the patients' representatives was important, perhaps even determinative, here. They could speak movingly of their experience, either direct or secondhand, of high-quality care at Healthco and what it had meant not just to the sick person but to a much wider group of concerned friends and relatives. They were committed to making that as generally available as possible and therefore wanted to hold the inquiry to the meta-issues of Healthco's position in a wider environment. They therefore acted as a counter pole to the staff, especially some of the less-skilled staff, who clearly felt more comfortable with the nuts and bolts issues such as conditions of service and the details of the caring package.

I saw this tension as both healthy and creative. The question was whether the work group could use it to fashion an appreciative protocol that would do justice to both sets of concerns; be both broad and specific enough to allow the questions to be aired within an appreciative mode; and be intelligible not only to the staff but also to the patients.

At the start of the fifth session of the work group I put this question directly to them. Having explained the nature of the protocol (and why it is called that and, deliberately, not an interview schedule)[102] and the way that it would be used in forming the basis of conversations with most members of the staff and many patients, I was delighted by the immediate response from the group: "You mean put them through some of the same kind of conversations we had in the small teams a fortnight ago, only a bit more pointed now that we know what we are driving at?" It was Paul, the ex-investment banker who spoke, but he was articulating the thoughts of most of the group.

Having seen the strategy quite easily, they found it much harder to nail down questions that could form the appreciative protocol. This is not untypical and I tend to play devil's advocate at this point, picking away at the form of the questions to make sure that they *really* know and approve what they are trying to get at.

The point in so picking is not wordsmithing. (That can too easily become a bane, as two of the case studies will bring out.) It is to test, almost to test to destruction, that the group as a whole thoroughly understands the field of inquiry, of experience, of data that each part of the protocol is designed to illuminate. I emphasize this because my colleagues and I have found repeatedly that a sloppily thought out appreciative protocol may generate some great conversations, but the relationship between those conversations and the substance of the inquiry may be marginal at best.

The danger of this insistent picking is two fold. One is the patience of the group. The less academically minded soon get bored of what they may begin to think of as intellectual games. I sometimes try to get round this by formalizing and sharing the role of devil's advocate. This usually not only sustains interest, but also drives home the point of the exercise more sharply. (It can also be a lot of fun, which helps.)

The second danger is more insidious. Because the protocol has been subjected to this detailed analysis by the work group, the temptation is to approach the first round of appreciative conversations with too-rigid a set of expectations of what should come out of it. This can lead to either an over-mechanistic approach to the conversations or else to a lack of spontaneity and openness to the unexpected on behalf of the interviewer. I shall demonstrate one possible counter strategy shortly.

For Healthco, I used a variant of the devil's advocate approach. I divided the work group into two sub-teams and asked each sub-team to examine half of the emerging protocol to make sure that it expressed what they wanted it to express, that it was not ambiguous, that it would enable the interviewer to move with the flow of the conversation and yet support him or her and keep the conversation within the scope of the inquiry. Each sub-team heard the comments of the other and we put into a bin for later refinement the suggested alterations we were, as a group, uncertain about. In fact only four changes ended up in the bin and all but one of these turned out to be relatively trivial.

5. Turf wars

The issue on which there was heated disagreement turned, interestingly, on the role of the auxiliaries. It became apparent that the nurses—or at least their representatives on the work group—objected to a line of conversation that could be construed as comparing the *nursing* input of the auxiliaries with those of the nurses. Even the word caring was suspect, presumably for the same reason. A turf war had broken out. How could it be handled within the appreciative mode?

I asked the work group as a whole to go back to fundamentals. What were we trying to do? We were trying to elicit from all sections of the company and its clients their best experiences of the company at work. Suppose it were true that some patients, perhaps even many patients, experienced the best care at the hand of auxiliaries. What, I suggested, we needed to know was what that best care consisted of and what it was about auxiliaries that enabled them to give it. The nurses were less than enthusiastic with this approach, arguing that it was the auxiliaries' job to help the nurses, not to nurse or care for patients. "That is what their job description says," said one of the nurses fiercely.

The terrain of the argument was becoming familiar. Were we concerned with a legalistic interpretation of best practice? Or an existential one? Or, to put it another way, was best practice to be defined in terms of people fulfilling to the letter the terms of their job descriptions, or in terms of the quality of life in the workplace for both staff and clients? I had thought that the latter interpretation had been read into the text of everything I had said and all the learnings we had been through since the work group started its labours. And I am sure that, before this particular issue came up, everyone would have agreed enthusiastically. What we were witnessing, then, had little to do with the *knowledge-base* of the nurses in the group; it had everything to do with their insecurity and anxiety which was being projected on to the auxiliaries. Their insecurity was biasing their reading both of the company and of the appreciative approach. The result was that the auxiliaries were being monstered into a threat to the nurses' employment. We were in the land of the unconscious and it was threatening to be destructive indeed. The question was simple: how did we avoid this wrecking the whole process?

At issue here—and sooner or later this comes up in nearly every appreciative inquiry—was the maintenance of the appreciative mode. If we were to be sucked into fighting turf wars by proxy, then there was no possibility of either conducting a genuinely appreciative inquiry or of helping Healthco move forward as an entity. We needed to find a way out of this but not by squashing the fears of the nurses; nor, for that matter, by endorsing them. Rather we (and by that I mean not just me, but the work group as a whole) had to enable the nurses to see that what was at stake was something that transcended the concerns they were expressing without ignoring or belittling them. How to achieve that?

In this particular case, it was at this point that the patients' representatives came up trumps and thereby fully justified the (contested) decision to include them in the work group. Without using the language, they made a powerful case for preserving the plurality of readings. Seen from the point of view of the client, they argued, what mattered was not the qualifications or uniform of the person at the bedside, but their timeliness and their competence. Blushing a shade I had hitherto thought beyond the physical repertoire of the human face, the investment banker put it this way: "Look, if you want to go to the loo, it doesn't matter a fig who takes you. What does matter is that they are there when you need them; that they are sensitive, helpful and competent; and that there is a degree of trust and empathy between the patient and the helper. If what we are about is establishing the baseline for what makes Healthco special, it is not how many nurses it has nor how well qualified they are—important though those considerations might well be. It is who will help you most *helpfully* when you need it." The long silence that followed this intervention spoke volumes.

It would, I think, be false to claim that the nurses' representatives were instantly enabled to see the point of the text metaphor or to take an appreciative view of Healthco as a company by this intervention. They did, however, find that the group as a whole was now sufficiently rooted in the appreciative approach to resist the expression of their anxieties *in a hostile or confrontational way*. Of course, they needed to be able to talk of their fears, anxieties and jealousies—and would, as we shall see, do so. But they had learned through this episode that the most constructive way of airing their concerns was through the appreciative process in which the best that Healthco could become was the overriding consideration. Without abandoning their own text, they had to read the wider text with an appreciative eye.

I have recounted this episode in detail because I believe it is not untypical; that is, one group or another will often seek to use the protocol to advance a particular line of thinking. I am not necessarily implying that this is deliberately manipulative; it might be, but more often I think it is an unconscious process whereby the real fears of a group of participants break to the surface and demand attention—attention they must be given, but not by that route.

6. Organizing the interviews

With this issue if not exactly settled, then at least laid to one side for the moment, we were able to agree the protocol with little further delay. Aware of the passage of time and the need to keep the momentum going in the rest of the company, I suggested that we pass immediately to the detail of arranging conversations with the first swathe of participants. Because of the dispersion of Healthco's units and the complications of shift work, we would need to give staff plenty of warning. And we could use the intervening time to apply the protocol in the work group itself.

The first strategic issue to be addressed was whether we were going to interview across or within functional groups; that is, were caterers to interview caterers or doctors or, for that matter, directors?

This can be an awkward issue to handle, since whatever the theoretical advantages of cross-functional conversations—and I believe them to be very strong— the class system is alas still so insidious in its effects that a relatively under-skilled person may be embarrassed or diffident about talking, at this level of depth and reflexivity, with someone he or she will see as a superior. Equally, it has to be said that someone who sees him- or herself as superior may well resent being asked questions that could be regarded as personal or sensitive in other respects by an inferior.

Perhaps it says a lot for the underlying quality of personal relationships at Healthco that these issues were not raised in the work group. Geography took precedence over sociology—or it was about to when I pointed out that it would be a pity if we reinforced the atomizing effect of Healthco's structure by confining conversations within the units at which members of the work group were based. "The Balkan problem," sniffed the investment banker. Exactly.

In the end we came up with a simple scheme whereby each member of the work group would interview three people in their own unit and three people in the unit closest to them. The whole staff was arranged in six functional groups and a proportionate number of names was chosen at random from each group to give a balance by geographical spread. Additionally each member of the work group would interview two patients at each of the units in which they were carrying out staff interviews. The patient representatives on the work group were regarded as based at the central unit and were to have exactly the same interview load and distribution as the staff members—that is six staff and four patients.

Each member of the work group was responsible for contacting his or her interviewees, though we did agree to a central paragraph of a letter that explained, in the broadest terms, the scope of the interview and how the recipient of the letter had been chosen.

The work group clearly found it refreshing to be able to get its teeth into this degree of detailed planning. "It makes it all seem real," said the accountant.

7. The work group uses the protocol on itself

It was made much more real when, at the next session, we went back to using the protocol on each other in the work group.

A procedural point: I sometimes let the work group use an early draft of the protocol on each other, partly because it quickly reveals the shortcomings of the draft, partly because it gives a greater sense of urgency to improving it, and partly because it exposes the work group early on to the actual practice of running the interview. With Healthco, I let them beaver away at the protocol, refining it as far as they could, going through the devil's advocate process of checking, before they used it on each other because I wanted the minimum discontinuity between the dry run in the group and the interviews in the rest of the company. That did not forestall further refinement after the dry run of course, but it did minimize the risk—which sometimes happens—that the instrument that was eventually used was widely different from the instrument used within the work group.

This relates to another procedural point. How much training should the work group be given in the actual business of using the protocol? I am not sure how much can be *taught* in a didactic sense. Most people learn fastest by doing, and so I tend to give only a quick introduction before sending the work group off to interview each other. It is, I find, the debrief that follows this that brings out the important points and which people actually remember and implement.

Certainly this was the case with Healthco. I introduced the session with only four quick points: (1) confidentiality (give an undertaking and keep it); (2) a time contract (only revise it, if you feel you really must, after explicit negotiation with the interviewee); (3) listen to what is not being said as well as to what is (but don't double guess the interviewee); and (4) be yourself, let the conversation develop, don't be the slave of the protocol (but do make sure the meat of the protocol is covered).

Each member of the work group was to interview one other member and, therefore, each was to be interviewed once.

If time had allowed, I would normally prefer to have doubled this. One interview, seen from both sides of the table, is enough to learn a lot; but double that exposure more than doubles the learning that comes out of the experience—at least for most people. It can also be extremely instructive, within the bounds of respect for the undertaking of confidentiality, for two people who have interviewed the same person to compare the data they acquired from the interview. The object is not to test the consistency of the information, but rather to look at the flow of the conversation. If the interviewee was more forthcoming or more comfortable with the appreciative mode in one interview, why was that? Was one interviewer more spontaneous, more sensitive to the memory-material that was being revealed, and, if so, what can be learned from that? (One needs to be slightly careful when making these comparisons, however; the very fact that it is a *second* interview based on the same protocol undoubtedly has a contaminating effect, unknowable in scale or direction.)

8. The debrief

In fact, the work group interviews at Healthco seemed to have gone smoothly. The debrief did, however, bring up some significant questions. A hardy annual that comes up as regular as dandelions was the issue of negativity. If a respondent starts airing their dissatisfactions, and then perhaps becomes locked into whinge-mode, what can be done? Is it the responsibility of the interviewer to try to move them back into appreciative mode? As I have repeated many times so far in this book, it is not the essence of the appreciative approach to manipulate people into blocking out or denying their negative feelings—or, for that matter, their critical judgements. That would be both unethical and counter-productive. The essence of the appreciative approach is, rather, to help people see those negativities within an appreciative context. For example, in the case of the Healthco interviews, a respondent may need to be helped to move from a statement such as: "The nurses do not get to know the patients well enough *as people,*" to: "Our care is at its best when every nurse relates to the patients in her care as a whole person." Or, to take another example that came from this session, the statement: "We have so much damn paperwork, we never get a chance to spend quality time with the patients" needs to be reframed as: "If paperwork can be kept to the barest minimum consistent with running an efficient organization, the nursing staff will have more time to do what they are best at: caring for their patients."

A final example, this time from one of the representatives of the patients. There was a series of complaints about noise which made it difficult for patients to rest—traffic noise, doors slamming, too-loud televisions in neighbouring rooms, staff talking and laughing outside the door and so on. "I was so sympathetic to all this," said the interviewer, "that I let it go on. Indeed, I found I was encouraging it. It came as a shock to realize how far I had lost a grip on what was going on. I didn't seem able to get back into appreciative mode for quite a time and then it seemed very crude and ham-fisted." This is almost classic. When someone's story touches a nerve in us, we want to respond empathetically to what they are saying, rather than keeping an eye on the process of the interview itself. Here a simple reframing early on in the diatribe against noise would have sufficed. The patient would know she was being heard, that her criticisms were not being dismissed, but she would have been held in appreciative mode. Thus the reframing could have been: "I hear you saying that Healthco is at its best when it offers a comfortable, peaceful, noise-free environment for the seriously sick to rest. Is that right?" The trick is not to dismiss the negative comments, but to reframe them in such a way that the interviewee knows that they have been heard but is encouraged to stay with the appreciative expression of his or her material.

But what, I was asked, if the interviewee shies away again and again, and seems only to be happy when complaining or making personal attacks on other people in the organization? Let me say at once that in most organizations there is a tiny proportion of unhappy people who are thus afflicted. But it is a *tiny* proportion and one should not rush to the conclusion that one has, by some irritating quirk of misfortune, stumbled across one such as an interviewee. If that is indeed the case, and they seem literally incapable of ever getting into—never mind staying in—the appreciative mode, all one can do is to hear them out as patiently and compassionately as one can manage. To repeat: that is exceedingly rare. More often people will, as it were, drift into whinge mode and *if their comments are not reframed quite quickly*, they will infer, probably unconsciously, that the interviewer either agrees or at least is interested in this type of material. Thus encouraged, they will become, like an avalanche, increasingly unstoppable. One of the unfortunate by-products of that is that the conversation will be reported to workmates as the following: "And I told him that we are all sick and tired of Mr. X and his sexist innuendo—and he quite agreed with me." The inquiry team is thus represented as having colluded with the criticisms and that in turn sets up a pattern of expectations for the action phase.

The reframing needs to be done with some care or it will have the effect of closing off areas of conversation, or seeming to rebuke the interviewee in such a way that s/he becomes excessively guarded in what s/he says thereafter. Above all, perhaps, it is critical to let the interviewee know that negative feelings, sour relationships, criticisms of policy or people are not ruled out, but that they are more helpful to the inquiry—and by extension to the organization as a whole—if they can be framed in an appreciative way.

A second common issue that arose in the Healthco debrief was a reluctance to engage what one might call the organizational imagination. I mentioned this in chapter 2, when we were reviewing the sources of appreciative inquiry. Sure enough in Healthco, many of the less skilled employees on the work group found that they could talk about their memories, but they were tongue-tied when asked to use their imagination. "They could read the text of the past but they were blind to the text of the future. Was it *our* fault?," the interviewers wanted to know.

My first response was to rid the discussion of the notion of fault. It is no one's *fault*. It is a regrettable fact of our culture that we are seldom asked to visualize a better, brighter, more fulfilling role for our organizations or for ourselves within it. The question we need to ask is not about fault, but about enablement: how do we, as interviewers, better enable our respondents to exercise a faculty they all have, albeit rusting in their mental backyards?

There are two standard procedures—and some unstandard! The standard approaches are, first, to ask if the respondent has ever visited another company (or whatever) where they have seen things they would like to introduce in their own workplace. Or have they heard tell of such...? This earths the discussion, moving from the abstract and speculative to the actual.

Second, it sometimes helps (as one of the case studies shows) to encourage an intergenerational comparison: "If your grandson was to work here in X years, what would you want it to be like for him?" Again this tends to make the question more rooted, and by attaching it to someone with whom there is, we presume, a strong affective link, we give it more urgency. I find these earthing strategies are much more helpful than tooth-fairy stratagems: "If you had three wishes for this company...." That leaves it in the realm of the abstract. It is, it seems, *too* open.

I will mention only two unstandard procedures. The first is a mini-fantasy exercise. If you were taking the Queen round Healthco, and showing her everything in a real in-depth tour, what would you most like to hear her say about Healthco to her Lady in Waiting as she left in her Rolls Royce? I find the symbolic power of the monarchy, at least in the British psyche, is such that it will often trigger ideas, aspirations, hopes that otherwise remain unexpressed. Those of a psychoanalytical turn of mind can work out for themselves why that should be. I only report here that it is sometimes effective.

The second is another fantasy exercise, of a more somber hue. I ask people to imagine that they have just retired. As they review their work life, what would they wish had been different—for themselves and those they worked with? And what memory makes them feel that they have accomplished something enduring in their working lives? This approach has to be used with a good deal of care and sensitivity; a few people find it disturbing. But it is meant to disturb, to disturb the hardened skin of conventional thinking, fatalism and cynicism that disables so many people from thinking creatively and imaginatively about their workplace.[103]

A coda on all these attempts is to make good the imaginative deficit. Usually as a defensive ploy, respondents will often say, "How could things be better? Well, they could double our money for one thing...." In other words they take refuge in semi-jokey distractions. Fair enough. A little patient probing, staying within the appreciative mode will usually (but not guaranteedly) shift them into a more reflective response.

A third issue that was raised at the Healthco work group debriefing was the question of recording the data. "I found that if I made extensive notes, I lost eye contact and empathy," said a housekeeper from one of the units in the Midlands. "But if I maintained eye contact, I had to make such abbreviated notes that I'm not sure how accurate whatever write-up I produce will be in terms of what the person actually said." The murmurs of assent round the table showed this to have been a common experience and I blamed myself for not having given it proper coverage in the initial introduction.

Sometimes the *very words* of the respondent are particularly telling, communicating affective truth in a way that notes will never recapture. The duty to *listen actively*, however, is paramount and will crucially affect the way the conversation develops. Indeed it is that quality of listening that differentiates an appreciative conversation from a standard social-research type interview. Some kind of compromise has to be struck between these two ideals, and different compromises are right for different interviewers (as is suggested by the fact that I nearly always find that people change their techniques radically over the experience of half a dozen sessions). My basic suggestions are two: leave yourself time to make short but precise notes between topics in the protocol. During that time you are deliberately breaking the contact with the respondent and you may need to make that explicit and make equally explicit the restart of the conversation. The respondent often values a short pause, too, and you may want to encourage him or her to use the time to reflect on what has been said and see if there is anything else that he or she wants to add.

Second, write up much more extended notes *immediately* after the interview while your own notes make sense and while you can remember the details of the conversation. And I mean immediately, not at the end of the day and certainly not after the next interview (which will inevitably become scrambled with this one in one's fallible memory). And that means timetabling an appropriate space into the schedule (and allowing for the fact that the interviews may well overshoot their allotted time, despite an agreed time contract).

So much for the mechanics; what of the substance? If the protocol has been prepared with the care that the Healthco work group demonstrated, questions of substance should not be too troublesome. (And it was clear in the debrief that the questions that came up were indeed about mechanics rather than substance.) For the preparation time, the devil's advocacy and the testing and retesting of the protocol are designed exactly to elucidate not only what is on the paper, but also what *is in the mind of* the work group. It is where work on the protocol has been skimped that confusion develops over what the questions are really all about. And when that happens, as it did in one of the case studies reported in part 3, I am inclined to take the bull by the horns and go back to work on the protocol. At the very least there needs to be a further session of the work group to look at the protocol again and make sure that everyone is clear what the central issues are. Without such a check, one can find the work group later confronted with data that are oranges and lemons. That may produce squash; it does not produce clarity.

From the point of view of the interviewees, the debrief brought up one fundamental point. It was put like this by the woman who was one of the patients' representatives: "I found myself thinking, 'Why *should* I tell you what I really think?' I know it is for the good of the whole community in the long run and all that, but I detected within myself a reluctance to let my defences down. I could play along with the process happily enough and put on a, I hope, creditable performance. But what I *really* think... I'm not sure."

Here we are face to face with the issue of trust. Why should the interviewee trust either the interviewer, whom in all probability he or she has never met before; and why should he or she trust the whole process? As we are beginning to realize, so much of our economic and social life depends upon unstated, untested leaps of trust that normal life in community is impossible without trust—and much is done everyday to undermine that trust.[104] The question, then, is well taken. What can the interviewer do to build trust and thereby encourage the respondent to be as honest and forthright as possible?

I suspect that that is a mistaken way of framing the question, though it was the way it emerged in the debriefing. Apart from the obvious things like being open about the process, being non-judgmental, affirming and interested, answering fully and truthfully any questions that are put about the interview and giving a clear undertaking of confidentiality, there is rather little that the individual interviewer can do to establish or enhance trust. Trust is built into and around the process as a whole by the sensitivity with which the micropolitics of its origins, its initiation and its implementation are handled. To put it crudely, if the inquiry is dumped on a reluctant organization by a coffee-plunger management, or if its early work is conducted in secrecy with no communication to the rest of the organization, trust will begin to ebb away however unwarrantedly. And once that ebb starts, it is almost impossible to reverse.

More than that, it is a paradox that senior management will often think in terms of introducing an appreciative inquiry (or, for that matter, any other outside intervention) when trust in their leadership is already minimal. One of the key tricks the facilitator is therefore obliged to pull is to distance the process from being identified with management as soon as possible. As I hope was clear from the story of Healthco, that does not mean a populistic or anarchic anti-management stance. But it does mean making it quite clear to everyone in the organization that the process has its own independent integrity which the facilitator will defend to the point of resignation. To that degree, the mainspring of trust in the process has to be in the integrity—personal and professional—of the facilitator. Solemn thought.

After the debrief, the work group was keen to start the main batch of interviews. Most of the members admitted to being a little nervous but felt they had learned enough from the intra-group conversations to do a competent job. None of us knew at that point that a cloud no larger than a man's hand was already on the horizon. It will grow larger in the next chapter.

98 I am aware that this is in direct contravention of the approach favoured by Belbin *et al.*, which puts prime emphasis on the *innate capacity* of the team members to work together and complement each other's skills. My own experience is that this is a counsel of perfection, and accordingly hard to implement in a system that is deliberately at least semi-democratic. See R. M. Belbin, *Management teams*, London: Heinemann, 1981.

99 Although appreciative inquiry does not depend upon or necessarily follow any model of group dynamics, I find it helpful to have at the back of my mind the Tuckman model, perhaps especially as modified by Woodcock. See B. W. Tuckman, "Development sequence in small groups" *Psychological Bulletin*, 63, 1965; and M. Woodcock, *Team development manual*, Farnborough: Gower, 1979.

100 A variant of this is the so-called "Wall of Wonder" when an individual's or, better, an organization's history is charted in terms of peaks, troughs and middle ground over time. This can be an effective team-building exercise, but, in my experience, its real strength is in getting a group to focus on the history of its organization and realize that what one person might construct as a peak may be constructed as the reverse by others.

101 Given all that we now know about the relationship between role ambiguity and complexity on the one hand, and personality types prone to stress on the other, it might well be argued that a facilitator's job also includes helping those demonstrating aggression at this early stage at least to talk through their confusions and anxieties about their role. At the time, this did not occur to me. If it had, I suspect I would have replied that, as soon as the appreciative protocols began to emerge, the general anxieties of the group would diminish. As we shall see, this was broadly true.

102 We tend to use the rather cumbersome word protocol to emphasise the fact that the list of questions is not and should never be used as an interview schedule. It is, rather, a list of generative questions which will open, if one is fortunate, a whole conversation, which will include feelings as well as facts. If the protocol is used mechanically, *as though it were a schedule*, the conversation is unlikely to take off and the data will be highly restricted.

103 This is a variant of an exercise in Anthony de Mello's *Sadhana: A way to God.*

104 The role of trust in all organizational and therefore all economic life has been given much prominence recently by the so-called new institutional economics. The two classic references are Francis Fukuyama, *Trust: The social virtues and the creation of prosperity*, London: Hamish Hamilton, 1995; and Douglas North and Robert P. Thomas, *The rise of the Western world: A new economic history*, Cambridge: Cambridge University Press, 1973.

Chapter 7
Progress—and diversion

1. The appreciative interviews

At this point the facilitator can feel rather like a parent sending off the eldest child to primary school for the first time. You have done all you can in preparation; now all you can do is wait and hope. I believe this is a mistake. Look at the process from the point of view of the stakeholder who is not on the work group and is not slated for an early interview. He or she knows something is going on. He or she hears vague rumours, some of them clearly embroidered in the telling. This is bound to influence the way he or she reads the organization. At worst, the appreciative inquiry becomes one more management plot against the workers, or one more example of a failure to communicate properly. If trust is as important as I suggested at the end of the last chapter and if, for better or for worse, it resides finally in the integrity of the facilitator, then this is the time when the facilitator needs to communicate with the non-active stakeholders and keep them informed about what is happening—and what are likely to be the next steps. This is not to seek to influence the way they participate in the interviews. It is designed only to build and maintain trust in the appreciative inquiry process.

For Healthco, however, this relatively simple process was complicated by the fact that we had, after much discussion in the work group, decided to leave open the question of how many interviews we would do and even who would do them. Some members of the group were aware that doing 10—and writing up fairly detailed notes on them—would pose a problem in terms of finding time, even though management had agreed that they could be done in paid time. (In fact many were done in unpaid time.) The thought of doing more, perhaps another 10, was not palatable.

Furthermore, I was concerned about the way we were going to process the data once it had all been collected. The more data we got, the more sophisticated a process we would have to use and the less detail we would surface. The bigger the photo, the grainier the texture.

At the suggestion of the accountant and the banker, we had therefore decided to do the first round of about 100 interviews, which would represent roughly a third of the staff and about 5 percent of the patients over the last six months, and then see if a wholly consistent picture was emerging. If it was, there would be little point—except in terms of PR and morale—in doing more. If the data were highly dispersed, on the other hand, we would have to find a way of enlarging the inquiry.

This pragmatic approach now made it hard to know what to say to the rest of the potential participants. Some of them wanted to know when they were going to have their say. The only honest answer was, "I don't know whether you are."

I wrote a one-page letter to everyone we had written to before, describing the steps we had taken and the reasons for them, putting special emphasis on the work the group had done to prepare themselves for the interviews. I then made a point of visiting every unit and talking with as many people as I could find, especially those who were not (yet) scheduled for interview.

To my surprise, I found a marked difference in the feel of the staff (I spent much less time with patients) compared with my last exploratory round of visits. Maybe this was because they had become accustomed to my role and were beginning to feel they knew me as a person. I hoped it was because they were satisfied with the way things were going and had faith that something worthwhile was going to come out of it. What struck me, however, was the level of interest in the inquiry. Nearly everyone I met knew someone who was to be—or had already been—interviewed and it was evident that there had been numerous coffee-time conversations about what should or should not be emphasized. A methodological purist might worry about the degree of contamination this informal lobbying represents. Overall, I took the view that, once the actual conversation was underway, the interviewers would be able to move the participants beyond any primed speeches quite rapidly.[105]

Those who had been interviewed were generally excited by the experience. It is common to hear people saying things like, "That's the first time any one has sat me down and asked my opinion about how things are done round here." What I was hearing at Healthco was subtly—and encouragingly—different. "Wow!" exclaimed a usually reserved speech therapist. "That made me think. We could have gone on for hours. I'd like to go back and have another bite at the cherry. Ever since the conversation (sic), things have kept popping up in my mind and I find myself thinking: 'Why on earth didn't I say that when I had the opportunity...?'."

That raises a point that is sometimes debated by practitioners. Is there a net gain to be had from precirculating the protocol to interviewees? Many find, as did this speech therapist, that the conversation is so rich, they cannot lay everything out that they would like to. They then feel that they have not done themselves or the process justice, and that in turn can have a negative impact on trust. Nonetheless we do not encourage precirculation for three main reasons. First, we are not interested in prepared speeches—and even less in speeches articulated or inspired by others. Second, the letter setting up the interview has given some warning of the nature of the conversation, so the shock of the new should be minimized. Third, we usually tell interviewers to finish the conversation by saying, along with the thanks, that if the participant, on reflection, feels he or she has misrepresented his or her real views, or wants to add a major new thought, this person should feel free to write to the interviewer within a specified time period. Rather few in fact do so but sometimes real nuggets come in this form.

2. The interviews completed: A quick and dirty start to analysis

When the work group reconvened, having completed their interviews (except for a handful of stragglers), morale was high. It was especially noticeable that those who had hitherto been reserved and nearly silent in work group sessions were now keen to tell us of their experiences. Again and again, we heard two themes repeated: how highly motivated the staff were (and this came from patients as well as from staff); and how isolated they felt. It might seem odd that such an unappreciative comment should come out of a round of appreciative conversations. It is not; it bears witness to the fact that the appreciative approach does not bury negativities, but allows them to be addressed in a non-destructive form. For example the kind of data that sparked the comments about isolation were responses like, "It has been such a pleasure and encouragement to meet other paramedics since this inquiry started..."; or, from a medical consultant: "The highlight of my work for Healthco is the twice-yearly meeting with all the other consultants. That is real quality time, both personally and professionally. I only wish we did it every two months. How much we would all get from that...."

I was conscious that we were in danger of cherry-picking the data and therefore of reducing our capacity to analyze it sensitively. We had two major tasks. The first, which needed to be done quickly, was to get a sense of the internal coherence of the data to determine whether there was any point in doing more interviews. The second, more substantively, was to see what the data were actually saying about the key issues so that we could begin to form provocative propositions. Behind these two questions lurked a purely practical one: how could we assimilate 100 interviews, reports on which averaged about four pages? We decided on a double strategy. The three of us who did not have full-time jobs at Healthco— the two patients' representatives and myself—would read all 100 reports, checking the dispersion of the answers. Simultaneously, the rest of the interviewers would read 10 reports each, thus acquiring a random knowledge base of 20 (10 plus their own 10). But what exactly were we going to look for?

I had given much thought to this over the last couple of weeks and had prepared a list of sensitive issues which I thought could be either reduced, however crudely, to a five-point scale or simply listed to reveal any obvious clusters. The resulting table looked like this:

- How can patient care best be improved? Keep a list of suggestions.

- To what type of patient can Healthco offer the best help: recuperative/geriatric/long-term care/EMI/no special group?

- Is the wide geographical dispersion of units a source of strength?

- Is professional formation and career development seen as a positive attribute of Healthco?

- Are intra-staff relationships within the various units a source of strength?

- Are staff-patient relations within each unit a source of strength?

- Are staff relationships with senior management a source of strength?

- Would you see Healthco's management structure as a source of strength?

- What do you think are the most helpful forms of bureaucratic control?

Looking down this list, I was concerned whether I had inadvertently shifted back into old-paradigm, analytical thinking. The repetition of "source of strength" hardly caught the spirit of appreciative inquiry with its emphasis on delight, on joy, on creative energy and enthusiasm. I was aware of the need for some kind of benchmark to test the consistency of the data but began to wonder whether that whole notion itself was not some hangover from a former style of thinking.[106]

It would, I reckoned, take less than 15 minutes a report to score, in a quick and dirty way, each of these questions, and while that implied the three of us spending three days on the job, I was confident that it would be sufficiently interesting to justify the effort. In fact it became so absorbing that we three admitted we had taken over twice as long.

Remember that what we were attempting at this first round of data analysis was strictly limited: to see if there was an emerging pattern of responses that gave us confidence that the random sample we had chosen was representative of opinion in Healthco as a whole. If we found clear clusters of issues and opinion, we were reasonably safe in assuming so. If, by contrast, there were no clusters and the issues that seemed important or peoples' opinions on those issues were widely spread, we would have to consider a further round of conversations, with all that implied in terms of delay, expense and complication of the data analysis.[107]

In the event, we found that on some issues—e.g., direct contact with patients— there was near unanimity; on others—e.g., the need to strengthen career development paths for both administrative and caring groups—there was a clear voice; while on others, among them some of the most sensitive—e.g., expansion into permanent care for EMI patients—there was a much wider dispersion of opinion.

3. Widening the conversation

The question, then, was whether further interviews would clarify these contentious issues; or would we find that our sample, already quite large in statistical terms, was reflecting a reality, that the stakeholders were divided on the issue? The work group debated this question until one of the nurses suggested we look at it in another way. "What are we trying to do?" she asked. "We have a pretty good idea where opinion is centred in the company, but we are not just doing a public opinion survey. We are about change, about embedding excellence. Surely we need to give *everyone* a feeling that they are involved in this—and whether their ideas alter the broad conclusions we have in the material is… well, not irrelevant, but not the whole point. What we want is their involvement, their enthusiasm, their openness to change."

A number of people agreed with this, some putting a slightly different spin on it. "A lot of people have talked about what's going on, either with us or with people who have been interviewed. So there is a high level of awareness of the possibilities. We are more likely to carry people with us if they think they have been heard." "And anyway," someone else added, "We are surely not looking for some kind of average opinion. We are looking for the ideas no one else has thought of—for the surprising, the unthinkable. They may be here, in this batch. But there may be more out there. Shouldn't we go out and look for them?"

The reservations about time, data-overload and momentum inevitably resurfaced. We were moving into a logjam, represented by either/or thinking. Either more interviews and loss of momentum, or more momentum and less participation. These simple trade-offs, so beloved of accountants and economists, nearly always need challenging, and it is part of the appreciative approach to look beyond "both/and" solutions, because so simplistic a response fails to take the harsh realities seriously enough. Rather, in keeping with a constructionist view of the world, we have to ask how can we construct a reality here that transcends the duality set up by the original trade-off. Here, could we not come up with a quick, light procedure that would enable everyone to participate, one which, while remaining in the appreciative mode, would surface key data, but not swamp us with material that merely duplicated what we already had? I put that question to the work group; it was important that they take responsibility at this point.

We discussed a number of possible ways forward—focus groups, shortened interviews, cascaded interviews, invitations to submit written ideas on the basis of the protocol. All were sensible; any might have worked well; none was exciting or innovative.

It was the Vietnamese lady who, despite having a Master's degree in public health from an American college, worked as a cleaner in one of the EMI units who eventually found a way through for us. "Look," she said, "the biggest question we have to answer is how do we make ourselves, as a company, the best we can be in the future. I mean the mix of patients, the skills and style of the staff, the admin and so on. Well, why not just ask everybody? Tell them what we have found already and then have a grand competition, with a juicy prize for the best entry: 'How I would like to see Healthco in seven years' or something like that. I suppose the language we have been using would put it something like, 'What is the best reading of the text of Healthco you can imagine?', though I don't suspect everyone will understand. Is this a mad, bad idea?" She trailed off into a vulnerable silence.

She must have been astonished at the response. Within minutes the work group, without any reference to me, had the competition organized. The investment banker had promised a fortnight's holiday in his Tuscan villa as a prize, with free flights for two. We had three volunteers, coordinated by the lady representing the patients, to produce a synopsis of the work so far and we had a tight timetable. And, more interestingly, we had agreement that the entries could be in any form—from a poem to a picture to a taped interview to a telegram. The publicity was to emphasize three things: we were after ideas based on our current best practice; form of entry or sophistication of medium and expression were unimportant; and although it was set up as a competition, what mattered was to take part in rewriting the script, not just to win.

It was this last point that caused me some unease, which I eventually shared with the work group. If the appreciative approach is about collaboration, was not a competition the very antithesis of that? "That's either/or thinking," came back the speech therapist as quick as a whip. "And *that* is certainly unappreciative! Think of it as a competition to stimulate collaboration in the future. Or a competition born out of a collaborative process. If it became really serious and divisive, then I could see your point. But a bit of fun? A balloon on a string?"

History was to prove both of us wrong; but that bit of history still lay below the horizon of time.

The summary of the data that had come out of the interviews included a collection of comments from those who had taken part as either interviewers or interviewees. Many people told me they found this the most interesting and challenging part of the whole document—which, by a Herculean effort of compression, was confined to eight pages. What these comments showed—and I am not inclined to believe they were manipulated in any sense—was the energy-expanding effect that the process had had. Yes, there had clearly been initial reticence to speculate about the future, to leave it to "them," to abdicate any responsibility. But when the interviewers persisted, sometimes using the techniques I described in the last chapter, the emotional response was: Wow! Somebody cares what *I* think. I *count*. I can choose. By making this point, the work group hoped to generate the same sense of being taken seriously in the competition. Certainly it would have been hard to see this as a front for a predetermined set of decisions. The road was open indeed.

The result was that the package of reports on the process so far, the invitation to the competition and a letter from the work group were in the hands of every employee and all the patients of six months standing within two weeks of the meeting at which the idea was first mooted. Three days later the bomb dropped.

4. Another agenda

The call came from the personnel director. He sounded embarrassed. "Err... umm. I think you should know that we have been offered five homes catering for EMIs, plus a very favourable financial package. The board will be responding within 48 hours to meet the vendors' deadline. I'm sure they will go for it. We'd be crazy not to."

I was aghast. There followed a tense conversation which left me angry, confused and deeply concerned. I had always dreaded this. It is a classic dilemma. Any intervention takes time, and the more participatory, the more time it takes. And therefore the greater the danger that life will cut across process. But need it blow it out of the water? Peter Reason has written about the chaos of the emergence of any participative process, and of course that is exactly how it often feels—with all the inner terror associated with the disintegration that chaos threatens.[108] This latest development, however, felt like chaos squared and I needed to work hard at Reason's deeper analogy: that any living form *has* to move between chaos and order if it is to survive and evolve. That evening it was not easy to hang on to that perspective.[109]

What was an appreciative way through this? Was there one? Was my integrity being called in? Resignation time? I knew all the theory about real empowerment only being possible within the context of new organizational forms, but this did not look like a new organizational form.[110] It looked like more of the old—only more so.

I met with Paul, the investment banker ex-patient on the work group, because he was the one person who would understand the conflicting pressures, and who, I thought, had already gained a sufficient insight into the appreciative inquiry's potential to want to preserve its momentum. He was in sober mood. "Could scarcely be worse timing, heh?," he grunted. "Do you have any ideas?"

I told him I had been wracking my brain to see how we could maintain the process in the face of what I took to be an inevitable board decision to go ahead. "It's not that they are *wrong*," I said. "Not in terms of the substance of the decision and their criteria. It's not even that all the staff and patients are opposed to expansion in that sector. The majority are, I suspect, some vehemently. But not everyone. It's just that... hell, I feel I have been put in an impossible position relative to the staff and the patients. Many of them have come to trust me. And I really like and admire them. They will feel I have let them down."

"In my experience," Paul said gently, "it's always a self indulgence to personalize these things. What we need to do is to find a third way. I've been *so* impressed by what we have found. Those people are gold, many of them. They really care. I sometimes wonder if the board people know what they've got... Typical." He seemed to drift off into his own world.

To cut a long—and only tangentially relevant—story short, Paul came up with the idea of *all* the stakeholders being given the chance to buy the old Healthco and run it as a kind of cooperative. He thought he could get the financial engineering right; and he could see why it would be in the interest of the board of Healthco to sell out—so that they could expand rapidly in the EMI sector and establish a position as market leaders. We did not know, however, whether they would indeed agree to sell; nor whether the stakeholders would be prepared to invest the quite significant cash that would be required as equity finance.

Clearly, this had great implications for the inquiry, implications that could hardly have come at a less convenient time. For here was a whole new raft of possibilities, of very far-reaching consequence, that had not even been in people's consciousness when the exercise was started. We were three-quarters of the way though a process that was designed to involve everyone (through the competition) and the ground had suddenly shifted. I began to think that Peter Reason's remarks on the creative role of chaos were a good deal too reasonable. However creative, chaos is extremely uncomfortable, especially for a facilitator who likes to keep things nearly under control.

5. A risky shift?

From my point of view, the situation was complicated by the fact that once Paul had the bit between his teeth, he showed that, however rhetorically supportive of the appreciative approach, he was, in his guts, stuck in old-paradigm thinking. That realization and a glimpse of its implications came out of a later conversation when he began to talk about using the inquiry to sell the idea of the cooperative, and about grafting-in the process of the competition.

My heart sank.

"Look, it isn't a question of grafting it in. Don't you see? That's just the mirror image of what Roger and company are doing—making the decisions and leaving everyone else to sink or swim with them. The whole point of the appreciative inquiry is to find the best, the most creative ideas among the stakeholders, build a consensus around them if that proves possible, and then go with that."

He interrupted. "But we have—or may have—the most creative idea here. All you have to do is to build your consensus. You people talk of the risky shift and reckon it comes out of well-functioning groups. Well, your work group is functioning well. Maybe they are ready for a risky shift."[111]

"But the idea is yours. It is not theirs."

"Well, now you mention it, I'm not so sure that is true. Sure, no one said in the reports I read: 'Why don't we restructure as a cooperative?' No, I admit that. But there were glimpses, glimmers. People saying, 'You remember that the best relationships and the best quality of care came when everyone felt equally involved.' Someone even said—and I couldn't figure out what they meant at the time, so the phrase stuck: '...when we all had a real stake.' So it is there in embryo. You just have to be the midwife."

"OK, OK. It's great that you think it may be bubbling below the surface. But we have to give it time, give it space to emerge in its own right. We have to ensure that these people actually *own* whatever comes out of the process."

The central problem, then, was how to integrate these developments with the rather leisurely pace of the appreciative inquiry, and, without in any way manipulating the outcome, allow the competition to throw up the idea of a much wider pattern of ownership, a formal separation of the EMI side from the rest, and a choice of path forward for those staff who wished to exercise it. At all costs it seemed important not to close doors, to keep options open, to maximize the potentialities of the future—and to keep faith with the process. The possible readings of the text seemed suddenly to have multiplied beyond anyone's expectation. The trick was going to be to get everyone to read the new texts with the imagination they demanded and then decide what was their preferred reading.

The practical question, however, was how to advise the board to communicate the news about the offer. I drafted a very carefully worded letter that the chairman could sign. It steered a course between the Scylla of presenting the deal as done, and the Charybdis of encouraging the staff to believe that it would be decided on a majority vote of employees. And it deliberately drew attention to the competition as a way for the staff to make their views known, not for and against the deal as such, but in terms of their wider vision of what they would like Healthco to become. I would have liked to share it with the work group, but as long as knowledge of the deal was privileged, I knew I could not properly do so, and, accordingly, feared how they would react when they learned that I had deliberately kept vital information from them.

I need not describe the details of the discussions over the next days, nor the intricacies and frustrations of Paul's attempts to put together a financial package along the lines he had half-outlined. I want instead to concentrate on the effect of these developments on the appreciative inquiry. As I hinted above, the flow of information to the staff soon emerged as the key issue. With more delay than I would have liked—since entries for the competition were already beginning to dribble in, and, more sinisterly, rumours that something big was in the offing were starting to circulate—the chairman signed the letter I had drafted and it duly went out to the work group's mailing list. The work group met on the day of the mailing, so I was at least able to tell them a few hours before they received the letter.

6. The work group reacts

Their reaction varied from the incandescently enraged to the intrigued. The enraged faction was small, and had, I think, not fully taken on board how open the situation still was (primarily because Paul's expectations of unforeseen delays were amply justified). The intrigued group was more tricky to deal with honestly and openly. I did not think that it was proper for me to *propose* establishing a cooperative, but as a member of the work group with skills in this area, I did not see why Paul should not at least rough out some of the possibilities. The work group, of course, wanted more detail, more assurances, more figures, but Paul showed both his professional mettle and his internalization of the appreciative approach by constantly playing the questions back to the work group.

His diplomatic handling of the questions, in a way that educated the work group without assuming one decision or another and simultaneously challenged them to relate their responses to the appreciative inquiry process, enabled the group to come to terms with the new circumstances without feeling threatened or demeaned. They were having to learn a new and unexpected way of reading a familiar text. No wonder they found it hard. By the end of a very long meeting, however, there was an undertow of excitement, almost of euphoria. Out of the corner of her mouth in the car park, one of the senior nurses said to me, "This is it. It's now or never. It could not have come at a better time."

That was so alien to my own recent way of thinking that I kept chewing it over in my mind. She was right, of course. It had thrown our plans for the appreciative inquiry into temporary confusion (or chaos), but it had given the whole process an edge, a purposefulness that the next days would demonstrate.

7. Keeping the conversation alive

By now entries for the competition were coming in at an accelerating rate. The four of us who had been nominated as judges had agreed not to look at any of the entries until the closing date, still a week away. My contacts among the staff and the members of the work group, whom I called on an almost daily, assured me of a high level of interest and the probability of some unusual entries.

"Whatever else comes out of it," said the speech therapist, "it's done wonders for morale in my unit. It's generated a lot of humorous banter, but behind that, you can sense a feeling that people appreciate being given an opportunity to think some of the big issues through. Chat over coffee is about little else. And no, I don't think the take-over thing has muddied the waters too much. People see that they can affect the outcome even of that—at least they can in aggregate with other members of staff. And that has given them a real lift."

I asked if there were people who remained trapped in their own negativities. "Not here so far as I can tell. There are various levels of skepticism, as you would expect. But no one is saying it's all a con. They wouldn't put in the work if they believed—or even half believed—that."

Paul was keeping his cards close to his chest—which I welcomed. I did not want to become identified with whatever alternate strategy he was developing until it was clear that there was a real head of steam behind it among all the stakeholders. He was, however, clearly anxious about timing. If the appreciative inquiry was to be integrated—in however chaotic a way—with the board's moves, time was no longer on our side.

It was largely for that reason that I decided to start the work group on the provocative propositions before the competition entries were submitted, sorted, judged and analyzed. Perhaps that phase of the task, in some ways the most demanding of all, would help us all see, with a new clarity, the depth at which we were working. Without their perceptual shift, their radical rereading of the script, I doubted whether the inquiry would achieve its potential. Given the pressures on both of them, however, it was an open question whether they would be able to find the mental and emotional space to make that rereading.

---

105 This raises the wider question of the extent to which appreciative interviews can be subverted by pressure groups within an organization. The pressure group, which might be formal (e.g., a works council or a trade union) or quite informal, might brief a number of their members to reiterate a party line. In my experience this threat is more theoretical than actual, not because it does not happen, but because the interviewing process takes it, as it were, in the side. If you are constantly being invited to tell stories about your best experiences, it is difficult to go on making predetermined speeches. I do not deny, however, that this *could* be a problem. I can only attest it has never yet been so in my experience or that of other practitioners whom I have interviewed in researching this book.

106 To be honest I am still in two minds about this, and long discussions with colleagues and fellow practitioners have only muddied the water. Some practitioners would skip this process altogether on the grounds that a 30 percent sample is adequate and one needs to trust the results. Others would merely read through the data and form a subjective judgement about whether there is any need to extend the sample. Others still would try to be more precise than this rather crude approach makes possible. My own, still-provisional, view is that, especially in an exercise such as this, it *is* worth trying to see if any pattern is beginning to emerge, but in that process it is worth trying to hold the appreciative tone as one interrogates the data.

107 The statistically minded will ask what constitutes a clear cluster. Without pretending to a degree of scientific precision which would be misleading, one naturally has at the back of one's mind the log-normal distribution and what that implies. In a process as open and, in one sense, as unstructured as appreciative inquiry, however, it is unrealistic to look for 95 percent of responses falling within two standard deviations, even if precise meaning could be attached to standard deviations in this context. Pragmatically, we were looking to see if, on these key issues, more than 65 percent of respondents were giving comparable answers.

108 See Peter Reason (ed.), *Participation in human inquiry*, London: Sage, 1994, pp. 76ff. With the fear of chaotic disintegration often goes a tendency to split and project our deepest anxieties onto whomever close to us will bear them. Here, I knew I had to be careful not to project my anxiety onto the board.

109 See Peter Reason, *Participation: Consciousness and constitutions*, American Academy of Management Conference, May, 1995, and cf. P. Reason and J. Heron "Research with people: The paradigm of co-operative experiential inquiry," *Person Centred Review*, 1 (4) 1986, where they wrote, "From our early inquiries we came to the conclusion that a descent into chaos would often facilitate the emergence of a new creative order." As Reason comments in his AAM paper, there is a striking parallel between this creative side of social chaos on the one hand and the subtle interplay of chaos and order in biological systems. He helpfully quotes Brian Goodwin's fascinating book, *How the leopard changed its spots*, London: Weidenfeld, 1994.

110 See R. M. Kanter, *Address to the National Conference of the Institute of Personnel Management*, Harrogate, UK, 1992.

111 He was referring to David Stoner's work which showed that groups tend to move to a more extreme position than the average of their individual judgements. This finding has been tested in a very wide variety of milieu and been found to be broadly true. See H. Lamm and D. G. Myers, "Group-induced polarization of attitudes and behaviour," in L. Berkowitz, (ed.), *Advances in Experimental Social Psychology*, 11, New York: Academic Press, 1978. Actually, I think he was misusing Stoner's ideas: the work group had not had a chance to formulate a position on the latest developments at this stage so it was anachronistic to say that they were ready for a risky shift. Interestingly, however, as we shall see, there *was* indeed a point at which they seemed ready to make that shift.

Chapter 8
The provocative propositions

1. Organizing the preparation of provocative propositions

I thought I now had no alternative but to ask Paul to share his findings with the work group as a whole. It seemed futile to seek to interest them in provocative propositions without sharing with them the outlines of what may prove the most provocative idea of all. Paul duly addressed them in his most city-like tones.

"There is no doubt in my mind that the vendors are serious. Nor that this represents an amazingly good investment for Healthco. I therefore assume the board of Healthco—of whose deliberations I am wholly ignorant—will go ahead. That will be regretted, even resented, by many employees and by some, but by no means all, patients. If those who object can come up with another way forward that would meet their legitimate objectives of maintaining focus on patient care within a profitable business, it might be possible—and I say might advisedly." Paul was revelling being back in his city boardroom. "It might be possible to put together a plan whereby Healthco sold to a group of staff and patients a majority holding in the non-EMI side of the business to allow them to expand the EMI side faster than they would otherwise be able to. The market is wide open; it will be filled. Healthco would be well advised commercially to make sure it fills as much as possible of it. It is preferable to be a market leader than a market follower. I am now confident—which I was not a week ago—that we can put together the necessary finance to allow staff and patients to effect the buy-out on terms that are onerous but not killing. But that would depend on the people concerned putting up sufficient cash to balance the loan finance. I have taken the liberty of speaking with a number of your wealthier patients and I am reasonably confident that sufficient equity—that is cash up front—would in fact be forthcoming if all the other pieces could be put in place."

There was silence round the table.

The mood had changed. I introduced the subject of provocative propositions, but was immediately interrupted.

"We've just heard the daddy of all provocative propositions," said Naomi, one of the nurses. "Talk about reading a new text! Why don't we just get on and discuss that and see how we are going to sell it to the staff? If they are going to have to put up real money, putting their houses on the line and so on, it's going to take some selling, I can tell you. They may be committed, but there are limits."

In the light of what Paul and I had seen in the entries to the competition, I came within an ace of losing my cool. "Look, could we all please stop thinking of selling things to the stakeholders. That is completely contrary to the appreciative method. It is standing participation on its head. Yes, there *will* come a time after we have analyzed all that the stakeholders have told us and we have presented provocative propositions, based on that analysis, when we shall need to build a consensus round at least some of those provocative propositions. But that is emphatically not selling to the staff or to anyone else. That's something dreamed up here or in the boardroom. For all that we know at this moment, there might be no interest in going the route Paul has outlined. All Paul has been doing is prospecting *one* possible way forward, if, but only if, we are convinced that the data support a provocative proposition along those lines. If they don't, then that avenue is closed, and Paul will, I'm afraid, have wasted his time. He has always known that."

Naomi was not to be so easily contradicted. "Come on, Charles. You know, I know, everyone round this table knows that there is bound to be a huge level of interest throughout the company for the kind of thing Paul is talking about. Aren't you being a touch pedantic, a bit academic in pretending that it might not emerge? OK, I guess the theory says we should wait until we have analyzed the data, tested the propositions, built a consensus and all that stuff. But this is the real world, not a classroom simulation. I thought the virtue of appreciative inquiry was its flexibility. But here we are, with our backs to the wall—or rather the clock—and you are insisting on being inflexible. You seem to be stuck with the old text, which a lot of us who work here want to reject."

There were murmurs of agreement around the table.

"Fair point, Naomi. And I apologize if I sound pedantic. Or academic. Or inflexible. And you may be right that an idea like this might have support. It was because Paul thought he could detect the germ of the idea in the round of interview reports you all did that he went ahead with my blessing and encouragement. So of course I accept that it—whatever "it" turns out to be—may come through. But look at it this way. In justice to everyone involved—and especially to those who have put stuff into the competition—isn't it more in keeping with what we are about to wait and see what *they* have to say before we start telling them what *we* think? I share your anxiety about time, especially in view of what Paul has just told us. But I have much greater anxieties about seeming to pre-empt a careful process—and thereby call the whole thing into question—for the sake of a week or 10 days."

"Then what are we doing here?," demanded a man who worked in the pharmacy in one of the most distant units. He spoke rarely and never this aggressively.

"I wanted to make sure that we all know the steps we shall have to take over the next few weeks," I said. I sounded uncertain. "We need to be clear about data analysis, about how we are going to frame the provocative propositions and how we are going to communicate them, test them and establish a consensus around them—or at least some of them." At last they were ready to get down to work. I was conscious that it was the nearest I had ever come to losing my self-control.

We agreed that the four judges of the competition would produce individual summaries of the major emphases revealed by the entries. Simultaneously, a small work group of four would reread all the interview reports and produce a similar set of summaries. These would be circulated to all members of the work group. We would then have a meeting of the whole group and see if any kind of clarity was emerging. We agreed, too, that if the co-op idea, as it had been unbeautifully christened, seemed to be strongly present, then, given the huge significance of that, we would probably want to limit the number of other provocative propositions to no more than three or four. The absorptive capacity of this organization, like any other, was limited; and absorbing a change of ownership, of board and structure, was going to make demands on all grades of staff, probably more than most of them yet realized.

As often in the past, I found that people in the work group wanted an instant formula for the distillation of the provocative propositions. "What exactly are we looking for?," asked Derek, the accountant. He was used to dealing with ratios and quotients and trial balances. He felt uncomfortable in this less-secure world.

"You are looking for repeated themes which, together, point to a possibility that currently lies just beyond the grasp of the company. You are *not* looking for a majority view nor a way-out odd-ball, but for a gathering set of ideas that, pulled together, given coherence and shape, will command an 'Ah, yes...' from a large majority of stakeholders who will recognize it as building on the best of the past but unlocking a new future."

He looked as convinced as a raw recruit about to go over the top.

"Could I have that written down?... So that I can have it in front of me as I wade through all this stuff?"

I was conscious that the group had moved from euphoria to a paranoid position in the space of two hours. They were feeling persecuted by the volume of work that was coming on them and they wanted to stay with the fun of the competition. I was the bad guy who was making them take the process seriously, being pedantic and denying them the satisfaction of making rapid progress down an exciting new road. Any facilitator will be familiar with these moments; never have I experienced it so strongly. Until now my relationship with the work group had been not just amicable, but almost familial. "The favourite uncle," as someone had put it. That, too, had its dangers I had been aware. Now that I was being demonized as the pedantic taskmaster, separating the group from its own energy, I was going to have to handle the relationship with great care. That was going to be made the more difficult by the fact that I knew, perhaps even more acutely than most of the members of the work group, both how demanding this phase of the work is and how little time we had at our disposal. Like driving on a busy road against the clock, one is uncomfortably aware of the twin dangers of going too fast and of not going fast enough. Pacing the group right would, I knew, add to their sense of being persecuted. The only antidote in my repertoire was to offer the group as much containing as I could manage; that is, to let them know that I knew how they felt and that, however real and unpleasant their feelings were now, they would survive them.

Morale was therefore low when the work group broke up, ready to start reviewing the data. I suspect they felt underbriefed and overburdened, but I knew that to try to reduce the inspection of the data to a formulaic process would rob both the data and its analysis of the freshness and creativity which each member of the work group could bring to it.

Perhaps some facilitators would have opted for a computerized word or phrase search on the written reports, and if the numbers had been significantly greater, such a procedure would indeed have become inevitable. I try to put off this computerization threshold for as long as possible precisely because it loses so much of the creativity of each stage of the process. Something is already lost by the very business of writing a report on the interview. Then, in the case of a computerized search, one needs to identify key words or phrases for which the computer searches and however carefully and comprehensively one does that the fact remains that one is forcing the data into a predetermined mould. That does not deny that much of value will be discovered—and discovered more scientifically, more accurately and more quantifiably than will be achieved by non-computerized means. But it does mean, that against those very real gains, one has to set losses of the idiosyncratic, the unusual, the surprising, the non-standardized. Yet it is, we find, sometimes exactly those odd-balls, which a computer search will usually miss, that provide a key that unlocks a new richness of meaning.

2. Extracting appreciative data from the art competition

For Healthco, then, I was conscious of the demands that were being placed upon the members of the work group who were going to have to look at the written data from the interviews. There were times over the next days, however, when those demands seemed to pale into insignificance by comparison with the task confronting those of us who had to judge the competition. A quick review of the entries sparked three questions: (1) how to find the real meaning of totally different species of entry (which ran from a fully programmed computer game to a highly abstract acrylic canvas measuring six feet by eight); (2) on what criteria to assess what they were seeking to communicate; and (3) how to distil from this mass of creative effort—with 116 entries—the kind of material that could be incorporated with the interview output and eventually form provocative propositions? We quickly decided that we would, at least in the first round, split the task: Paul and I would focus on the meaning of the entries, both individually and in aggregate, the other two would try to decide on a short list of three potential winners.[112]

It was hard to come to the artifacts with no preconceptions, just as it is hard not to put one's own constructions on the data that come in from appreciative interviews. There the stronger the story, the less the likelihood of one projecting one's own agenda. Here, the stronger the artifact (which is not to be confused with the cruder the artifact), the less room it left for our own prejudices.

We were both conscious of how much was riding on the co-op idea. We therefore needed as rigorous a methodology as we could devise to ensure that we were not led to see in the artifacts what we wanted to see in them—or what we knew, consciously or unconsciously, others wanted us to see.

I felt it was also important that we keep the appreciative mode alive in this process of analysis. To my dismay, I was finding that increasingly hard as deadlines shortened and tension rose; how much more comfortable to slip back into old-paradigm thinking! And I knew if that was *my* feeling at this stage, it would be magnified for the others. We were in danger of trying to read the text with crazed glasses. I broached the topic with Paul, half hoping he might see a way through more clearly than I did. He did not but he gave me an important clue.

"You talk about interrogating the text of an organization," he said. "Well…hmmm…let's interrogate the entries about what they tell us about the best of Healthco."

This led us to formulate a very specific criterion that could be put formally like this: As we look at this artifact, what do we think its creator is seeking to communicate about what he or she sees as the best that Healthco is and the best that it could become? If the answer was that it did not seem to communicate anything—or that it communicated so general a message that it allowed us too great a degree of freedom in the interpretation—then we would simply ignore it.

We debated about whether to predetermine categories—quality of care; interpersonal relations; relations with the board; administrative sensitivity and so on, items that we expected to come up from what we had seen in the interview reports, but we quickly came to the conclusion that that was to move too rapidly to a form of closure. Unconsciously, I think we were both longing to be surprised, and we therefore wanted to do nothing that would jeopardize that surprise.

As I went, rather self-consciously, through the piles of paintings, poems, songs, videos, essays, messages, carvings, the two themes that forced themselves upon me were, first, something about wholeness, harmony, integration, that cluster of connotations of health that goes far deeper than the absence of illness. It was as if the entries—and the people from all walks of life, disciplines and levels of seniority within the organization who had expressed themselves in their creation—were saying something like: Healthco is not about recovery from disease or the curing of symptoms; at its best it is about a quality of life that has to be enfleshed in the daily routine of the organization itself. I had expected to see much about the quality of *care*; what I was actually seeing was about the quality of *life*. Or more challengingly, I was being told that the quality of care is optimized by the quality of life that is lived within the organization by all its participants—from the illest patient to the most skilled physician to the kitchen porter. This seemed to me a more profound insight than anything that had, so far, come out of the interviews.

The second impression was something about detail: that little things matter. That was easy to see in some of the paintings and in a couple of wood carvings, but it was expressed most beautifully in a poem about a man dying of AIDS. One quatrain lodged with me immediately and stays with me still:

I look into the eyes of death and know
The smallest things are now too huge
To fumble. My every breath, my simplest move
Touch him in his deepest part. Forgive.

I had initially to work hard to translate that into the language of the appreciative inquiry, but it suddenly became unnervingly clear. Healthco is at its best when it gives space and value to the little things. The big things—the co-op idea, for example—might be important in their way, but what really matters to both patients and staff is having time and encouragement to care enough to get the details right, to be aware that the simplest move touches people around us "in their deepest part." If we are forced, by time pressure, by the need for profits, by administrative overburden, by deadening routine, to forget that, we do indeed stand in need of forgiveness. The formal side of organization is therefore to be judged by the way it honours the details, especially the detailed interaction between staff and patient, as it were at the apex of care, but below that, between any persons or groups of persons connected with the organization.

It would not be true to say that there were no entries that picked up on some of the issues we had been discussing in the work group. There was, for example, a marvellously libellous bawdy song which began with the lines

Daisy, Daisy,
I'm half crazy
All for the love of a loo.

140

It went on to poke fun at the way decisions about capital expenditure (the loo) were made when there was a conflict between patient desires (not strictly needs) and the desire of the directors for profit maximization. The moral seemed to be that if patients were shareholders, such conflicts might not be resolved, but they would be aired from quite different perspectives.

And there was a remarkable entry from the two groundsmen at one of the most distant units (which was submitted via a video). How they had found money or time to construct it was a mystery, but it was in essence an Indian water garden, a kind of horticultural parable, making the point that the life of any organization (symbolized by water) becomes decreasingly effective the more it is divided between competing ends. One might see this as another statement about the need for harmony and integration as above, but what was striking—apart from the provenance and the sophistication of design and execution—was the refusal, made explicit in the unvarnished commentary on the voice-over, to come to any half-baked conclusions. However often a stream is divided, water remains water; the form of its channel does not change its chemical composition. Perhaps the creators of the garden were telling us that organizational structure is in the end less important than the people who make up that structure.

At the end of a day locked into a large common room with the entries, Paul was as mind blown as I.

"Hmmm…. Ye gods!… Most impressive… but what… where do we go from here?"

I asked him what clues he had come up with.

"Well, I'm clearer about what is not there than about what is. There's not a huge head of steam for the cooperative thing. That's plain. A few point in that direction, a few might be *interpreted* to do so, but that would be largely in the eye of the beholder. There's less than I expected directly on the quality of care issue, and, interestingly, very little anti-feeling about expansion into the care of EMIs. If you look for analogous patterns with the interviews, yes, they are there, but less strongly than I would have expected. There's much about the quality of relationships at all levels; there's much about administration and the need to simplify it; there's much about what I call patients first which overlaps with the quality of care thing, but which is essentially about financial decision-making. Trust seems to be an issue, too. I suppose that is part of the quality of relationships that a lot of the entries seem to be about, but I was very struck by some of the poems and songs and a short story that was making the point that just as the patient puts his trust in the doctor, so the doctor puts his trust in the nurse and the cleaner and the cook and the person who types the path lab report and so on. Sorry, I'm rabbiting on. It's so rich and yet so hard to pin down. You begin to long for a good old-fashioned head-count that says at the end of the day: 'x percent want a co-op; y percent want to go into EMI care; z percent want nothing to change.' Would that life were so easy!"

We spent the next day working through the entries again, this time collaboratively, checking with each other what we saw, what impressions each artifact left with us, what we thought it contributed to the inquiry. This proved an astonishingly enriching experience for both of us and we wished that we had had the whole work group with us—though recognizing that if that wish had been granted, we would have taken at least 10 times as long, and possibly come out with quite different results. Nonetheless, we felt sufficiently confident of our reading of the entries by the end of the second day that we could write a short report for the rest of the work group outlining the appreciative indications that we had been struck by, and comment on the things we had expected to find, but which did not, on our reading, appear to be strongly reflected in the entries.

On the vexed issue of the co-op, we had this to say: "We know that there was a lot of discussion throughout the organization about the possibility of the staff and patients jointly buying a controlling interest in the existing Healthco. While that idea is not wholly unreflected in the entries, it is our shared view that there is very little evidence that it has gripped the imagination of the great majority of those who have submitted entries. Further and perhaps more telling, where it is reflected, it is referred to tangentially or parenthetically or subordinately. It would certainly be hard to argue from the work we have seen that there is a strong desire to move in that direction. We believe many of those who have taken part in the competition see that as a subsidiary issue of less interest than the more central issues of relationships, mutual trust and the care of patients."

I asked Paul how he felt about that. He shrugged. "At one level, sad. It would have been an interesting way to go and would, I think, have addressed some of the underlying issues—such as a residual hostility to the idea of a company making profits out of caring for the sick. But I agree that there is not enough... hmm... oomph behind the idea as reflected here to make it viable. And I don't just mean in terms of numbers. I never expected that. But if there had been a core of really committed people who were ready to bring creativity and imagination and enthusiasm to it that would have been different. But it ain't there—yet. And so that's that."

On matters of substance which might go forward into provocative propositions, it was not hard to isolate half a dozen over which we had no difficulty in agreeing and another four or five where we found that our readings were quite different. Our report concentrated on the former, but we kept detailed notes of the latter, resolving to bring them forward if they chimed with what came out of the reflections on the interview material by the rest of the work group. We therefore listed the following points:

1. Quality of relationship at every level of the company is vital and needs time and resources and a far higher visibility in the thinking of management. Trust is a key element of that quality.

2. Administrative systems work best when their purpose is clear to everyone who has to operate them.

3. Transparency of decision-making about investment in patient facilities (in the broadest sense) increases acceptability to both patients and staff about inevitable conflict between care and profit.

4. The devil may be in the detail—but so is the glory.

5. The sum is greater than the parts in the context of care. Therefore mutuality, shared respect and appropriate information flows need attention throughout the company. A special priority for cross-unit interaction seems to be called for.

6. Healthco exists to serve the sick and vulnerable, of whatever type that vulnerability may be. (This one surprised us both, but came through the entries strongly. There was not only a sense of wishing to expand into the care of EMIs; on the contrary, plenty of entries seemed to recognize that here was a form of human need that was underserved in the community at large and which Healthco was well equipped, in terms of experience and skills, to meet.)

Paul and I shared a sense that in what we had written we were in danger of somehow failing to communicate to our colleagues the depth and subtlety of thought that lay behind many of the entries. "We're doing a kind of lowest common denominator exercise," Paul commented gloomily, "and I always hate that. There's too much of it around."

I agreed and I was conscious too that such a coarse distillation is, in an important sense, contrary to the spirit of the appreciative approach. Be that as it may, it is nonetheless true that in any appreciative inquiry, one always finds oneself in this position, just as our colleagues working on the interview material were distressed at the simplifications and distortions that inevitably come out of that process. That is why, as I was to emphasize constantly to the work group in the next phase of the inquiry, we try to avoid working in a too mechanical or closed way. We need to keep in mind the complexities and multi-valencies of the raw material and allow our own imaginations and inventiveness to play with them. Paul, I thought, was beginning to see the significance of this play, however contrary it ran to his professional formation. I looked forward to seeing how the rest of the group were faring.

3. The analysis of the interview data

Some of them, it transpired when we next met, were as stimulated by their material as Paul and I had been by ours. It was clearly going to be a tough task to concentrate on a smallish number of central issues, and I feared that I would again be seen as the persecuting parent who would not allow them to play with the ideas—although it was, paradoxically, I who was encouraging, with the reading the text metaphor, the notion of play. That very paradox would make me seem all the more sadistic. I was therefore very explicit about the group itself deciding who was to chair it throughout this phase and how the ground rules of discussion were to be determined. Oddly, the latter question turned out to be easier to settle than the former. For once there was a smell of cordite in the air while they discussed who should take the chair. It soon became clear that it was an issue of control: as the climax of the process approached so Roger and the accountant, Derek, seemed to be attempting to ensure that control rested in safe management hands. A small group of the more vocal staff, mostly nurses and paramedics, were warmly opposed to so cozy an arrangement and sought to establish their own control.

We looked set for a long and distasteful fight. We were spared that only by Mary, the patients' representative, who, in her quiet and perfectly elocuted way, pointed out that it would be appropriate if she or Paul chaired the sessions. "We have no axe to grind, except the most fundamental axe of all: that patients' interests are always respected." As Mary had been judging the competition rather than looking for the raw material of provocative propositions within them, she seemed a natural choice. Perhaps because she was both so courteous and so well able to wrap an iron fist in layers of the softest velvet, she turned out to be exactly what was required to steer us through some technically demanding and occasionally acrimonious discussions.

In the event, the list of issues that came from the interview group was remarkably parallel to the list that Paul and I had prepared. Certainly there were marked differences in language, in emphasis and in style, with more attention to implementation and concrete suggestions about what is to be done. More explicit was the ambivalence about profits from health care and, even more so, anxieties about job security, wrapped in appreciative language though both of these were. Very similar to what we had found, on the other hand, was much material on collaboration, mutuality, respect, trust, interdependence, the positive contribution of the support staff, even though they may never come into contact with patients.

4. Assembling the data—and its emotional impact

When we tabled our report, it was greeted with disbelief both because of the broad similarities with the interview material and, more predictably, because of what it said about the cooperative. The group that I had mentally labelled the Diggers derided the whole appreciative inquiry as a waste of time because it had not produced the result that they had come to desire (without, as Paul pointed out, being clear about many of the implications).

Standing back from the now-heated exchanges between Paul and the Diggers, I realized that we were heading for the most serious crisis yet, just as we approached the most creative and significant part of the process. It was not so much that the Diggers represented a smallish minority (there were six of them) nor that they were well coordinated, coherent and cohesive. The role that a vocal minority can play in making a majority re-examine its own assumptions and logics is vital as an antidote to group-think or the domination of a small cabal.[113] It was much more that *some* of what they were saying—that the point of provocative propositions is to provoke, not to reflect majority opinion—was quite correct and needed to be heard by the work group as a whole, for some of its number would have settled too easily for a quiet life with a revamped *status quo.*

The Diggers' disenchantment with the process was just about handleable; much less so was their unconscious abandonment of the appreciative mode. To try to form provocative propositions while they were stuck in what was sounding increasingly like an old-fashioned shop floor haranguing match was not only dangerous, it was a denial of everything I thought we had all been committed to. For me, then, the central issues had now become, first, holding the work group in appreciative mode and, second, allowing them to use the energy they were wasting on berating Paul on the more constructive task of framing provocative propositions. Conscious as I was of some of the negativities that were still sticking to me as the demanding task-master—now reinforced by my identification with the death of the co-op idea—I could not help wondering how far the mauling that Paul was getting was actually intended for me. (I smiled at the thought of Paul, banker to his finger tips, as sacrificial victim.[114]) If there was that level of hostility among even the small number of Diggers, how could we find a way back into appreciative mode that would allow the group as a whole to move forward? For it was not a matter of closing down their anger, disappointment and frustration, but of flipping those emotions over so that they became a positive charge that could serve a useful purpose.

5. Containing the emotional response

I needed to find a way back to the main track of the inquiry that would keep as many of the Diggers as possible with us. Should I try to reason with them? Should I resort to some kind of moral or inspirational suasion?[115] These might have worked at the substantive level: what was required was an intervention that would allow them to re-enter the appreciative mode. Throwing caution to the wind, I launched a major containment exercise.

"Look," I said, speaking as slowly and quietly as I could manage, "you guys are disappointed and angry. You had set great store by introducing what would have been a revolutionary concept in the history of British health care. It was exciting, innovative, offering you a chance to have much greater say on the future development of Healthco—and perhaps to right some of the wrongs you are familiar with. So it was a hugely attractive possibility, that would have served many of your emotional and practical needs and those of your colleagues and all our patients. So no wonder you were committed to it at the emotional level, even though at the superficial level you knew that it had to acquire support from a significant minority of the staff and patients."

"It would have done if it had been sold properly," interrupted one of the Diggers.

"Ah, well," I replied, hardly believing my luck that he would play so directly into my hands. "That's really the issue, isn't it? You feel let down because they did not buy what you had already bought. But as I have said many times before, the appreciative method is not about selling anything. It is about liberating what is in people, about actualizing what they have already learned from their own experience. That is not to deny that sometimes it is right to sell an idea whose time has come. And maybe the co-op idea's time has come and it *should* now be sold. But the appreciative inquiry is not the process for that."

The same Digger interrupted again. "You're being too purist again. Appreciative inquiry is, I thought, about change, about change for the better. Here was a potential change that could have revolutionized this place. And now we've thrown away the opportunity."

"No we haven't. The people who have taken part in the competition have told us—Paul and I think unambiguously, and the evidence is there for you all to inspect and see if you come to another conclusion—that they are not yet ready to go down that road. They are not saying or we don't hear them saying, 'Never. No way....' but they are surfacing far deeper issues that would need to be addressed whatever the pattern of ownership and control of the company. That surely is the strength of what we are doing in this inquiry: we are getting at the core issues that determine how this place operates and the quality of life it enables for all its stakeholders. To that extent, the issues raised by the cooperative are seen by the staff and the patients who took part in the competition as secondary. They want us to address the primary issues."

"There's nothing more bloody primary than who runs the company and what they run it for." It was the same Digger again. I suspected he was beginning to feel deserted by the rest.

"Perhaps. And at least some of that *is* addressed by your material and ours. Surely what we need to do is to pay attention to that material and frame provocative propositions that do justice to it and which, maybe, leave open the questions of

146

ownership and control for the moment. They are not going to disappear off the agenda in a puff of smoke. But if we are going to be fair by the data we have before us, we cannot pretend that there is sufficient support for it at this stage to warrant making it the explicit objective of the propositions."

He was silent, withdrawn, morose.

More containing: "I know how hard it is when you have glimpsed something that really excites you and then feel let down by your colleagues and perhaps by your facilitator. It's hard to get back into appreciative mode when all you want to do is to storm out and kick the cat. And of course you end up resenting the process, because, if it had been different, you may have had a better chance of pulling off the radical innovation. It's the price we pay for an essentially participative process. Sometimes we have to wait for people to catch up. And waiting is the hardest thing in the world for action-oriented people. But it is a sacrifice that trust has to make to caution. Never easy; often painful."

One of the other Diggers spoke: a 30-something senior secretary in one of the new EMI units.

"Well, I guess I can go with that if you are saying we are not obliged to bury the idea for good and all. Of course, we shall never have as good an opportunity as this again, but if people are not yet ready for it, if we have a lot more talking, explaining, educating, encouraging to do before it will fly, well, perhaps it isn't as good an opportunity as it looks anyway."

"I'm not the thought police," I smiled. "My hunch would be that people will go on talking and thinking about this. If it catches fire, then it may well be inextinguishable. Who knows? Obviously, it is not part of the appreciative inquiry process to kill off *any* ideas that might be in the pot. It is our job to go with the flow of what is there that is new, exciting, energy generating *and* fairly well established already, though perhaps seldom articulated or even brought to consciousness."

"And," chipped in Paul, "if we get the provocative propositions right and all that flows from them, we can nurture that process. I was as disappointed as anybody about the way things went. After all, I had put a lot of work in to it and put my credibility on the line with people I cannot afford to antagonize. But I am beginning to think that a period of reflection, of growth into the idea, of letting it take root would be better than trying to cobble something together against the clock before everyone, or at least a significant core, is really ready."

The murmur of assent showed that he had defused the frustration of the Diggers. We could move on.

After this spat, the first time real anger had been expressed in the work group, and, perhaps even more revealingly, the first time the group had divided on clear ideological lines, there was a sharp change in mood. How far the containing had enabled that; how far it was a natural reaction; and how far it was a guilt-induced correction, it is pointless to speculate. I could not help thinking of the Diggers' behaviour, even at the time, in Kleinian terms: as a swing from the paranoid-schizoid position—persecuted by both colleagues and facilitator and splitting the emotional response and dumping it on Paul and then on me—to the depressive position, in which they were seeking to make amends for the damage they had done. If that was right, it would make it all the more important to hold them in that depressive position as long as I could. That would not involve playing on their feelings of guilt—that would be nothing but destructive. Rather it meant accepting the gestures of reconciliation that they made and allowing them to feel, as they resumed the appreciative mode, that they were indeed recreating a healthy and sustaining relationship.

6. The provocative propositions emerge

And indeed they were, for they went about the business of forming the provocative propositions out of the material we had severally contributed with a quiet purposefulness, guided with precision and economy by Mary and the minimum of instruction from me. It was as if the experiences they had been through had already given them a natural insight into what the provocative propositions needed to be and needed to do, and they could, individually and as a group, now see quite clearly how they were going to do it.

Within an hour and a half, then, the main shape of the provocative propositions had begun to emerge; and the Group insisted on an extra meeting the following weekend to polish them up and get them into a form which could be circulated immediately to all the people on our mailing list. Coincidentally, they would thus become public property within a few days of the expected board announcement about the take-over.

Perhaps surprisingly, the propositions that bore most directly on the co-op idea neither originated from the Diggers nor proved especially contentious. There were two of them and in their semi-polished form they emerged like this:

Healthco is a profitable company and funds further expansion and improvement from its profits. It limits the proportion of profits paid out in dividends and other returns to capital to a maximum of one-third of net after-tax profits, investing the balance in the enhancement of patient provision.

and

Healthco's success in providing a patient-centred environment where the quality of care is paramount depends upon the quality of working and living relationships among all employees. Healthco therefore recognizes the need to foster mutual respect, collaboration and the acknowledgement of interdependence throughout the company and to that end is committed to four days a year when every full-time employee is exposed to cross-functional job experience.

I expected that Roger, the personnel director, would have great difficulty with both these propositions. In fact he was relaxed about the first, on the grounds that if the take over was going ahead, there would be no possibility of paying more than a third of profits as dividends for a very long time. "And after that," he finished enigmatically, "who knows?"

It was the second that caused him much more concern. "Do you mean to say that we shall be committed to four days a year when the clinics are taken by gardeners and the meals cooked by paramedics and the accounts kept by consultants?"

"No." Mary spoke from the chair. "But as I understand it, we would be committed to four days a year when the consultants might be accompanied on their rounds by a gardener or, for that matter, a gardener might have a consultant in the greenhouse. Who knows? The consultant might even be allowed to prick out the lettuces, though I doubt if the gardener will be allowed to insert a drip."

"Dear God." Roger was having some difficulty with this image.

"An extreme example, no doubt," Mary continued suavely. "But you get the idea. If we are serious about mutuality, it surely makes sense that everyone should understand more about the work of their colleagues on whom they rely, often without realizing it. We were told constantly in the interviews that what makes Healthco special is—or was—this sense of people supporting each other."

Roger shook his head in disbelief, but remained silent. I suspected he was already thinking how the board could deflect the propositions or at least make them less provocative.

That was going to provide the last major challenge.

---

112 I shall say nothing about this aspect of the process. In retrospect, it almost certainly was not a good idea to set it up in terms of a competition. Judging a winner turned out to be not only meaningless, but also quite invasive of the spirit of the enterprise. The strongest thing that can be said for it is perhaps that it stimulated many people to be involved in a way that perhaps nothing else would have done.

113 See for example, C. J. Nemeth, "Differential contributions of majority and minority influence," *Psychological Review*, 93, 1986, pp. 23-31.

114 I should not, however, be taken to imply that the way groups select and then seek to destroy a scapegoat is a risible issue. Far from it. See, for instance, Rene Girard's classic study of this process in *The scapegoat*, trans., Yvonne Freccero, Baltimore: Johns Hopkins University Press, 1986.

115 On the power of this see G. A. Yukl and C. M. Falbe, "Influence tactics in upward, downward and lateral influence attempts," *Journal of Applied Psychology*, 75, 1990. Yukl and Falbe show that earlier experimental work by Kipnis *et al.* understated the effectiveness of moral suasion whatever the direction of influence.

Chapter 9
Action

1. Building consensus among the stakeholders

The 10 provocative propositions were circulated to staff and patients exactly eleven weeks after the first meeting of the work group. Just over two-thirds of the employees had been directly involved in the process, and although the proportion of patients admitted over the last six months was lower, we had contributions in one form or another from nearly 40. The proportion of stakeholders taking part was, then, by the standards of most medium-scale appreciative inquiries, acceptable, and the openness of the art competition (as it had, somewhat misleadingly, come to be called) had ensured that everyone who wanted to make a contribution had had the opportunity.

We did not, therefore, expect serious difficulty in winning a hearing for the provocative propositions. Building a consensus around them might, however, be more of a challenge. The method we chose was simple. Within a fortnight to a month of the circulation of the propositions, each member of the work group would convene a focus group in his or her place of work. Patients resident within the catchment area of each unit would be invited to the same meetings. Size would be limited to 20 (bigger than optimal, but we could not expect work group members to run more than two focus groups each) and duration to 90 minutes.

It became clear that I needed to train the work group to run these focus groups. The notion of selling the propositions reared its ugly head again, this time with slightly more justification in that we were after a consensus around the propositions and that consensus would need construction and, therefore, a degree of restrained and subtle advocacy. I tried to make the point that the appreciative way forward was not to bludgeon people into accepting the propositions, but rather to present them as *their* creation, the distillation of their input—and then to invite their ownership of them. It was about presenting a reading of the text and inviting others to share that reading, or to adjust their own reading in its light.

It was Sheila, the senior secretary who had been one of the Diggers, who spoke. "But what if they say, 'Nothing doing. We don't like these provocative propositions,' or, more likely, 'We like some of them but not all of them.' I can easily imagine hearing one of the consultants saying, 'I simply don't have time to spend four days a year in the potting shed.' "

"Fair question and not unlikely at all," I smiled. "All I think you can do is to keep taking them back to the basic approach, keep explaining that what we have tried to do is to take their wisdom on what makes Healthco healthy. This is what they have told us. If someone wants to opt out—well, I guess we can't force anyone. But they need, in the end, to be obliged to accept responsibility for what they are doing, which is to turn away from something that a lot of people here think, rightly or wrongly, gives this place a special feel. I must say my experience is not what you seem to be fearing. Sure, people will express reservations about the detail. And they will want to monkey about with the wording. But usually I have been surprised and delighted at the level of enthusiasm and energy which the provocative propositions—if we've got them right—generate."

We agreed that I would be a roving observer, attending such of the focus groups as I could, but not taking part and only answering questions on process. Some people asked me not to be embarrassed about coaching them afterwards if I saw them making mistakes in the conduct of the groups. Roger pointedly did not ask me to attend the board meeting at which he would make his presentation.

The focus groups were better attended by people who had not participated thus far than by those who had. I asked some of the work group members how they interpreted that, for I found it puzzling and counter-intuitive. The general impression was that the people who had contributed, through either the interviews or the competition, were broadly satisfied with the propositions: their questions tended to be nitty-gritty ones about implementation. The people who had not contributed, by contrast, were either curious or found the style and wording of the provocative propositions too opaque.

This opened a disconcerting line of inquiry of its own. I spent a day analyzing who had been interviewed and who had submitted some artifact to the competition. Despite our best endeavours with the interviews—we had no control over entries to the competition—it looked as though participation in the process had been skewed quite heavily toward the higher-skill groups and therefore away from the less educated, less articulate, less middle-class professional groups. I was puzzled about this because we had made a strategic decision with the interviews to represent each function proportionately, so a social skew should not have happened. Conversations with some of the work group and a further check on my own data showed what had happened. *Within* each function cohort, the less educated who had been randomly selected for interview tended to decline the invitation and give their place to someone, in the same cohort, better educated or more articulate, or both. In a word, the less educated had disenfranchised themselves and were now turning up in disproportionate numbers to see what they had missed. And because they had missed out on the earlier conversations, they found the provocative propositions complex and mystifying.

I was angry with myself for not having spotted this obvious (in retrospect) quirk in the process. Although I was confident that it would make no difference to the outcome, I felt a carelessness in the design had compromised the participatory nature of what we were about—*and I had only just noticed it.* I regretted not having checked at the interviewing stage whether we were being sufficiently sensitive to the reticence of some groups who imagine, perhaps, that they have little to offer. In the meantime, a number of the work groups were reporting that they were having great difficulty keeping the focus group meetings to 90 minutes because so much of the time had to be devoted to explaining, sometimes over and over, what the provocative propositions meant and what implementation might imply.

"When they do get the message," said Derek, the accountant, "they are excited, sometimes a bit nervous, a bit apprehensive even. But I'm picking up no hostility, no opposition. They even cheered the one about the minimization of admin overburden—but maybe that was for my benefit!"

At the next work group meeting, his experience seemed to have been widely shared. Were there, I wondered, any of the 10 propositions that could be eliminated because they had not commanded such acceptance? A quick trawl round the group identified two possible candidates: one about training and professional formation which seemed to have elicited no comment at all (perhaps it was too anodyne); and one about greater interaction between units (fine in theory, not a high priority in practice). I asked the work group if they wanted to eliminate them. The consensus was they should stay formally on the agenda but that we should give them a low priority in terms of implementation unless there was a groundswell of opinion that started agitating for faster progress.

2. The reaction of the board

At the same meeting of the work group, Roger reported on the board's discussion of the provocative propositions.

"It went better than I had predicted in that there was real interest in some of the ideas—and by that I mean exactly what I say. This was not tokenism nor an attempt to placate the workforce. Rather to my surprise, the chairman, no less, was keen to explore the detailed implementation of some of the propositions— for example on a dividend ceiling; on having another look at our administrative systems to eliminate anything that isn't absolutely necessary; on building trust. I have to tell you that his interest is primarily the bottom line. Obviously cutting excessive documentation is a way of cutting costs. Having a dividend ceiling could be wonderful PR. Building trust is the latest in-word in the management schools so it must be good for the business. That may sound crude. I don't mean it to be. It is how Bill thinks and it is because he is so single minded that this company has been able to grow so fast, as we have just demonstrated with the takeover. There were some things he was less keen on: he was pretty skeptical about job-swapping or whatever you call it, as am I. But in general the door is wide open."

3. Preparing for implementation

We accordingly arranged for the whole work group to meet with the whole board to rank the propositions in implementation priority, but before that meeting I suggested that the work group do some homework of its own. They needed to be clear in their own minds what were their own priorities, to have given some thought to the details of implementation, and to have the arguments marshalled that would speak to the likes of Bill.

"So far we have gone with the process in its own terms," I said. "That is, it has been a satisfactory argument to say, 'This is what people are telling us from reflecting on their experience in appreciative mode.' OK. But now, we are going to have to add on to that—not abandon it, but add on to it—an argument about it (whatever that is) being demonstrably good for the business. The two arguments are not incompatible—not if the appreciative stuff has been honestly done. But there is a big difference in language and style of presentation. We need to be ready for that."

As I had noticed before, an external challenge did wonders for the internal cohesiveness of the work group. Without reference to me they put together three sub-groups to work on sets of the propositions, setting themselves three questions:

- what exactly needs to be done by whom to make it happen?

- how easily could this be done within our present structures?

- what benefits will it bring and in what time period?

I would have preferred them to reverse the order, because I think a glimpse of the benefits motivates people to find ways around the structural obstacles that one always encounters. If you start with the obstacles, you can easily get lost in a miasma of organizational in-fighting, the very reverse of the appreciative mode. Perhaps mistakenly, I did not press the point, resolving to suggest it if I saw any of the sub-groups beginning to get stuck on the first two questions.

In the exercise, the only contentious conversation in the sub-groups was about a proposition that read like this: *Healthco values the people who work in the company and seeks to maximize job security in return for the loyal service of its staff. Further, it takes pride in matching tasks to skills and temperaments in the belief that a contented workforce is a necessary precondition of the highest quality of care.*

As so often with provocative propositions, you have to scrape away the superficial gloss to discover the provocation. This was actually all about Healthco guaranteeing that none of its existing staff would be obliged to work with EMIs if they did not choose to do so. There was perhaps more grassroots emphasis on this proposition than on any other single one because fears were widespread that the company would seek to restaff the homes it was now committed to buy with a core of its existing employees. And given the reputation of some of the newly bought homes for low-quality staffing, such fears were entirely understandable. They were reinforced by the rumour that the long-term plan was to switch all the existing units to EMI care, with the implication that you either worked with this type of patient or you did not work for Healthco at all.

The implementation of the proposition clearly implied a guarantee from the company that no one would ever be required to work with a type of patient not of their choosing. Or to put it baldly, the company was being asked to guarantee that no one who did not want to would have to work with EMIs. And that implied that the company was being asked to forego the extra profit margins it would certainly enjoy by switching some or all of its existing units to that type of patient.

It happened—I think entirely coincidentally—that Roger was in that sub-group. He argued that the board would be sympathetic to the preferences of the staff, but that it could not allow its hands to be tied by the issue of a guarantee. The staff on the sub-group, who, equally coincidentally included two of the Diggers, were adamant that a guarantee was required. They knew well enough that the real issue was job security and that only a public guarantee of no forced reallocation would meet the fears of their colleagues. We were moving to deadlock.

I therefore put in action my reserve plans to shift them back into appreciative mode by looking at the benefits. I was aware, however, of the need to do so cautiously. I, therefore, made the issue purely procedural.

"You seem to be getting stuck on the second item on your agenda with this proposition. Time is running on: we meet the board the day after tomorrow and you have no other meeting scheduled. So may I suggest, for the sake of completeness, that you leave this discussion here and move on to the third item on your list. If time permits, you may want to come back to this question. If not, you will just have to report to the work group as a whole, at its session immediately before the meeting with the board, that you could not agree on this issue. That's OK. It isn't the end of the world."

The relief was palpable. And the enthusiasm of the discussion of the benefits was, counter-intuitively, equally shared between Roger and the Diggers.

The discussion ended with Roger saying, as much to himself as to anyone else, "Yeah. Yeah. We've got to do something. Not a public guarantee. The board will never buy that. But we have to find another way. I'll go away and think about it some more."

He was as good as his word. He brought to the final session of the work group, before the encounter with the board, the suggestion that the board declare company policy to be that no member of staff of three years' unbroken service or more be obliged to work with a category of patient for which they had not been trained. If no appropriate work was available with other types of patient, the company would offer either compensation for loss of employment at one and a half times official redundancy rates or training for work in a form of employment that did not demand intensive patient contact. It would be false to claim that this offer won over all the Diggers with enthusiasm, but Roger had shown that he was capable of moving toward them and that he had accepted that there was a general problem that needed addressing. Although we did not have time to come to a detailed agreement, it was clear that compromise was now possible, and, more important perhaps, the work group did not enter the meeting with the board in a spirit of antagonism or persecution.

4. The work group meets the board

In fact the board meeting was something of an anticlimax. Following the pre-arranged and necessarily somewhat stilted plan, one member of the work group spoke for six minutes on a proposition, giving its potted history, recounting some of the stories that lay behind it and the organizational impact of its implementation. I had coached the speakers in presenting this material appreciatively; that is to avoid speaking about the problems that the proposition addressed or the difficulties that implementation would bring, but rather to go back to the original best practice or peak experience data we had and speak about the organizational benefits to be garnered from implementation. By and large they had learned this lesson well; indeed, when the board member who was to respond inevitably slipped into problem language, Adrian, one of the Diggers, corrected him with great sensitivity.

"You speak about the problems," he said. "We do not of course deny those. But if that is where we start the discussion, that is where we will finish it. We shall be overwhelmed by the problems. Let's look at the opportunities and the benefits and then see what needs to be changed to realize them."

Bill, the board chairman, shot me a half-amused, half-irritated look that said: "You've coached these buggers a bit too well. When do we reach the real world?"

His way of reaching for the real world, in which he was followed by all but two of the rest of the board, was to ask insistently, "But what will it cost?" Of course there are costs associated with any change and I do not wish to imply that the board was being obstructive by focusing on this issue. Maybe we should have done more work on that aspect before we met with them. The reality, however, was that the costs associated with any individual provocative proposition were small and mostly insignificant. Perhaps the most expensive proposed innovation was the job-swap arrangement which, it could be argued, implied an indirect rise in the salary bill of about 1.5 percent—not huge, but enough to raise the finance director's concern.

What had looked as if it might develop into a defensive sparring match actually, thanks in large measure to skilful chairing, became a tightly focused discussion with three major topics: benefits, costs, timeframe; and two subsidiary topics, who would take lead responsibility and through what channels would they work?

It was a long and exhausting meeting. By its end, however, we had ranked the propositions in order of priority of execution. We knew who was responsible for making them happen and with whom they needed to consult, and we had identified the benefits we expected to flow from their implementation. We had put the two questionable provocative propositions into cold storage, not least because the executive demands on some of the key players were already formidable; and we had agreed to delay implementation of two more until the first round was up and running.

5. Embedding the appreciative approach

We held over to a later meeting one of the delicate but fundamental questions that practitioners of the appreciative approach always emphasize—how to *embed* a monitoring and evaluation function in the implementation of the provocative propositions, so that there is in place a feedback loop which, maintaining the appreciative mode, allows the organization to adjust its learning to its actual experience. At one level, this has become the stock in trade of the learning organization in the style of Peter Senge,[116] but at a deeper level, it requires that the whole organization so internalize the appreciative mode that it becomes second nature to look out for best practice and ask how it can be built into the texture of organizational life.

Concretely, Healthco needed to find ways of tracking the benefits associated with the provocative propositions, not by the accumulation of yet more administrative overburden, but by processes that encouraged staff at all levels to get into the habit of reflecting on their experience from an appreciative point of view. In Healthco's case, they had the unusual advantage of also being in close touch with their customers, an opportunity which, handled sensitively, offered a rich resource of feedback information which was currently much underused.

From the point of view of *process*, I was uncertain how best to get this final piece of the jigsaw in place. I worked out a number of ideas to put before the others. In brief, these were, first, the formation of appreciative circles in which three or four colleagues would routinely meet, perhaps once a month and certainly across units, to look at the month's work, identify the best, look for benefits from the provocative propositions and report to a sub-committee of the work group who would continue in existence for that purpose.

The second option was to reconstitute the focus groups which the members of the work group had run as part of the consensus building around the provocative propositions. And the third option was to put round a simple questionnaire every month, with questions like, Where have you seen Healthco at its best this month? Are there ways in which we could generalize that? Or, the company is committed to proposition X; where have you seen that commitment being delivered? In your own experience, what benefits did it bring?

It came as no surprise that in a private meeting, Bill, the board chairman, summarily dismissed the third option. "If we've got one provocative proposition declaring war on bumph," said Bill testily, "don't for Pete's sake let us be party to introducing more."

He was marginally more enthusiastic about the appreciative circles and the focus groups, though with less frequent meetings than I had proposed. "Too many damn meetings in this place," growled Bill. "People forget that meetings cost money."

When we took the ideas to the joint meeting of the work group and the board, the same lack of enthusiasm was evident, even among some of the freer spirits of the work group. I had to admit that I had not gotten it right. After a brief brainstorming session, however, we had a much lighter, more flexible and more feasible solution. A monitoring group of three—one director, one senior administrator and one nurse or paramedic—would send a note round to all staff and patients every three months, calling for written submissions *and giving notice that they would be visiting randomly to seek comments, reactions, answers to appreciative-style questions that would be included in their note.* Thus everyone would be put on notice to prepare for the visit. Only a small number would be visited, but everyone would have the opportunity to write in if they felt, on reflection, that they had something worth sharing.

6. Two years on

Like all case studies this one has to finish before the end of the story can be written. Some loose ends can, however, be gathered up. The work group was discontinued after the second meeting with the board, though the Diggers continued to meet occasionally in a pub, and were scrupulous about inviting the rest of the group to join them. Adrian told me they found it much more useful as a way of keeping the spirit of the inquiry alive than the monitoring group.

That view was contested by Sheila who was soon put on the monitoring group after it had made a rather shaky start. "The proof of the pudding," she said. "The fact is that we have made major headway on all the provocative propositions we have implemented. The anxieties about the expansion into the care of EMIs have evaporated completely. You never hear it mentioned as an issue now. I would say relations with the board are better than they have been as long as I have been working with Healthco. And the job-swap, for all the initial skepticism, has become really popular. I can't say we have yet seen consultants with dew strings round their trousers planting the antirrhinums, but I have had both a surgeon and a boilerman shadowing me (at different times, of course) and they and I have both enjoyed the experience. And for the surgeon, it actually had a quick pay-off: he knew a patient was in financial difficulties; he knew, because we had talked about it when he was with me for the day, that I keep a list of charities that have helped us in the past. And so within 24 hours we could get that sorted out to the patient's great benefit. And I've spent a day in the boiler house—so I moan a good deal less when the heating breaks down! I know that Bert will be running round like a scalded cat trying to get it up and running. So yep, we are more or less on track."

What I wanted to know was whether it could be honestly said that the appreciative mode of thinking had taken root in the unconscious mental processes of the company. At the most recent of the very few pub meetings that I have attended, I asked the people round me. Naturally I got a range of responses.

"But I'll tell you this," Adrian concluded, "certainly what has taken root is that it is no longer acceptable to start a discussion by saying, 'The problem is...' or 'The difficulties I see are...' Someone is bound to say, 'Well, that's not a very appreciative way of putting it...' There's a danger that it becomes a kind of cretinous political correctness. But behind that, there still lurks, over two years on, an acknowledgement of the power of language, of the importance of reframing the way we look at the world, or how we read the text. And I'll drink to that."

---

116 Peter Senge, *Learning organization, sup. cit.*

Part 3
The practice of appreciative inquiry

The case study of Healthco has given as full and honest an account of an appreciative inquiry in action as I am capable. It was, as I explained, something of a pastiche, and it deliberately included a number of the things that can go wrong. Few inquiries are absolutely straightforward—life has a habit of intruding into process!

Now it is time to turn from the laboratory, where we have tested the theory of part 1, into the real world. I have chosen a wide variety of case studies for this part of the volume, some (like that kindly contributed by Carter and Johnson) almost classical in their proportions and style, others, such as the one on an organization working with street kids in Africa, at the other end of the scale.

I start, however, with something rather different. Chapter 10 is the record of a conversation I had with the celebrated Dutch practitioner, Joep de Jong. Rather than have Joep write another detailed case study, I thought it might be more revealing to ask him to reflect on his whole experience of using appreciative inquiry in a very busy and diverse practice. We thought it would be good to relate his general experience to two cases he was deeply involved in at the time of the conversation, but, as a contrast to the Healthco study, I wanted to be able to stand back a little, and gain perspective and allow the fundamentals to sediment out of a rich brew. I hope the reader finds it a palatable and rewarding taster.

Chapter 10
A Dutch practitioner's experience of using appreciative inquiry

Joep de Jong, founder and president of LBC International, has worked with the appreciative approach from the early days of its development. His company has applied the approach in a wide variety of organizational settings in both the public and private sectors. In this interview he reflects on that experience, using two recent interventions as examples of his company's approach.

1. Uses of appreciative inquiry

CME Joep, tell me about some uses to which you have put appreciative inquiry.

JdeJ Let me mention two projects that we have been involved in over the last couple of months. First, quite near here, we were asked to help in the merging of three secondary schools. These schools merged formally 2 1/2 years ago. As they were very different kinds of schools, with different traditions and a different ethos, it was clear that it was not going to be easy. The government department concerned gave little help—and such help as they did give was of a traditional type. That is to say, they took a narrowly organizational perspective on such things as the division of work among the staff, the use of different buildings and areas of executive responsibility. That's all right in its way, but what was lacking was intensive work with the three individual directors who were now jointly responsible for one institution. They were given no help in understanding each other, in learning to cooperate, in recognizing each other's strengths and areas where they would need help. Almost inevitably, after a year and a half, it was so obvious that the new combined institution was not working that the government department concerned recommended that an interim manager be installed over the directors to sort out the problems and then, perhaps, hand it back to the directors to carry on. That was obviously going to be an expensive solution. It was also a solution which had within it the seed of its own destruction, in that the fundamental problems of the three directors learning to work together were most unlikely to be solved and might even be exacerbated. Luckily, some of the people responsible saw the shortcomings of this supposed solution and called us in at that point to see if we could come up with an alternative.

Having become acquainted with the staff and having immersed myself in the institution, I had a feeling that there was nothing intrinsically wrong with the individuals or with the basic plan of merging three institutions.

163

The difficulty was that there was no shared vision, there was no common objective, and there was hardly even a common language or a common culture. An external company had produced a statement of objectives but that was experienced by the individuals concerned as something that was being imposed upon them—and, as you would expect, it was ineffective. I saw that our objective was to gain the trust of the directors and their staff, and then begin to use an appreciative inquiry process with them so that they could develop a shared language, a shared vision, a shared understanding of what they were and what they could become and then commit themselves to that.

So that's the first recent experience. The second is about one of the largest Dutch computer dealers. This is an almost classic story of its type. Two very successful companies, each employing between 30 and 40 people, each growing very fast, decided to merge. The commercial logic was compelling, at least seen from an accountant's perspective.

Naturally, it didn't work. Because the merger had been driven by accountants, it simply didn't function at the operational level. Consequently, all the senior management were fired and a new manager was brought in. He appointed two change managers, known to be willing to take risks and reshape the business. You can imagine the effect that had on morale. Six months later, the owners of the merged company began to realize that the staff's lack of motivation was undermining the company.

We were initially brought in to do some sales training with the staff of the two merged entities, to get them to sing from the same song sheet. Out of that came an invitation to look more widely at why the company was struggling. We recommended the use of an appreciative inquiry process. That recommendation was accepted. We put 70 people through the process in a month, in five two-day sessions, and that seems to have been astonishingly effective. Now we are looking at the follow up because people want to build on the provocative propositions that they have developed, and we shall be doing that within the next couple of months.

CME Why do you think appreciative inquiry worked in those two situations in a way that other interventions that you might have used may not have worked? What was special about appreciative inquiry?

JdeJ First, appreciative inquiry shifts the focus from the difficulties, the troubles and the problems. That is crucial in the two applications I have described where people were feeling alienated, demoralized, demotivated. I believe it is crucial to shift the staff of organizations from problem-focused orientations to an appreciative sense of what has worked.

Second, a provocative statement that comes out of the appreciative inquiry process is a statement about the future, couched as though it were already real. Forming it is therefore a challenge to people to socially construct their own desired reality. I find it's extremely important to have people develop for themselves something that they can use as an anchor or as a symbol if you wish. They need to focus on something that they have identified for themselves, on something they wish to work toward. If you can get people into a state of mind where they believe in the goals they have set themselves, they then move toward it.

CME   OK, you've told me what you find special about it in terms of your clients, but what do you, yourself, enjoy about using appreciative inquiry?

JdeJ   What I enjoy is allowing the appreciative inquiry process to put the responsibility and the power where it should be: in the hands of each individual or group of individuals. It's putting power back into the hands of the people at the heart of the organization, rather than telling them—or even allowing management to tell them—what they should do. Once you give people responsibility for setting their own course within the boundaries that you've specified, it's very rewarding to see people actually take up that responsibility and start working with it. For example, during the second working session with the computer dealer I was telling you about, my colleague and I found that we could actually leave the group without saying anything and just let them get on with it. They would be able to take care of themselves. That is the greatest joy I personally find in appreciative inquiry.

And that relates to the other thing I like about using appreciative inquiry. It emphasizes that people have a great responsibility for each other. People should take care of each other in a way that combines love—in its broadest sense—and respect. What I enjoy about appreciative inquiry is that it gives space for those emotions. It gives room to the love, trust and respect that you want to show other people and allow other people to show each other.

CME   I'm interested that you talk about love, trust and respect. I guess some people in the business community would be surprised to hear that kind of language coming from an organizational consultant. Have you encountered any resistance to using that kind of language in the context we are talking about?

JdeJ   Yes, people do, at times, feel awkward. When I say, "What it is all about is that you've got to love somebody else," sometimes there *is* some resistance. But that's why I dress it up in terms of a model so that it isn't just emotional language but it is language about emotions *rooted* in organizational reality. And I will usually start with trust rather than with love.

CME   Yes, I follow that, but there will be nonetheless clients who resist the kind of language we are talking about. That raises questions about the selection of clients. How do you choose between clients who you think will respond positively to what appreciative inquiry is all about and clients who simply won't relate to this kind of process?

JdeJ   We will only work with clients who we think will respond to appreciative inquiry. Sometimes we have potential clients come in saying, "Just name the price; we want you to work with us." But we then have to decide whether we really trust the client to work in the appreciative mode and to go on working in it after we have gone. Otherwise, I feel that we are being hired to perform some sort of trick, like a magician putting on a show. Everybody laughs and enjoys themselves and applauds but there is no serious follow-up.

CME   So what's the decisive factor?

JdeJ   As we use it, appreciative inquiry is about looking to the future. If a company isn't prepared to allow us to engage them in looking into their future, I guess it's not worth their being a client or us working with them. We're not interested in short-termism. If the medium- to long-term future is not in a company's vocabulary, appreciative inquiry is not the process to use, and we will not be interested in working with that company.

CME   We've come across companies where there is a lot of conflict, a lot of bitterness, where the very notion of holding people in a loving, trusting relationship seems impossible in view of the current levels of conflict. How would you react to an approach from that kind of company?

JdeJ   We are usually called in to help in situations that have already got out of hand. I suppose we're the last resort! A lot of organizations have been through traditional solutions like problem-solving, decision-making, idea-working, re-engineering. They've been to the big names. They've been charged a lot of money. But nothing, fundamentally, has changed. They call us in as a last gasp.

What we have done in every situation, whether it be the school that I talked about or whether it be the computer dealer that I talked about, is to start by building some understanding, some sharing of experience that explains the past, both in practical terms and in emotional terms. One of the ways we approach that is by using the wall of wonders.

CME   What do you mean?

JdeJ   We find that getting people to review their history in the organization, especially getting them to identify the things in the past that have given them satisfaction and a sense of enjoyment, has always been very helpful. By concentrating on the things that have been good in the past, they are able to talk about the past including the bad things that they might otherwise find difficult to talk about. And it raises the issues that are current for them at the moment. Once they have been through that process of recollection, of identifying the good as well as the bad, we usually find that the conflicts become much more manageable. Maybe they don't wholly disappear, but they become more manageable. It's a relief to be able to talk about it and see it in a wider perspective. I want to emphasize that we do it this way round. We don't go into the appreciative process hoping to get some understanding out of the appreciative inquiry. Rather, we spend sufficient time and trouble reviewing the past, letting the issues emerge, identifying the nature of the conflicts, putting them in a wider perspective *before* we go into the appreciative inquiry. We find it's necessary to build understanding *first.* They don't have to like each other at that stage. They actually don't have to like each other at all. It's a matter of building an understanding and getting some respect for each other as a prior condition of moving together into the appreciative process.

Working with the 70-plus people from the computer retailing company, we discovered that, if we took the time and trouble to do this preparatory work, the negative feelings almost disappeared. That came to us as a surprise. We thought we would have a lot of difficulty with the interviewing process because people would not stay in appreciative mode. To our surprise, it didn't work like that. We found that almost automatically people had an understanding of why some of these issues were so painful and they were ready to move on beyond them into appreciative inquiry.

2. Appreciative inquiry and negativities

CME You will have had, as I have had, people criticize appreciative inquiry because they say it ignores the negative experiences, the negative emotions and therefore misrepresents reality. Do you have a view about that?

JdeJ Yes, I definitely do. I think that kind of criticism only comes from an abuse of appreciative inquiry or a misrepresentation of what appreciative inquiry is about. It's not about jollying people into being positive. The appreciative inquiry process is a matter of being, a state of thinking, a way of doing. It doesn't mean that you're without pain, without sorrow, without grief. When people are in deep trouble, there is very little sense in telling them—or getting them to tell each other—how bright the future will be. That's just re-arranging the deckchairs on the Titanic. For example, when we worked with the computer dealer, they were in serious financial trouble. It was no good for us to go to the finance director and tell him how wonderful the future would be. We had to get the full facts of the financial crisis that was upon them out on the table *before* we could move into appreciative inquiry with any kind of integrity. We had to acknowledge the problems—not *deal* with the problems. In such cases, we will be quite explicit that they should take their financial problems to their bankers, their development problems to their development engineers, their design problems to designers. But when they are having problems with their people—and problems with people will almost certainly underlie all the other problems—they can come to us. I find that by being as honest and open as that overcomes a lot of resistance. I say, "OK, it doesn't solve everything. Appreciative inquiry is great, but if you have cashflow problems, appreciative inquiry is not going to solve your cashflow problems. It would be great if it did but it doesn't! It addresses different issues—people issues."

Now, that doesn't always mean that it's plain sailing. Sometimes, management decisions can cut right across what we are trying to do with appreciative inquiry. For example, in our work with the computer dealer, one of the groups was assembling in the car park, waiting to move to the training location. One member of the group was called into the manager's office and fired on the spot. Now, imagine what that did to the rest of the group. It's very hard to get them into any sort of appreciative inquiry mode. We managed, but I would say that I wasn't feeling too comfortable about the result. They went through the process. They enjoyed it. They did the work. But there was inevitably a high level of mistrust. We had been talking about trust. We had been talking about the future, and what had happened is that one of their colleagues, whether right or wrong, got sacked on the morning of the first day. How can you hold people in appreciative mode under those conditions?

On the other hand, some of the groups we worked with were so enthusiastic and so caught up in the work and in the spirit of the appreciative mode that they achieved minor miracles. The difference is obvious. The group that had experienced one of their members being sacked might go through the process in a quasi-mechanical sort of way and will, perhaps, get something from it. Other groups that came in with their tails up, determined to make the best of it, did a fantastic job. The crucial difference was that some groups could trust each other and the company as a whole, and cared for each other and the company as a whole. Others, probably through no fault of their own, were unable to make that kind of emotional commitment.

CME Do you have any hints to other practitioners about how you enable a group to make that shift so that, instead of being defensive, competitive, distrustful, they move into a quite new area of emotional geography as a pre-condition to appreciative inquiry being successful?

JdeJ   It's not a trick. It's almost another way of living. It's a state of being. You have personally got to live appreciative inquiry. It's no good going in and saying, "I've got this great trick for you, we have this mathematical formula and now, if you apply it, you'll be happy for the rest of your life."

CME   Sure, sure. I see that. But is there anything that we can do as facilitators to increase the likelihood of a group clicking into appreciative mode, rather than having to feel their way cautiously and mistrustfully into it?

JdeJ   I think you have to show yourself as someone who lives appreciative inquiry. At the same time, you have to be able to connect with them. Like a lifeboat rescuing a sailing yacht, you have to move in the same direction, at the same speed and be on the same wave. And that takes time. It takes sensitivity. It takes patience. It takes all those skills that facilitation is all about. But those skills alone—without an inner commitment to thinking and living in the appreciative mode—will not be enough.

Or to use another analogy, if you go to Rotterdam, you see huge tankers being pulled and pushed by tugs. The tugs won't necessarily all be pulling in the same direction, but they will be pulling in a way that is concerted, in a way that delivers a coherent force, to shift the tanker in the desired direction. For me, the fascination of appreciative inquiry is—to stretch the analogy a bit—getting people off the decks of the tanker and into the tugs so that they take responsibility to move the tanker and play their part with all the other tugs to bring that about. As a facilitator of the appreciative inquiry process, you are encouraging the tugs to operate in a coherent way without forfeiting their own individuality or negating the specialness of the contribution of each. But that again takes a lot of explanation, a lot of patient listening, a lot of encouragement.

If you just go in as a facilitator and say to the group, "Well, OK, we're going to do this appreciative inquiry process. Now let's get on with it," you don't do justice to the group. You're not showing love, compassion and respect for them. And therefore you are very likely to run into serious trouble.

CME   Yes, I guess so. And you deserve to do so because you are functioning non-appreciatively yourself.

JdeJ   Exactly; that's the crucial issue. As a facilitator, you have to allow the group to go its own way. That's difficult and sometimes painful. Certainly, it's very different from our traditional ways of teaching and training, when ultimately we are always in control. Now, of course, as a facilitator you will always be regarded as someone who is controlling some of the process but in yourself you have to be prepared to let the dynamics of the process take over so that what is really inside people comes out.

CME Certainly that's our experience in the Cambridge Partnership. We have had to learn to trust the process. If you are constantly being anxious about the process and trying to control it, that communicates itself to the group with the result that the group gets anxious. And if they are anxious, they'll never stay in appreciative mode. For us, I think the bottom line is to learn to trust the process and then just sit back and let it happen.

JdeJ Exactly, but that's very difficult. As a human being, it's very difficult to put enough trust in the group to say, "Well, you can do this"—especially when they get stuck! Even then, one has to resist the temptation to push the group in a certain way. You may want to engage with them, as for example in the conversation about what is making them get stuck, but you can do that only if they trust you. And you can't *tell* them to trust you. You can invite them to grant you their trust. And if they do, then you can help them work their way through, even when they get stuck. But if their trust isn't there, it is a terrible abuse of the appreciative inquiry process for the facilitator to end up in a dominating role.

CME I agree entirely, but I think it's time to move on. Tell me what you find is the best way to help an organization define the precise focus of the inquiry.

3. Defining the focus

JdeJ Well, in a way, that's very easily answered. It's part of an appreciative question. "Tell us about a great experience. Tell us a story about a really positive experience within this company," and we listen very carefully to what they tell us because that will already begin to define what the inquiry is to be about.

But we follow that up by telling them that we don't know where it's going to lead. The precise focus lies in the future. Indeed, we tell people that by the time we're finished, 50 percent of their people may have walked out because they have found this isn't the place where they want to be. So we have to let go of the outcome. And the company has to let go of the outcome. So, in a very real sense, there can be no focus predefined before we start.

For example, in the work that we did with the computer company, two of their brightest people decided that they were not in the right company. They saw that for themselves. We could see it plainly enough. And that's fine. I would say that's a very positive outcome of the process, both for the individuals and for the company. It enables both sides to handle the parting in a mature and generous spirit.

So, to answer your question in a word, how do we define the focus. The answer is that we don't.

CME One of the difficulties we sometimes run into is that companies or organizations think they know what they want the inquiry to produce. As the inquiry develops, it actually becomes quite clear that the *real* issues are somewhere else and then we have gently to persuade them to allow the process to develop in the direction it wants to develop. And management may feel uncomfortable about that, and want us to try to draw it in another direction with which they will feel more at home. Does that ring any bells for you?

JdeJ Yes, yes; that makes sense to me. We start with the people who work toward an organizational goal. In that sense we're engaged through appreciative inquiry in a kind of team-building. That's what we say companies should really focus on, where it will have a positive contribution. We believe that if they take that seriously, companies will end up as more effective organizations, building better products, building up market shares, increasing customer satisfaction.

CME You said earlier that the questions that are asked in appreciative inquiry are crucial; indeed, I think I remember you saying that it all boils down to one question. Do you have any stories you would like to share about drafting the questions?

JdeJ We build three questions into the protocol. As I already said, question one encourages the telling of a great story from the past about the company or about the individuals concerned or about the present situation. Obviously, if appreciative inquiry is being used in the context of a counselling session with a small group or even with an individual, then we start with telling a story about that group or that individual.

The second, which we find works particularly well in companies, could be put like this: "Tell us what assets you bring to this situation." For an individual, I guess we would rephrase that something like this: "Tell us about your strengths. What can you bring to the party that will make this process work, which will help this company or this situation move forward in a positive way?" People often find this difficult. We Europeans—perhaps unlike Americans—find self-disclosure difficult. As a matter of fact, I often find that even in Europe it comes as a relief to people to be able to say—to be *encouraged* to say, "Well, I'm good at this" or "I'm good at that. This is what I bring to the party." I find this has a very positive contribution to the process as a whole.

Then the third question would be to focus on the future and might be put something like this: "Tell us what you would like to be different in this company in the future so that it would be improved. What would you be prepared to put your energy into to achieve that?"

These are the three basic questions in any protocol we would work with.

CME So you would draft the protocol, would you?

JdeJ Yes.

CME You don't get them to draft it?

JdeJ No, we draft the protocol. That is one thing that I do like to stay in control of because I find it is very important to get the questions right. My fear is that if you got the group to draw up the protocol, they would probably—anyway in our society—fail to emphasize their own strengths. They would feel embarrassed about that. I fear that they would revert almost immediately to a problem-solving mode. And for me that would be a real retrogression. What I want them to do is to have something they want to change for the better which will help them as a group or as an organization serve the customers' needs better. Once a group is used to working with appreciative inquiry, however, I can readily see that there may be a lot to be said for getting them to draw up their own protocol.

4. The appreciative interviews

CME We have agreed that the interviews are central to the whole process. Would you like to share your experience of helping people interview each other within the appreciative mode? As you said a moment ago, they quickly sink back into problem-type thinking. What is your experience of helping people stay in the appreciative mode during the interviewing?

JdeJ Well, I think this takes us back to what we were talking about before, the foreplay if you like. I find that if I get into the interviewing process too quickly and I haven't dealt with some of the organizational issues—by which I mean acknowledged them, heard people's reactions to them, rather than solving them—then the tension and the *mis*trust tend to linger on. Once we have said that we are aware of the issues but that there are different places to deal with them, the atmosphere becomes easier and makes it much more possible to hold them in the appreciative mode. And as I said before it takes time and it takes facilitation skills. This foreplay, this pre-work, is a kind of rehearsal before we get into the main perfor-mance of the actual interviewing.

CME   But you say you were doing this in two-day slots. I'm surprised that you can do it in two days, and if you are doing a lot of pre-work as well, estab-lishing trust in the person handling the process, two days feels pretty short.

JdeJ   Well, maybe; but it works. The first day is nearly all pre-work using the 'Walls of Wonders.' We may not get into the appreciative inquiry until the beginning of the second day. But our experience is that, if the pre-work is done properly, the appreciative inquiry process goes much more smoothly, you can take it much faster, and the level of trust and mutual care is so high that you get high levels of motivation so people really apply themselves to the process.

CME   What about the data analysis? You've had your interviews, they've gone very well, you've managed to hold people in appreciative mode. Do you have stories about how the data analysis works in practice?

JdeJ   We allow as much time as we possibly can—as long as the group wants—to analyze the data. That means retelling the stories. They have to share those stories. We had a striking comment twice in the past couple of months from senior managers. They have said that with appreciative inquiry they get data in a couple of days that had cost them a fortune a year ago when it was being done by a big company that had spent months gathering this sort of data. Indeed, they said that the whole exercise was worth it just to get the data that come out of the stories, quite apart from the provocative propositions and all that follows from that. So I believe the analysis of the data—and I bridle slightly at the word analysis; let's say retelling the stories—is crucial and I get them to come back to the stories again when they present their provocative proposition. So it's a two-stage reiteration.

5. The provocative propositions

CME   Let's move on to the provocative propositions. You say they come out of the data more or less automatically. Some practitioners find that very often groups—particularly groups in pathological organizations where there are really deep-seated unresolved issues—find it difficult to be provocative. They tend to produce mom-and-apple-pie type propositions that everyone can assent to but which don't upset anybody. Is that your experience? Or do you find it quite easy to get groups to be both provoca-tive and realistic?

JdeJ   I find that we have less difficulty with the provocative propositions when the group represents a vertical cross-section of the organization rather than a horizontal cross-section. To put it bluntly, the higher up the hierarchy you go, the longer the future perspective tends to be. Manual workers may look six months, maybe even two years ahead; senior strategy managers may be paid to look 10 years ahead. It's the mix of these perspectives that seems to be particularly productive. And I think one reason why it's productive is that there is a debate about how far it is sensible or even possible to look ahead. The 10-year managers are challenged by the six-month manual workers, and vice-versa. And interestingly, the debate that goes on between those two groups—which, fundamentally, is about who has the power to decide how long the horizon is to be—is often as productive as the results of the debate. We see that as part of the appreciative inquiry process itself, enabling the short-horizon people to talk to, to challenge and to be challenged by, the long-horizon people.

Second, we find that the state of the organization makes a big difference. If it is facing a major financial crisis such as threatened bankruptcy, then it's very hard to ask that organization to look ahead and plan creatively for an 18-month to five-year time horizon. There is a parallel with Maslow's hierarchy of needs. We find that once the company grows beyond the survival level, they start looking at the competition and the need to meet that competition. Then they start looking at their own markets and extending the market. Then they start looking more critically and more creatively at the company itself. Their capacity to generate genuinely provocative statements seems to correlate with what level in this development hierarchy the company is at.

CME   If you find an organization—and let's ignore the survival type because that, as you say, is understandably very reluctant to face the distant future—that is unable or unwilling to generate genuinely provocative statements, how do you enable them or encourage them to be a bit more adventurous?

JdeJ   I find it difficult to be clear in my own mind what it means to be provocative. Sometimes, what looks like a rather anodyne statement may contain within it seeds of ideas that are very demanding for the person who made it. So I don't think you can judge the level of provocation without looking very carefully and empathetically at the individual from whom it comes.

But let me try to answer your question. How can we stimulate them into being more provocative? As a facilitator, I try to get to know the team I'm working with really well (and that relates to the pre-work we were talking about earlier) and I try to judge how far it is reasonable for them to go. If, in my own judgement—and of course I accept that this is a subjective decision—they are letting themselves off too lightly, I can become quite directive. Indeed, I can become quite fierce! For example, I might say, "I feel I'm your coach, and I feel you're trying to get out of this too easily. You're trying to win the game by one-nil because that's all that is required to say that you've won, but there is this paying public that expects you to win by 10-nil, so that's what you've got to go for. Mediocrity or getting by is simply not acceptable here." And if I do get fierce like that, I'm not just playing emotional games with them. It's because I believe passionately in the capacity of the people I am working with and I believe that my contract with them requires me to stretch them as far as I can. My intervention and my work with a group is a very expensive business: it's not only my fee, but it's their time and the opportunity cost of that time. So, even at that very basic commercial level, I feel I have an obligation to give good value for money—and mediocre getting by, satisficing kinds of output, are not acceptable. And they are not acceptable to me professionally, emotionally and morally.

CME Once you've got your provocative statement, you've got to get people in the organization to commit to that. How do you find that works?

JdeJ Well, the road to hell is paved with good intentions. What I find is that if you just leave the provocative propositions hanging in the collective conscious and people don't do anything about them, inevitably people go back to their traditional habits, their traditional ways of working. Those come most easily to them. It takes a lot of effort, a lot of time to go on living in an appreciative mode and there are times when you don't feel like that. That's true of individuals. It's also true of organizations. So one of the things we do is get them to make a token or an image of the statement and then hang it up somewhere so that everyone can see it. Then they have a constant reminder, not only of the provocative proposition itself, but of the process that lies behind the provocative proposition.

CME What kind of token or image are you talking about?

JdeJ Well, it could be a picture, a painting, a symbol. For the computer company, we had them make their own drawings. In other circumstances, we've had people work with clay. Sometimes, I'll take the propositions and the data behind them and give them to an artist and say, "Please make me an image based on these statements, based on these data," and then I will give the picture to the organization. It's a very personal gift from me, as an individual, to the people I've been working with, which is designed to describe the way the organization feels at the psycho-emotional level.

This seems to have worked really well with the computer dealer company I told you about.

As an additional benefit, I find that it helps the people in the company to tell their potential customers what the company is about. Because it helps them plug into the positive emotions they experienced during the appreciative inquiry process, they can talk about the company with more enthusiasm, more commitment, more dedication, more imagination— and that energy communicates itself to their potential customers.

It's amazing how creative people can be if you give them this opportunity. Sometimes they draw things that have clearly been influenced by models that I have used in the course of the appreciative inquiry. For instance, I often talk about a tanker being manoeuvred by tugs because I think that's a very helpful image, and so it's not surprising that that image re-emerges in the pictures they draw. Some people draw images from nature, sketching trees, trees bearing fruit, trees which are obviously having difficulty surviving, even trees that are withering and dying. I've had groups do mime plays. I haven't told them to do that; they've just done it by themselves. One group came up with the idea that they were some sort of a zoo with all different animals and they asked each other, "What sort of animal are you?" and they pretended that the environment was a forest because they felt very good in a forest. And then they discovered that one of their number was a sealion and that posed the interesting question about how a sealion can prosper in a forest. Now, this was a very subtle way of them facing really difficult issues that they may have found impossible to face directly. Let me emphasize that this was all self-generated. All I had said was that they were to communicate their statements to the organization as a whole in any way they liked. And they chose these highly creative, indirect, almost allegorical forms of communication. That's very powerful and, I think, genuinely transformative.

CME Do you know whether they have gone on using right-brain activities as a result of what they discovered through using these kinds of activities?

JdeJ I don't know. But I do know that the follow-up has been very positive. I had a meeting with one of the managers last week and she said, "It's surprising that some of the members of these groups have such fond memories of what happened two months ago. When they see each other, they start to smile in a very spontaneous way and enjoy recollecting what happened."

That's one of the main reasons for being so enthusiastic about appreciative inquiry when consulting with companies. You actually release so many forces of goodwill if you give people the space to do so. And a corollary of that is that I prefer to work with the whole organization, involving everyone, even if the organization is, at the beginning of the process, fairly traditional and hierarchical. They soon learn to abandon the rigidity of the hierarchy and to move, almost naturally, into a much flatter, more mutually cooperative style. Certainly that was our experience with the computer dealer I was telling you about. Their people were in two locations and were being directed in a very hierarchical way from a distance. After the appreciative inquiry, they decided that in future the people on the remote site would work far more independently, telling the main office what they needed and, of course, reporting what they achieved. It brought about a fantastic change in attitude in the way they were working.

6. Implementation

CME Let's move on to the action phase. Do you have any stories about moving from the challenging statements into the action-planning phase of the process?

JdeJ Yes, we've done this with a major drinks company and the schools I mentioned and we're beginning it with the computer company. After we've got the token or the symbol in place to remind them of what they're committed to, we insist on working in a very organized and disciplined way. And I say that in such strong terms because often there is a feeling that appreciative inquiry is a very *un*disciplined process. I strongly disagree with that. I think it's an extremely disciplined process which can, at times, look a bit chaotic, but which at a deeper level is highly structured. It's fundamentally about constructing reality. And people have to be very disciplined, very organized, very committed, if they are going to construct that reality concretely as well as conceptually.

In more practical terms, we favour encouraging groups to take little steps at a time. Many of the provocative statements are very broad brush. That's fine. But it can also be very intimidating. That's why we start by encouraging them to define and then implement small changes that they can manage and that they can see in place quite quickly. The skills involved are not necessarily new. We use a wide range of techniques that are well known and well appreciated in the management literature.

The other issue is accountability. I find it's very important for people to know who is responsible for implementing what. And of course that will only work if the people who are accountable actually *own*—have full ownership of—the provocative propositions in the first place.

We've begun to experiment with putting the pictures of the people who generated provocative propositions around the symbol or painting that expresses that provocative proposition. This is a way, some people may even think quite a crude way, of holding those people accountable for that provocative proposition in public.

CME   Do you ever find that people start very enthusiastically with the implementation of a provocative proposition—find they run into some kind of difficulty and then back off? Have you ever had that kind of experience?

JdeJ   I would put it a bit differently. Once they've developed the provocative proposition and moved back into day-to-day business, they tell me that they use the provocative proposition as a kind of encouragement to get back into the appreciative way of thinking, rather than using the provocative proposition as a compass to steer their every action. The proposition—and the paintings or symbols that reflect its function—is something that gives you confidence, hope, belief in the future, and it's that emotional state that enables you to deal with the day-to-day rubbish that routinely crosses all our desks. I don't believe that people can be *constantly* engaged in the realization of their provocative proposition. But they can change their way of conceiving of themselves, their colleagues, their organization, their day-to-day work in a manner that makes it more probable that the essence of the provocative proposition will become reality.

CME   Can you illustrate that from either of the two cases you mentioned when we started this conversation?

JdeJ   Yes, particularly in the merged schools I mentioned. The key issue there was the level of distrust between the three members of the management team. They all had nearly identical profiles; they were all school leaders; there was little diversity but the appreciative inquiry process did allow them to develop a genuinely shared vision. Now, in the day-to-day work—and I'm still monitoring this closely—they have found a more disciplined way, for example, to organize their weekly meetings, and when the meetings go awry, each accepts the responsibility to say, "OK. Let's stop here for a second because I'm not feeling comfortable with what's going on and it's not in accord with the provocative proposition we agreed. So let's take one step back and let's approach whatever we are doing from the perspective of that statement." And I find that really works. That changes the atmosphere and the perspective from which they are discussing their particular problem. Everyone accepts the responsibility to go back to the letter and the spirit of the provocative proposition.

CME   So you see the provocative proposition as acting as a kind of overarching metaphor for the quality of life of the organization, rather than incorporating a strategy that can be reduced to tactics and implemented step by step?

JdeJ   Yes, I strongly agree with that. I believe appreciative inquiry really comes from the individual and it's not just another organizational development tool, although of course you can use it to support that. But the individuals build the organization. They are the organization. And therefore the process of change has to start with the individuals.

CME   That raises a question that I wanted to invite you to comment on. In our experience, after an appreciative inquiry process, people are full of confidence, enthusiasm and energy and the question I ask myself is how long is this going to last? Staff come and go. The external world changes. The energy levels that appreciative inquiry has generated at its best may not be indefinitely sustainable.

JdeJ   Yes, that's true; I agree with that. I suppose I visualize it as a traditional bell-curve. Out of 100 people, I'll have five who always drive the organization, I'll have five who will always resist and I'll have 90 in the middle who will do what they're asked. What I'm doing with appreciative inquiry is, for a limited time, moving a number out of the 90—and, I hope, quite a large number—nearer to the five who take the leadership role. I take the view that appreciative inquiry is a very successful way of moving those people along the spectrum. It changes the shape of the curve. Now some of course will trickle back into the middle of the distribution. That's inevitable. But if the appreciative inquiry process has really demonstrated the power of love and respect within the organization, that trickle will become a flood. But, I do accept that you may need to repeat the experience, precisely for the reasons that you identify.

CME   Have you talked to the computer firm about this? How did they react when you said that you thought that they might need to do another appreciative inquiry in, say, a year or 18 months' time?

JdeJ   They were very positive. Interestingly, they came and asked me to continue. Indeed, they want a regular slot over four to six months and a monitoring process to see that provocative propositions are acted upon. My experience is that companies are so excited by what happens that, rather than resisting a repetition or a booster, they ask for it—sometimes I think more insistently or earlier than they really need.

CME   So do you think companies can learn to do their own appreciative inquiry? Can the process become self-generating in that sense?

JdeJ   Look, anyone can learn to do appreciative inquiry. But that's not the issue. It's not how well you *master* the process, because anybody can master the process. What makes the big difference, the reason why it works in some situations and not in others, is the nature of the person who facilitates the process. As I said before, it's not a trick. It's not a set of organizational development tools. It's not, I believe, part of a normal consultancy package which you can sell with the right kind of patter and the right kind of enthusiasm. I don't believe you can do that with appreciative inquiry. You will not reason people into appreciative inquiry. It's about trust and respect and compassion and empathy and understanding, which the facilitator brings to the organization and which people in the organization catch from him as though he were infectious with those qualities. Now, it's very possible that a company will generate someone like that. I know of companies both in Holland and in the UK where that has happened. Someone has been through an appreciative inquiry process within their own company and has, as it were, caught the bug and has then been able to pass it on to others. In that sense, it can become self-generating. But of course that self-generation can't be guaranteed. It depends on finding the right person and then giving him or her the right skills (so that they do in fact master the process) and, above all, the confidence and the trust in their own intuitions to go with the process.

CME I suppose what bothers me is that some people could interpret what you're saying as almost a kind of fundamentalism.

JdeJ I'm not a fundamentalist.

CME But you know what I mean. There are appreciative inquiry practitioners around who believe that this is the final solution. This is the true faith. And this kind of exclusive expectation that appreciative inquiry will solve all organizational problems is not only wrong in its own terms, it will actually damage appreciative inquiry in the longer term.

JdeJ I agree entirely. That's why I sometimes use appreciative inquiry. I sometimes use problem-solving or decision-making techniques. I sometimes use team-building. Appreciative inquiry is sometimes appropriate but at times I would much rather leave it to one side and wait until the time is right to use it.

CME You've mentioned working from time to time with individuals with appreciative inquiry. Do you mean counselling in that context?

JdeJ Perhaps coaching rather than counselling. As you know, coaching is often used in situations of corporate rescue because something has gone terribly wrong, where a group will have to be helped through a very difficult patch. In those situations, I find it is important to help people identify what is significant in their lives. And in that context I find getting them to tell me stories about peak experiences or moments of great meaning-fulness for them is immensely rewarding. And by getting people to identify what is crucial for them, you can bring them back to that insight again and again and have them work through their present difficulties. In another context, I found this very helpful in dealing with people who are in mourning or in other forms of deep grief where they are psychically and emotionally lost. They almost literally don't know what they are doing or where they are going. And I guess the same would be true of people after a divorce or in situations of deep marital disharmony. Helping people in those kinds of situations get in touch with their deepest selves, their ultimate identity I suppose you could call it, can be enormously helpful, both for the individual and for those around them. Working with a bereaved family in this way—one that has great assets and great problems—I've discovered just how long an appreciative inquiry process can take. In the business world, we think in terms of a two- or three-day session with occasional follow-ups. In my counselling work, I've realized that the timescale can be much, much longer.

CME   Final question, Joep: how do you see appreciative inquiry developing in the future?

JdeJ   Well, my challenging statement for appreciative inquiry in the future would be in a sense what we were talking about before: that it become a self-sustaining process in organizations themselves. I look forward to the day when, in a medium-sized organization, one or two people are as it were permanent appreciative inquiry advocates within the company, constantly recalling people to the provocative propositions, to the process, to the spirit of the inquiry, to those three words that have come up again and again: love, respect and trust.

Chapter 11
Testing the appreciative approach—
to destruction?

A case study from three Mauritanian villages

1. The environment of the inquiry

There can be few less promising environments in which to apply the appreciative approach than a huddle of villages in the Western Sahara. The villagers are recently settled—or semi-settled—nomads who, having lost most of their camels and cattle during the great droughts of the late 1970s and early 1980s, came to the shattering conclusion that their traditional way of life was no longer viable. Growing cereal and vegetable crops from settled villages, and sending their young men off to find work in town (or herd a few cattle down to the banks of the Senegal river during the long, hot summer), they now have to rely, not on a series of well-known, reliable wells at oases used for generations by their ancestors, but on hand-dug wells in their villages, often of uncertain yield and always of dubious cleanliness.

Cool, airy tents have given way to mud and in a few cases cement-block houses. The most striking changes are not the physical, however. The need for social adaptation impresses even the most casual observer. Now parents want not just the weak or feeble who will never make warriors or tough herdsmen but all their children to go to school—and not just Koranic school but the full primary cycle and as much secondary as possible. They know they are going to have to compete in the modern world and they have to be equipped, against all the odds, to do so. The implications are stunning. All the young men have gone—either to school or to look for work—yet all the young women remain. In the village of Bourella, part of the study area on which this chapter is based, we found 17 adult men, of which only two were under 45 (neither unmarried) and 55 nubile women who were well aware of their slim chances of finding—or having found for them—suitable husbands. The great social gatherings for weddings, in which a whole clan would gather from hundreds of square miles of desert and which was the main chance young people had of identifying potential partners, are now neither frequent nor well attended. We had the sense of a village slowly dying on its feet, an adaptation that had not yet quite come off.

Not much to appreciate, then. But there is worse to come. When these villages were originally settled, the provincial government persuaded the United Nations Development Programme (UNDP) to build a number of minor dams to conserve the small and diminishing annual rainfall. As the water receded from these seasonal lakes it would recharge the aquifers tapped by the shallow wells and leave a damp and marginally fertile bed in which cash crops could be grown. Through some almost incredible degree of incompetence by the UNDP, the dam in the study villages was so ill designed that in two years the direction of the flow of water was reversed—away from its intended bed into another depression which, lined with clay, does not permit it either to recharge the aquifers or to recede and leave a suitable seedbed. Picturesque the new lake may be: life supporting it clearly is not. The result is that the wells in two of the study villages are drying out; the trees in the dambos are dying; the yields of cereal and vegetable crops in the old garden are declining to the point where it was hard to believe that intentional agriculture was actually taking place.

A harsh environment but one made the harsher by the fact that for many of the farmers there is a tax to pay—a tax that can be as high as 30 percent of the pathetic crop. This share-cropping arrangement is part of the relics of the so-called and much misunderstood "slavery" system that was formally abolished only in 1980. Historically linked with the incursion of the Berber "white moors" (maurs) from the North and their envassalling of the indigenous population, who adopted many of the life characteristics of their conquerors, including Islam, this relationship was more akin to the relationship between a medieval lord of the manor and his serfs than to that between a plantation owner and his slaves. There was the acceptance of mutual responsibilities, of a duty of care and provenance in both directions. Whatever the legal position now, of which much survives but in a desperately resource-poor environment, it is open to abuse. The white moor expects to extract his share of the crop, even as he accepts that, in the soudure, he may have to give some of it back to prevent the black moor from starving to death.

I hope I have managed to convey some of the realities—as they would appear to a Western-trained social scientist—of the area in which we were to test the appreciative approach to destruction. Here were some of the poorest people on earth, facing some of the toughest environmental conditions anywhere in the world, with a social structure that may have served some of them well in the past but which is now creaking under the strain of adaptation. In these conditions, did not talk of appreciation sound callous or even sick?

There is a final dimension that needs to be sketched into the picture. The international development agency with which we were working, World Vision, has an ambitious integrated rural development project in the Assaba region. Remote and poorly connected our study villages undoubtedly were (three hours of tough Land Rover driving from the nearest town), but the word had got around. World Vision had money. World Vision did things. It sank wells. It built schools and clinics. It trained local women in primary health care. It was a sugar daddy to be milked as hard as possible. And the proof of that was that it was bringing

Europeans, *who spoke a weird French*, into the village for a week—even European women. They must have a lot of money to disburse: play our cards right and we can live on meat and milk right through the soudure.

The consciousness of this raised level of expectations is part of the context that any funding agency faces—to its great peril. In our case it was doubly unfortunate in that it is normal for clients to emphasize their problems, difficulties and failures to wring from the funding agency the maximum benefits. In other words the regular psycho-dynamic of the relationship we were witnessing was problem biased from the start, with the victim on one side and the saviour on the other.

For all these reasons, then—the physical, the social and the psycho-social—we could hardly have designed a less-favourable environment in which to launch the appreciative approach. We knew we were taking a huge risk, though to be candid, the scale of that risk only dawned on us as we arrived in the villages. Before I give an account of the process in the village, however, I need to explain how we came to be there at all and what preparatory steps we had taken.

2. The background to the inquiry

World Vision's Assaba People's Project is a flagship enterprise for the largest church-related development agency in the world. It is a bit of a paradox: a Christian-based and funded organization operating in a traditional Islamic context where it is illegal to proselytize. Directed by a Swiss agronomist who speaks fluently the local version of Arabic (Hassaniya), it is staffed by Mauritanians who have been trained to a high level in essentially Western management tools. The project offers a maximum of 50 percent funding for community-based projects and nothing for individual schemes. Originally based in primary health care and health promotion—with a heavy emphasis on child survival—the project has developed to respond to the priorities of the villagers themselves.

The way these have been identified has involved the extensive use of PRA—participative rural appraisal—in which the fieldworkers are highly trained and in which they take a good deal of pride. PRA is designed to generate both facts for the project team and motivation and participation for the villagers themselves. As they go through the various participative processes that PRA generates—a village map; a seasonal calendar; a Venn diagram of inter- and intra-village relationships, a transect through the village (essentially a straight walk with your eyes open)—the villagers are encouraged to talk among themselves about the life of the village, about their past, their present and their future, about how it looks to different groups among them.

The World Vision teams give special weight to the marginalized in the villages—women, the young, the aged and infirm—since it is their voices that often get overlooked in the traditional processes of decision-making, where the village chief still holds great and sometimes seemingly absolute authority. PRA may go a long way to incorporate these voiceless people in the decision-making process, especially if it is handled, as it tended to be by the World Vision in Assaba, with that end in view.

On an earlier visit to the Assaba project it had struck me that, excellent as the work with PRA was in many ways (and a huge improvement on traditional top-down planning methods as it undoubtedly was), there were at least three dangers with it. The first was that it left too much power to set the agenda in the hands of the fieldworkers. Though the teams used the rhetoric of ownership and sustainability with sincerity and conviction, their own processes actually made it hard for the villagers to own either the process or the results.

Second, I was aware that PRA itself had become too much of a rote-learned technique. It lacked spontaneity, a sense of wonder and engagement. Data became the yardstick by which the process was judged and if the data were not hard, they tended to be ignored or at least minimized. Part of the reason for this is cultural and will not be easy to overcome. The combined effects of Koranic instruction and an old-fashioned rigid French education engender a mentality that does not easily play with ideas. It produces plodding clerks rather than singing poets. It is happiest when there is a precise set of rules to follow and reality fits the rules exactly. That this cuts across the whole genius of any kind of participative inquiry is immediately obvious, but it remains an unresolved tension—and it was to haunt the appreciative approach as much as it does PRA, as we shall see.

Third and most important, I was aware that, given the psycho-social dynamic between any development agency and its clients as described above, PRA is an open invitation to move into problem modes of thinking. Indeed, the World Vision field staff told us that PRA was effective at persuading the villagers to prioritize their problems. The catalogue of past failures and present unmet needs which PRA so readily unleashes has, of course, its analytic interest, but its psychological destructive power can hardly be exaggerated—even in the absence of a perceived advantage in crying up present discontents.

For these reasons, then, I had mentioned the possibility of introducing the appreciative approach to the field staff, not as a substitute for PRA—for I knew that that would be stoutly resisted—but as a complement to it or, as we later came to see it, as an alternative spirit in which PRA might be done. This suggestion grew in my absence and when I returned, accompanied by a trained colleague, we were surprised to find that the plan now embraced the training of all World Vision field-based staff from all their programs throughout the country, including sectoral experts in health, education, credit and small-industry development. Thrown into the mix for good measure was the government extension worker for the area in which we would be working, a Peace Corps volunteer working in a neighbouring village, a senior manager of World Vision, two female Mauritanian consultants sometimes hired by World Vision to carry out PRAs and World Vision's own PRA trainer.

We were to carry out a two-day training session in Kiffa, a small, dusty town in the south of Assaba, and then move in three large teams to the villages, where we would live *en famille* as guests of the villagers for five days to carry out the inquiry. My wife, my colleague and I would coach the teams but keep as low a profile as possible.

The training sessions were clearly going to be extremely tight, not least because the premises were far from ideal and many of the participants were fasting for Ramadan. Expecting high and sustained concentration from all participants was unrealistic. With the wisdom of hindsight, I should have concentrated more on a "how to" approach, and perhaps given some of the theory in the evaluation sessions after the return to Kiffa. I was anxious to give the group, large and diverse as it was, some reason for believing that the appreciative approach was qualitatively different from PRA and required a different mind-set. That was a mistake. It may have disarmed some of the suspicion and sense of invasion, but it added unhelpfully to the complexity and mystification.

Interestingly, however, it was the evidence of the Pygmalion effect that caught the group's imagination. If there was one moment when they shifted from a stance of reserved skepticism to one in which they were ready to give the approach a serious try, it was when they discussed the effect of expectations on performance—in their own experience and in the villages and communities among which they had worked.

This was reinforced when we moved from classroom work—lecture, small group discussions, plenary discussions—to role play and simulation. Two groups of about seven role played villagers—the chief, the Imam, the teacher, the urban-based son, an elderly villager, a youth, a young unmarried woman and a married older woman—and two groups simulated a group of fieldworkers carrying out an appreciative inquiry. I had forgotten the irrepressible sense of fun that is one of the most delightful characteristics of many Mauritanians. The lecture room was transformed into a village, with tents and mattresses. Village dancing, drumming and feasting got underway, and the World Vision team was kept waiting—"Let the Toubabs cool off a bit; won't do them any harm"—until the festivities reached a natural lull.

High spirits in this village had led the villagers to agree to give the visitors as hard a time as possible, so I wondered how the World Vision team would handle the appreciative protocol. To my surprise and delight, they showed themselves well up to the task, inviting the villagers to tell stories about the origins of the village, about their ancestors, about what their ancestors valued of their own times and what they would value if they were to return to the village today. (That later proved a culturally sensitive issue. Many Mauritanian Muslims regard it as distasteful to even imagine the dead returning to the present.) The villagers were taken by surprise at their own delight at moving into storytelling mode, and each sought to extend or develop the story of the last.

It quickly became apparent, however, that giving voice to the traditionally voiceless was not going to be an easy task. Neither of the women would speak in front of the men, and the other men tended to defer to the chief. They would certainly not express disagreement with him in public—i.e., in front of anyone except closest (male) family.

This became an important strategic issue for the conduct of the rest of the inquiry. It meant that we must find ways of either talking individually to all or nearly all the villagers in an environment which they regarded as safe; or we must break them down into small groups of people of the same social standing in the village where they felt comfortable to speak honestly and openly; or we must structure the self-interviewing process in a way that allowed everyone to speak in an unhindered, unembarrassed way.

Each of our groups of fieldworkers opted for a different one of these solutions. In Bourella, for example, the villagers elected a *groupe de travail* to work with the World Vision fieldworkers. This included the chief and his urban-based and quite-highly educated youngest son and two women, both related—as were most people in the village—to the chief. These women established a good relationship with the female members of the World Vision team, both fluent in Hassaniya. Together they went off, apart from the men, and spent long periods chatting to small groups of women, roughly in age cohorts. So far as they could tell, there was no embarrassment in the presence of the wife and daughters of the chief, even when some mild criticisms of the chief were voiced.

The many fewer men were interviewed by the male members of the *groupe de travail*, with the World Vision male team acting as coaches. Luckily, the chief was often called away on village business and so his presence—and his tendency to speak for others—was not, so far as we could tell, disruptive or intimidating.

In another village, Oum el Kheez II, by contrast, the World Vision team did all the interviewing in groups, trying to ensure that the groups were small and homogeneous enough to allow genuine freedom of expression. This was a particular issue in that village, where a small number of "black moors" (former slaves) lived on the physical margins of the village. It was specially important to protect their space and encourage them to feel both part of the process and sufficiently confident to share their own stories. It is at least arguable that the *groupe de travail* approach, which operated fairly well in Bourella, would not have succeeded in this mixed village.

It is worth emphasizing this plurality of approaches. There is no single formula which can be operated like a blueprint in all circumstances. In this case the two villages were within a mile of each other and, to a superficial observer, would have appeared near enough identical to justify the adoption of the same approach. In fact, not only were the villages very different in structure, demography, social composition and economic security, they were (or had been until very recently) locked in bitter intra-tribal conflict which had come to have the most far-reaching implications. That is the paradox. It was absolutely right to adopt quite different approaches in the two villages. But we only knew how right it was *post facto*. I would want to argue that this is one of the strengths of the appreciative approach. Because it calls forth from the team a special kind of creativity, adaptability, spontaneity and an ability to think on the hoof, it enables a dialectical process to grow between the developing sense of reality as the context discloses itself and the team's reaction to it. The contrast between that and the rather mechanical application of PRA techniques—at least as applied by the World Vision field staff—could hardly be more striking.

It is important to make one further comment on process before turning to substance. As implied in the last paragraph, the teams of World Vision field staff were required, by the context, to adapt the process as they went along. The appreciative approach was new to them. Only one of the World Vision personnel had ever been in the villages before and that to a minimal degree. For all these reasons, it was important to keep up an intense level of planning and reflection within the team. In Bourella, the team chose a senior Mauritanian program officer—whose own responsibilities were urban programming—as a facilitating chair, and for the first few days, routinely met before and after any serious contact with the villagers. The level of discussion and self-critical reflection at these meetings were among the most profound I have experienced in any working environment—not excluding the University of Cambridge. The chair handled the meetings with great sensitivity and skill, but more striking still was the high level of motivation and even fascination expressed by the group. They were quickly convinced that they were on to something—something unusual, exciting, potentially important not only for these villages but also for the whole work of the organization.

That having been said, they were also aware of a tension between the twin objectives of our study. Were we training the field staff in the appreciative approach? Or were we seeking to help the villages move toward some kind of action plan? Initially, I thought this was an unnecessarily fine distinction: why should we not do both? Later events were to show me the deeper wisdom behind the question. As we shall see, our failure to resolve it nearly jeopardized the whole exercise.

3. The inquiry

As I was based in Bourella, I shall give a detailed account of the process in that village. As I have already emphasized, significantly different approaches were taken in the other two villages. I shall cross-refer where that will be illuminating.

The exercise began with a village meeting. The drums were sounded and most people in the village, a dispersed settlement that covered about half a square mile, made their way to the chief's compound. Only later did we discover what an innovation this was: it was the first time in the history of the village that all the residents, most of whom belong to one extended family, had come together to discuss anything. There was a high level of interest and even excitement as the chief made a short welcoming speech to the World Vision team and the team leader replied.

The formalities over, the gloves came off. World Vision, the chief said, had been known to help other villages in the area and so everyone was expecting that it would help Bourella. That was fine. There was no need for us to bother with a long investigation. He was quite clear what the village needed. He did not quite say it, but his message was clear: Cut the cackle and hand over the cheque.

It took a good deal of diplomacy on behalf of the World Vision team to sidestep this demand, and to move into a genuinely participative and appreciative mode that would not threaten the chief's authority but would motivate all the villagers to own the outcome. One strategy they employed immediately was to start asking appreciative questions such as: When is this village happiest? How did this village come to be established? Who founded it? What makes people here glad to be alive? What would visitors to this village comment upon most favourably? When you have visited other villages in the Assaba, what has impressed you most about them?

It was striking how the chief's monopoly of the conversation broke down as soon as the World Vision team started playing with these questions. Everyone wanted to join in—and even the women, smirking behind their veils, were holding animated conversations among themselves, with much giggling and, we later learned, much earthy humour. To his credit, the chief was not in the least outfaced. Rather he seemed to enjoy hearing the praises of his village sung by "his people."

It then became relatively simple to suggest that the conversation was best continued in a *groupe de travail* and to allow the selection of such a group to emerge more or less spontaneously from the meeting as a whole. Though we shall never know whether the group that did emerge was in any sense optimal—was it in fact packed with the chief's buddies? were significant minority interests in the village excluded?—we never had any reason to believe that it was seriously unrepresentative or partial in its deliberations. Certainly it included two women, one of whom, interestingly, was of the "forgeron" caste—i.e., one of the lowliest castes—whom one would not normally expect to see being offered or accepting any kind of leadership role. Statistically, of course, women were grossly underrepresented given the gender imbalance in the village, but it is possible to be overly mathematical in this environment. The accomplishment was not to get arithmetic equality for the women, but a strong voice and a genuinely participative process.

After the chief had ended the meeting with a firm word to the villagers that they were to cooperate with the World Vision team and treat them as honoured guests in their midst—a speech we did not think was put on for our benefit—the whole meeting moved off into the desert outside the chief's compound to create the village map in the best PRA tradition. The villagers quickly latched on to the idea, and heaps of camel dung were assembled to represent the mosque or the school or Youssof's house. There was a good deal of back-chat and laughter, and furious debate about orientation and scale, but behind that a number of features began to emerge that gave the World Vision team pause for thought. For example, this was a village with an unusually large number of wells, most of them dug by hand by the villagers themselves. Did that betoken a serious water problem—or a highly developed sense of the money to be made from out-of-season vegetables? Another point: the village was an odd shape, somewhat representing a dog-bone. Why? Was this in response to physical features (e.g., water) or did it reflect social or political tensions?

These questions were not trivial and would be clarified in the course of the next days. The main achievement of the mapping exercise, however, was to break the ice, to get the villagers thinking about their environment, to get them to tell stories about the chief building the school with his own hands or the current campaign to improve the teacher's house so that he would stay in the village. The flow of stories had begun.

The *groupe de travail* met the following day to formulate the appreciative protocol. They quickly saw the point, in the light of the village meeting's conversations the night before, and were ready to continue the exploration of what the village had achieved. For us this was a most interesting development. Instead of presenting us a list of their problems and requirements—which was certainly the chief's starting point the evening before—they had, with minimal prompting from us, chosen to recount, with a mixture of pride and pain, the processes of adaptation involved in shifting from a nomadic lifestyle to settled agriculture plus a little herding. They began to realize just how much they had achieved in less than 20 years. A mosque and a school had been built. Wells had been dug. Gardens had been established. Homes had been constructed. Herds of camels, cows and goats had been slowly, painfully, rebuilt. Some basic health care had been introduced and one of the women trained as a primary carer. Children had been raised, and the infant mortality rate had allegedly fallen.

Interestingly, despite this emerging record of achievement, none of the *groupe de travail* nor any of the villagers we spoke to in the subsequent round of interviews, expressed any wish to return to a nomadic life. Indeed, nearly everyone was emphatic in their rejection of it. They had no wish to go back to what they remembered as a harsh, demanding, dangerous and insecure way of life. We were not, then, indulging in group nostalgia. These people are tough-minded realists. They know they face daunting problems in the present and in the future. But they also know that they have worked hard to adapt themselves to their settled life and that life, hard as it is, promises them more than the old ways could in an extended period of declining rainfall.

The *groupe de travail* distilled areas of the village life which they thought would serve as pegs on which to hang conversations with the rest of the villagers. It was assumed with the minimum of discussion that the women in the group, plus the women in the World Vision team, would speak to the women in the village, and the men, including the chief and his son, would visit all the male-headed households and talk to the men. In the event, the men clung much more firmly—indeed one might almost say desperately—to the schedule of appreciative questions, grouped around six village topics—the mosque, the school, water, cattle, gardens, construction—than did the women. And this suggests that we made a mistake at this point.

With the easy wisdom of hindsight, I now think that we should have spent much longer in training the men (and, possibly the women) in the flexible, spontaneous and playful use of the appreciative approach. They saw, I am convinced, the creative potential of asking appreciative questions and inviting respondents to switch into story mode. But, like many beginners in this approach, they lacked the confidence and the experience to prevent the interviews becoming increasingly mechanical and repetitive. That danger was probably increased by a decision that was never properly debated either by the *groupe de travail* nor by the World Vision team meetings: that each (male) member of the *groupe de travail* should handle the questions on one topic—water, livestock, construction, and so on. This actually imposed an over-rigid format to the interviews with the individual male householders and discouraged any of the *groupe de travail* from exploring beyond his brief. As this danger became apparent, the chair of the World Vision team tried himself to open the questioning by asking much more general and, as it were, speculative appreciative questions. But his participation in the interviewing process cut across the dynamic we were trying to unleash and although it produced some important contributions, it was, in process terms, a near-desperate manoeuvre.

It is of course an open question whether we could have achieved much if we had tried more consciously to train the *groupe de travail* in the appreciative approach. I find myself increasingly convinced that the only way to learn is by doing and I suspect there would have been a good deal of resistance to anything that, however skillfully disguised, looked like formal instruction. Maybe what we should have done, especially if we had had more time and had not been in the last throes of Ramadan, was to reconvene the *groupe de travail* after each set of interviews and go over the process more carefully with them. That is what we were doing in the World Vision team. Maybe we should have done it too with the *groupe de travail*. (Here we begin to see the emergence of the conflict between training the World Vision team and conducting an appreciative inquiry in the village. That conflict was to deepen—dangerously.)

Despite these hiccups, the World Vision team was excited about the quantity and quality of the information that was coming out, mostly in narrative form. "We would never hear all this stuff in a classic PRA," said one of the rural fieldworkers. Even the government extension worker, a most impressive and usually silent figure, agreed that it would have taken him months of living in the village to have gathered so much information and secure so good a feel for the resources and potential of the village. We were not especially concerned that much of the data we had were soft. We still, for example, did not know precisely how many people lived in the village. (Actually that is an almost meaningless statistic as it varies hugely over the seasons as men come and go, depending on both the movement of cattle, itself a function of the very variable pattern of rainfall, and the urban job market.) We concluded that if we decided we needed harder data later, we would collect them as we needed them, and probably with a great deal more help from the villagers.

One of the most striking things about the data we were getting was its consistency. We were hearing the same accounts of the past, the same aspirations for the future, the same sense of the potential of the present from all the households we visited. Was this some kind of group-think? Was it a carefully orchestrated response? Or was it a reflection of part of the reality of the lives of the villagers? They shared, after all, the same experiences and, perhaps through conversation among themselves over the years, had come to form the same hopes for the future. It was striking, for example, that most of the men we spoke with rated the permanent presence of a veterinarian in the village as one of their top priorities, although no agency operating in the Assaba nor the government offers such a facility. Even more striking was that not one single man mentioned any kind of health care for people as a priority. (A loudspeaker for the mosque was, judging by the frequency with which it was mentioned, evidently more desirable than a health clinic. Which of us, I wonder, would have predicted that?)

In the end, there is no way of validating this kind of data other than by listening carefully, asking questions, playing devil's advocate, cross-checking with other observers and with what can be observed on the ground. This was the stuff of the World Vision team meetings that had become so central a part of our discipline. Even if they did not finally silence the inner voice of scientific skepticism, they did all that could be done to check the reliability and reality of the story that was slowly emerging.

Another invaluable function of the team meetings was to check across the gender divide. The women were making much more creative use of the appreciative approach and were already beginning to move in the direction of provocative propositions that would be very different from the men. (For one thing they were more concerned about the health of their children than about the health of their animals!) The *forgeron* lady was emerging as a dynamic and creative person who seemed quickly at ease with the appreciative approach, engaging the other women in storytelling that revealed some remarkable insights into the life of their community. Two examples will suffice.

First, it became apparent how frustrated the women were by the lack of eligible men in the village—and the lack of enterprise shown by the men in finding them husbands. With so many nubile women and so few young men (we counted only five), they were well aware that, unless drastic steps were taken, many of them would remain unmarried for life. Such of their number as were married had met their husbands by fortuitous escapes to either Kiffa or Nouakchott—e.g., to be admitted to hospital for emergency treatment—but their sisters knew that the men would never sanction fishing parties to the wicked city, however well chaperoned and decorously conducted. What they wanted was economic development of any sort in the village because wealth, of however modest scale, would bring merchants into the village. And merchants were men. And men might be marriageable. This in turn implied less fascination with livestock—which walk to market tens of miles away—and more determination to develop handicrafts and a gardening cooperative and thus produce a surplus for sale. Notice the income associated with this was important but not dominant. The real motivation was men.

Second—and in some ways in contrast to the impression we got talking to the men, who seemed to know each others' minds intimately and to have reached a kind of mental commonality—the process of appreciative conversation revealed that one woman was a skilled tie-dyer without either cloth or dye or the means to acquire them, while another woman had both cloth and dye but lacked the expertise to use them. A two-woman enterprise was formed on the spot and began production within days. Would that have come out of a PRA? Possibly, but the World Vision team doubted it.

After two days of intensive interviewing—a word I found myself increasingly rejecting as being too rigid and formulaic—both men and women were ready to begin forming their provocative propositions (actually the women were about half a day ahead of the men). Slightly to my surprise I found they had no difficulty with the rather artificial rules that surround the provocative propositions— the use of the present tense, the stretching nature of the propositions and so on. Much less surprising was the fact that the women came to a somewhat different set of propositions than the men. Put shortly, the women's provocative propositions centred on their determination to do all in their power to improve the water supply; to develop food and handicraft production to guarantee the sustainability of the village over the long term; to develop the school and the mosque as the central features of the communal life of the village; and to send one more woman for more effective training as a primary health care worker.

The men set themselves a more difficult task. One of the priorities that was mentioned in nearly all of the interviews was the need for fencing to keep animals out of the grain fields and the gardens. Wire fencing is, however, very expensive relative to the present productivity of the land; more significantly, it bestows private rather than public benefits and thus presents a particular difficulty to World Vision which, in the quest for community sustainability, much prefers to fund projects of which the outputs are generally and necessarily shared. In much the same way, the men were clear that the key to the critical water issue lay in the repair of the dam about a mile away, but they knew too that the original design was so flawed and the damage subsequently inflicted by waterflow over the bed of the dam was so severe that this was likely to be a hugely expensive undertaking and one far outside World Vision's normal scale of operations—not to mention the little matter of the village's 50 percent contribution on which World Vision is wholly inflexible.

The men were therefore struggling for a provocative proposition that respected the realities of the situation but which also reflected the tone of their conversations over the last $2^1/2$ days. Like the women—and perhaps because of unobserved cross-fertilization—they finally chose the theme of sustainability as key to their leading provocative proposition. They saw this as desirable in itself, as one of the features they remembered with most pleasure from their former lives as nomads, as imposed upon them by their geography and physical environment, and as a value that they could all share. They thus formulated their first provocative proposition as follows: *This community is determined to produce as many of its needs as possible for itself and to take whatever steps are necessary to achieve that.*

As we shall see below, the *tone* of that proposition and the discussion it engendered was markedly different from where we had started with the chief's first public address to the World Vision team four days earlier.

It was when they discussed their second provocative proposition that I gained a deeper insight into the real needs and aspirations of the community. It was, in a nutshell, about survival. Just as the women were looking for men, at least partly so that they could sustain the village by starting families of their own, so the men were looking for ways in which to stabilize the population of the village and ensure its capacity to endure. That, I began to understand, was why the object of self-sufficiency and sustainability was so important; and now it emerged that that was what lay behind the imperative for improved education.

The reasoning may seem a little unusual: "Education is excellent. It helps people achieve a serenity of spirit. It encourages people to stay here." But the thrust behind that reasoning is clear enough. People who are well educated, not only in a technical sense, but also in a Koranic and spiritual sense, are not so foolish as to be tempted to the fruitless search for a well-paid job in town. On the contrary, they will stay in the village and use their education to improve the economic base of the whole community. So emerged the second provocative proposition: *We are determined to have a high-quality school which offers a full primary cycle and a well-furnished mosque to guarantee education in the village.*

At this point a surprising twist of events occurred. As I emphasized above, though the men were unanimous in their requirement for veterinary help, they had shown no interest in health care in any of the conversations we had audited. Yet when they came to discuss their third provocative proposition, it came out, with the minimum of discussion, as follows: *We are determined to improve the health of the village by whatever means.*

I can only assume that they had been shamed by the women overnight and realized that they would be given a hard time at the whole-village meeting scheduled for the next day if they got up and announced that they wanted to commit to a veterinarian rather than primary health. Certainly, I got the impression that they were a little embarrassed about it—hence the lack of discussion—and I thought it impolitic to press the point.

It was when we got to the last provocative proposition that the going became unexpectedly difficult. Water was such a dominant issue that we were all surprised by the indirect way in which it had been handled in the first proposition. The chair of the World Vision team gently fished to see if they wanted to say something more direct about what we had observed as their major and wholly understandable preoccupation. There was a long, rambling and peculiarly prolix conversation, in which no one seemed wholly at ease. It eventually emerged that the villagers of Bourella were locked in a tense struggle with the people of Oum el Kheez II over access to land in and around the dam. The worst of the breach had been recently healed by marriage between the two chiefly families, but the villagers of Bourella were still extremely unclear about what rights to access they would be able to make stick if the dam were in fact ever repaired. They were thus, it now came out, very ambivalent about the future of the dam. They know they needed it to work because only so could they be sure that the aquifers tapped by the wells of the village would be adequately replenished. But at the same time they feared that if the dam was restored to its former function, it could generate major conflict with a powerful chief and lead to their exclusion from the wet land. What they *really wanted*—hydrologically impossible as it was—was a secure supply of abundant well water in the village and as good a deal on the existing, non-repaired, dam as they could get.

For them to talk of these highly sensitive micro-political issues at all was hard. To talk of them as a group with the chief, and with strangers, including Toubabs, present was doubly so. I am confident that we would have heard none of this without the slow confidence building that had gone on during the appreciative inquiry.

In the end they settled for a provocative proposition that might have been drafted by the Security Council of the UN. It seems to say nothing. Behind the bland exterior there lurks dynamite: *We shall engage all our forces to develop our water resources.*

We approached the village meeting with a sense of excitement, not unmixed with dread. How would the men take to the women's propositions? How would they take to the women speaking up in such a forum and if necessary making demands of the men? How would the women react if the chief tried to override them?

In fact these anxieties proved almost wholly groundless; the real difficulties lay in other and quite unexpected quarters. The *forgeron* lady made a short but gutsy presentation laying out the women's propositions, with an added and unexpected coda: World Vision was welcome to cooperate with them if it wished, but their help was a secondary issue. "If you help, that's fine. If you don't, we shall do it by ourselves." I wondered if this was indirectly aimed at the men. If so, the chief replied equally indirectly.

He sketched out the men's propositions, with little of the reasoning that lay behind them as I have explained it above. He was clearly anxious to produce what old trade unionists would call a composite resolution, and declared that the whole village was expressing a priority for health care, literacy, water and income generation—a gross oversimplification of a complex set of issues but one that he thought politically safe.

At this point, one of the Hassaniya-speaking female expatriates on the World Vision team, herself married to a prominent Mauritanian, was invited, by the *forgeron* and her sisters, to speak up for the women. They evidently felt that the chief's synthesis and somewhat brisk manner were not doing justice to the depth and care of their own thinking. She made a long speech, punctuated by murmurs of assent from the women and with no visible sense of unease from the men. She spoke of the solidarity of the women and of their wish to open themselves to the possibility of learning new things—and, by implication, meeting new people—to improve their lives. The social cohesion the women had discovered in the last days, she said, had come as a delightful surprise to them all, for it made "all things possible in the future." The women were aware of having been let down in the past by NGOs, which came to the villages, made extravagant promises and then disappeared for good. She promised that a long road lay ahead. The women were determined to tread it, if necessary by themselves (i.e., without World Vision or the men), but, stepping from her role as spokesperson from the women to senior executive of World Vision, that organization would walk the same road with the women arm in arm.

The women were clearly delighted with this speech; the men largely indifferent. It was clear that the men were waiting to see what was in World Vision's box. They had patiently gone through a long and laborious process of consultation at World Vision's behest; they had clarified their objectives; they had even given way to the women on important points. What more could reasonably be expected of them? How would World Vision respond?

I was asking myself the same question. The World Vision field officer for the upper Assaba had been working in a third village and had serendipitously arrived in Bourella as the village meeting got underway. We all turned to him to give detailed responses to the implicit (from the women) or explicit (from the men) invitation to collaborate. At that critical point the conflict between the training dimension of the exercise and the operational dimension became all too apparent. The World Vision team officer explained *sotto voce* that the World Vision budget for the Assaba was under pressure, underfunded by donors, and that he could not make any commitments. For reasons that have still not become clear, he even felt unable to make any general statement about his willingness to discuss further with the villagers exactly what forms World Vision's collaboration would take, even where those would have been virtually costless, such as entering into further discussions with the UNDP about their plans for the future of the dam.

It is unhelpful to speculate about what was going on in terms of the micro-politics of World Vision at this point. But there is such an important general principle at issue here that it needs special emphasis. The appreciative approach generates enthusiasm, commitment, hope, solidarity and ownership among those who handle the process competently. World Vision had, through its lack of experience and inadequate planning (deficiencies for which I must accept a major part of the blame), put itself in a wholly untenable position. It had used the rhetoric of partnership and the shared walk in the context of persuading the villagers to make costly and demanding commitments. But it had then failed to honour its own rhetoric.

Astonishingly, the villagers did not seem to share my sense of frustration and anticlimax. Perhaps they had seen it all before. Perhaps they did not expect any hard commitments at this stage. Perhaps they really meant it when they said they were not especially concerned whether World Vision joined them: they would trust in their own resources. Whatever the reason, the fact is that informal feedback after the village meeting, which agreed to the provocative propositions, was positive—especially so from the women. Even the chief, who closed the meeting with a speech that at least in part reflected the appreciative spirit: "Everyone has muscles," he said. "Work is good because God wants us to work. The true worker is beyond criticism. There is plenty of potential in this village. Families can earn their livings if they apply themselves—and good livings, too." Even he told me privately that he was very happy with the process. The proof of the pudding would be in the eating in the following few weeks.

4. Conclusion

We knew that in taking the appreciative approach to the Sahara we were testing it to destruction. We also knew that many of those whom we were supposedly training in the appreciative approach would see it as a threat to their existing and hard-earned expertise in PRA.

Yet what had come out—almost *malgré nous*—was an extraordinary shift in the mentality of the villagers with whom we had been working, and perhaps an even greater shift in the paradigm orientation of most of the World Vision staff whom we had been training.

For the former, none of the expected reactions persisted. There was, in the last days, no overt suggestion of the Inshallah fatalism that is often said to be the bane of development in Islamic communities. There was similarly no overt sign of agency-dependency or of domination by deficiency thinking. There was a clear-sighted assessment of the needs of the village—in terms of water and income-generating possibilities—but these were put into a context of sustainable action by the villagers themselves by the generation of clear action proposals.

To that extent, the appreciative approach had achieved its objectives. Additionally we had a wealth and depth of factual information that ought to make it possible to generate a quality of partnership between the villagers and World Vision which each will find satisfactory and sustainable. The question remains: had we achieved more, both in terms of data collection and in terms of the motivation of the villagers, than would have been achieved by PRA?

As the concurrent work in Oum el Kheez had shown, that is to make a false dichotomy. There the World Vision team, assisted by Mette Jacobsgaard of the Cambridge Partnership, had chosen to use a wide range of PRA tools but had done so within an appreciative framework. Thus, for example, the plotting of the seasonal map had not focused on the hardships of the soudure but on the abundance of the rainy season and the steps that could be taken—such as preserving fruits and vegetables through various forms of sun-drying, smoking and salting—to prolong that abundance through more of the dry season. Likewise, the history of the village had been skillfully shaped into a history of the achievements of the villagers rather than a catalogue of disasters and conflicts.

The Oum el Kheez II team, then, like we in Bourella, had found that what made the difference was the form of the questions and the ensuing conversation, rather than the precise design of the research tool. Instead of studiously writing down hard (or usually quasi-hard) data in the conventional field-research way, both teams had learned to listen, to converse, to play—and then, afterwards to sift, test and examine the data from many different standpoints. Most of the World Vision trainees were in the end ready to agree that they had uncovered a richness and multilayeredness of information that PRA is unlikely to yield, even though much of the formal structure of the inquiry in Oum el Kheez II had been that of PRA. They may not have used the language of reading the text, but what they were saying is that they had learned how many texts there are and how illuminating it is to read them against each other.

We had all made mistakes. None of us had had the energy to maintain the very high level of intellectual input that marked the first days of the World Vision team's interactions in Bourella. Especially toward the end of the process, there was a sense of things slipping through lack of concentration (and perhaps a subconscious sense of relief that it was all going so well). Despite these glitches—and because of the lessons that can be learned from them—the appreciative approach has become a standard process in all World Vision's programming in Mauritania.

Chapter 12
Using appreciative inquiry as an evaluation tool:
An example from Africa

1. The setting

Two agencies working with street children in the capital of an African country I shall call Bengo were coming to the end of their mandate as experiments and needed an evaluation to enable their sponsors to come to a decision about their future.

Part of the background, however, was a clash of organizational cultures between the executives of the agencies and one of their principal stakeholders, a large UN-related organization which had played a major part in providing start-up finance. Unsurprisingly, the latter was primarily interested in classic measures of cost effectiveness and cost-benefit ratios. The former, by contrast, argued that measuring outputs in a program that was centrally concerned with a long-term process—essentially changing consciousness—was inappropriate and misleading.

Behind this familiar wrangle lay a deeper ideological conflict. The leadership of the programs—two expatriates and one Bengolese—had erected knowledge of the street into a fundamental principle of their work. By that, they meant that only those who had experienced the street firsthand, who had immersed themselves in the culture of the street, seen its horror, its degradation, its pyramid of exploitation for themselves could understand adequately the demands of their work and the strain on their staff. Seen in this light, a conventional evaluation, with external consultants jetting in for a few days, speaking to stakeholders and the wider circle of NGOs and government departments, interviewing the staff and perhaps a small sample of clients—such an approach was not only unacceptable, it also seemed like an insult, and especially an insult to the people of the street themselves.

Another dimension to the question—what sort of an evaluation will be acceptable to all parties?—arose from the fact that three of the sponsors of the organizations had their own institutional pressures to manage. The two Europeans who founded the organizations were both religious: one a Catholic priest from a very distinguished missionary order; the other a brother from an international community dedicated to teaching. Both their parent bodies were asking fundamental questions about whether their scarce personnel should be involved in programs as far removed from their areas of traditional work. That anxiety was raised to a higher power by the fact that both men were formally contracted to the Archdiocese of Bengo, and legally the programs were set up as programs of the

Archdiocese. If the powers-that-be in the Archdiocese became disenchanted with the programs, therefore, they could terminate them immediately. In each constituency—the missionary order, the teaching community and the Priests' Council of the Archdiocese—there were voices that were expressing doubt whether their respective bodies should be so closely involved in a program so far outside their normal areas of work, especially at a time when resources were tight and immediate needs clamant.

These doubts have to be seen against a wider backdrop. In most cultures where the phenomenon is well established—and in this connection Bengo is no exception—the term street children is at least as pejorative as it is descriptive. That is to say, street children are seen as criminals, preying on legitimate citizens, as centres of the thriving drug and prostitution trades, as shiftless, irresponsible and disease-ridden nuisances. On this account, improving the lot of such unwelcome elements of society is not only foolish but also socially destructive because it increases the flow of migrants from the deprived rural areas into the urban slums. In this sense, then, the whole notion of street children is socially constructed by the dominant powers of the society, of which the Archdiocese and the other sponsors were—or were thought to be by the founders of the two organizations—a largely uncritical part. To set an evaluation in the socially constructed world of the urban bourgeoisie seemed to the program leadership to be a contradiction in terms.

Fortuitously, appreciative inquiry seemed to offer a way out for all of the constituencies. To the UN body, it was attractive because it would give them a chance to learn more about a technique that some of their senior staff had begun to hear about. To the other sponsors—the three religious groups—its very intensity ensured that valuable evaluative material would emerge which could not readily be challenged by the leadership of the programs. And to them—the leaders and founders—it was acceptable because it recognized the relativity of interpretations put upon their clients and the work they were seeking to do with them.

For the program leaders, there was also a more practical reason for choosing appreciative inquiry as the evaluative method. The essence of appreciative inquiry in the context of evaluation is that it gives the organization as a whole a process by which the best practice of the organization can become embedded as the norm against which general practice is tested. In this sense, it is at least as much a teaching and training exercise as it is an evaluative one and therefore has a prolonged beneficial effect on the performance of the organization. This is especially true in an organization which is still unsure of itself, and of which the staff is relatively inexperienced, for the embedded evaluation to which appreciative inquiry gives access is much less threatening and judgmental than many variants of traditional evaluation for it invites the staff—and indeed, in theory, all the stakeholders—to reflect on their best practice rather than to admit their failures and unsolved problems.

So much for why appreciative inquiry came to be chosen for this somewhat unusual evaluation. In the next section I will describe the programs in some detail in terms of their content, and in the following short section I shall say something about the organizations delivering the services described. In section 4 I will describe the way the evaluation worked out and in the final section I will try to draw some general conclusions.

2. Working with street children

Orphanages run by religious institutions in areas of high deprivation have a long and honourable, if currently unfashionable, history in all the continents of the developing world. They have, however, a special appeal for Roman Catholics, with their distaste for abortion and contraception, and to that extent have contributed to Roman Catholic participation in urban programs from the early days of the missions. More recently, however, the inadequacy of this approach—essentially seeking to lock the stable door after the horse has bolted—has been widely appreciated and more proactive steps have had to be taken to try to prevent unwanted pregnancies, or ensure reproductive health, or both. This led, for Bengo, to Fr. Peter starting a project called Aidurb in a low-income area of the city to cater to the health needs of prostitutes and very young unmarried mothers. When the logic forced the program into a major involvement with contraception, as it had to, Fr. Peter was obliged to withdraw.

His acquaintance with the living conditions of the women he had been working with was, however, so disturbing that he could not walk away from the human deprivation that the street represents for the poorest, weakest and most vulnerable. Rather, he immersed himself in the culture of the street, living with it, in it and on it for a year, seeking to understand it at an ethnographic level—but seeking, too, for keys that would enable young men and women of the street to decide, freely and unconstrainedly, to leave the street and take up a regular living in the informal sector. He was joined in this search by Brother James, a Dutchman from a community known for its thoroughness, its uncompromising commitment to excellence and its intolerance of sloppiness in its members and their clients.

Between them, they developed the idea of a three-stage process which could be described as protection, conscientization and training. First, the young and vulnerable had to be offered what in other contexts might be called respite care; that is a temporary refuge where they could rest, feel secure and gather their forces to rejoin the endless battle for survival on the street. Second, they had to be enabled to value themselves, to slough off the negative imagery society at large placed upon them and learn that they could earn respect and even affection by adopting a way of being different from that they had learned on the street. Third, they had to be trained in a marketable skill, and trained to a level at which they could pass vocational tests to give them access to the best jobs in the trade of their choice. The religious were very clear about this from the start. They set their faces against the cheap pseudo-training that declares a man a carpenter when he can knock two out of three nails into the wood straight, or a motor mechanic when he can remove a sparkplug. There is almost a mystique of the artisanal values here. Accuracy, goodness-of-fit, precision, perseverance, hard labour, pride in a difficult job done well—these, the religious thought, gave a man (or, *mutatis mutandis,* a woman) proper cause for self-respect and therefore sufficient pride to reject the predatory values of the street.

Clearly, what the religious had in mind was a kind of transformation of consciousness that would shift a young person from the dog-eat-dog mentality of the street, with its norm of exploitation of the weakness of anyone outside the gang or "base," to a respect for self and others that makes trust and responsibility possible. Programmatically, such a shift implied the experience of what the religious, drawing on their own tradition, called unconditional love—the experience of non-judgmental acceptance of the young person for him- or herself which would invite a response of personal growth. But before they could be offered that experience, they had to be identified, to be befriended and drawn gently to a more sustained relationship in the safe place where they could afford to drop their defences, both literally and metaphorically. The idea developed, then, of a task-force of fieldworkers who would, rather like the religious themselves, spend most of their time on the street, meeting anyone who would talk to them, finding the young and vulnerable, getting to know their stories, building trust and acceptance until they could be invited to the refuge and find it a place to which they were happy to return. There another team of fieldworkers would get to know them, win their trust and watch them to see if they showed signs of wanting to leave the street. The religious were emphatic that the young person must take the initiative, must constantly express the wish to learn a trade, to achieve literacy, to accept the discipline that a three-year apprenticeship implies. There was to be no attempt to sell the exit route; indeed, life on the street was to be accorded equal value to life off the street.

If, however, a young person did express a wish to opt for the exit and could demonstrate—e.g., by regular attendance at literacy classes at the refuge, or taking an interest in the crafts taught there, or by regularly saving a tiny sum deposited with the housemother, or by showing genuine care for a more vulnerable peer—a capacity for change and development, then the plan was to feed them into a network of masters who would accept apprentices from the street, show them the tough kindness and understanding that would enable them to grow as persons as well as technicians and enable them to pass the relevant trade test in both the theory and practice of the trade.

That this is an expensive process hardly needs emphasis. The master expects a premium when the training starts and another, often larger one, when it is finished. The apprentice has to be fed, clothed and housed for three years; his or her tools have to be bought and his or her progress monitored by regular and fairly frequent visits by a fieldworker. Precisely because it is so expensive, the religious accepted that they could not make many mistakes. They therefore put in place, in agreement with Plan International, which helped finance the early experiments, a slow, thorough and costly process of checking the young person's story. That included a visit to the native village and, where possible, a visit to the parents and an attempt at reconciliation with the parents. (Most street children have been abandoned by, or have themselves abandoned, their parents. The law demands a parent's consent before a minor is accepted as an apprentice.) As the native village might be in another West African country and the parents might be exceedingly hard to trace, it easy to see how this checking process could gobble up time and resources. Sometimes it is discovered that the young person has told a series of total untruths, even though the staff thought that it had established an honest and trusting relationship. Such a child is not rejected, but nor is he or she accepted for sponsorship on an apprenticeship.

By the time of the evaluation, then, these three elements of the program were well tried—the initial fieldwork on the street, the refuge as a safe place where a change of consciousness could begin, and vocational training where it could continue.

To that initial program design had been added, almost by accident, a large residential facility for young pregnant and post-partum women. This was established as a separate charity, without the authority of the Archdiocese. To be admitted here required no previous signs of change of consciousness, but to be referred from the home to an apprenticeship certainly did. Such a reference was rare, however, because masters were, not unnaturally, reluctant to take on young mothers with small babies as apprentices. Most young mothers therefore had to leave the home after they had been delivered and had a few weeks of intensive training in mothering skills and, if they showed any aptitude or inclination, in basic sewing. Routinely, all mothers were given a full medical screening and, as the project was not officially under the aegis of the Archdiocese, all were fitted with IUDs unless they specifically declined.

There was clearly a difficulty in returning residents from the relative comfort, absolute safety and intense solidarity of the home to the precarious and dangerous life on the street. Many were reluctant to make that move; some had to be removed physically.

3. The organizations

From what I have said already about the founding of the two organizations, it will be obvious that we are dealing here with small NGOs of the charismatic variety; that is, heavily dependent upon the initiative and energy of one charismatic figure, supported by a group of willing acolytes. Here, the Catholic priest effectively ran the home for pregnant women, and the brother the refuge for boys. This gives a slightly exaggerated sense of separation; in fact, both religious were heavily involved in both projects, not least because they (the projects) shared the services of the fieldworkers in the sense that each fieldworker would refer (or accompany) clients to the appropriate locale. Although a Bengolese graduate was nominally in charge of the home and was formally accorded equal status to the religious, the reality was that she administered the day-to-day affairs of the home. Fr. Peter made all the major decisions.

Immediately, then, we are in dangerous water. The dangers are made the more threatening by two facts: first, the religious were both Europeans and as such the only whites involved in the projects; and second, they were both products of quite conservative missionary movements. Both these features need a little unpicking.

Race relations in Bengo are remarkably relaxed, partly because it was never a settler colony, partly because it has a long and distinguished history of higher education and therefore an elite that feels itself the equal of any white group, and partly because no one tribal group was obviously the favourite of the colonists (in contrast to Rwanda or Uganda, for example). From that it does not follow, however, that white leaders are indistinguishable from black ones, seen from either side of the racial divide. To put it shortly, whiteness bestows authority, and authority is not easily questioned or called to account in the local culture. Given that both whites still used their religious titles—father and brother—and given the respect, almost awe, in which these titles are often held, the tendency for authority to crystallize around the white leadership was marked, whatever the rhetoric to which we shall have to give more attention below.

This cultural fact reinforces a personality trait of both religious who are forceful, energetic, opinionated and, when provoked, prepared to be sharp to the point of brutal. More than that, the missionary formation of both men—the brother perhaps even more than the father—had taken place in the 1960s, at a time when independence was new in West Africa and when most missionaries were still trained to handle patterns of authority in the church which were centralist, hierarchical, male dominated and directive. Both men had, of course, revised their understandings of the nature of authority both in the church and in society at large, but the original conceptions were still occasionally observable, showing through the skin of a more democratic approach. It was nicely symbolic that in the chaos of the refuge, with its noise, its sporadic violence, its press of bodies and business, the brother sat in a relatively calm, well-furnished office with the only fridge and the only reliable source of electric power in the place. Fieldworkers were not encouraged to loiter there.

It was thus no surprise to find that all the financial affairs of both organizations were tightly controlled by these two religious. They raised the money from donors. They wrote the project proposals. They kept the accounts. They dealt directly with the auditors.

This charismatic approach was tempered by a set of deliberate derogations of authority from the religious. For example, they did not attend selection interviews for new appointees and, so far as we could tell, they did not seek to interfere with the recommendations made by their local staff. They did, however, have very considerable and perhaps dominant voice when annual contracts (on which all staff served) came up for renewal. Likewise they took pride in the fact that they did not police the fieldworkers, who were free to set their own work schedules in ways that would maximize their chances of meeting and getting to know the street children. (This usually involved a good deal of night work as then the children were resting and were easier to locate and more disposed to chat.) They did, however, insist that all fieldworkers clocked in and out at one of the refuges. Ostensibly a safety precaution, this had the not entirely unintended by-product of ensuring that staff did in fact turn up for work.

So much for the relationships between the leadership and the staff. But what of other stakeholders? Of these the most obvious was the Advisory Committee. On paper this had quite formidable powers and a membership that was clearly designed to plug the organizations into a number of key networks—the Department of Health, the Department of Social Welfare, and the Archdiocese. Two members of staff, apart from the religious, were co-opted members. Having met some of the members of the Advisory Committee and having read minutes of its meetings, the reality seems to have been much closer to what Father Peter frankly told us: "These are powerful people in their own worlds. When we need something doing, we tell them and they do it." In formal terms, then, the leadership tended to see the Advisory Committee as an extension of the staff, rather than as a body to which they were themselves accountable.

There is no point in exhausting this theme. I have said enough to show that, in organizational and social-psychological terms, we were dealing with a heavily authoritarian, personalistic or charismatic organization that, either consciously or unconsciously, hid behind a thin veneer of participative rhetoric. Two consequences followed. The two religious were close to burn-out, hopelessly overburdened with administrative concerns which did not play to their strengths. Yet their need to control the organizations was such that they did not dare to be out of the country simultaneously. Cox and Box was the order of the day at a time when both Cox and Box badly needed at least three months' total break. Second, both organizations were in danger of being unable to make the crucial transition from their present charismatic form to a sustainable institutional form. Paradoxically but not unusually, the very concerns that drove the religious to risk their own mental health were also the concerns that endangered the projects they cared so deeply about.

I am aware that by presenting some of the findings of the evaluation in this prefatory section, I am pulling the rug from under my own feet in the later sections. Of course, these conclusions dawned on us only slowly; they were revealed by a series of small signs and events during the three weeks of our work, and only began to form themselves as provisional conclusions about half way through that period. I mention them now, however, because I want to argue that the use of the appreciative approach in evaluation allows one to react to the reality that is emerging and embed in the evaluative process, itself a way of tackling what are seen as key organizational needs. This process will continue long after the formal evaluation has been completed, the report written and the consultants have departed. Indeed the vitality and creativity of that process is the measure of the success of the intervention, rather than the report and its recommendations. In this sense appreciative evaluation is the start of a process that allows the organization to self-steer toward its optimal future track. I shall illustrate that with reference to a number of more operational issues in later sections and return to this central theme, of the authority structure of the organizations, in the concluding section.

4. Appreciative evaluation in progress

Before the consultancy began, we agreed with Father Peter, who had visited us in the UK and to whom we had explained as carefully as time permitted what the appreciative approach involved, that the basic form of our work would be in three stages: a preparatory workshop with as many of the stakeholders as possible to explain the appreciative approach and prepare an appreciative protocol; a full week (actually eight days) of data collecting by the participants from the street children themselves; and a three-day seminar in which the data would be analyzed, provocative propositions agreed and action plans prepared. As this evaluation was to be paid for by international donors who might be interested in financing an extension of the projects in the future—or even, for one UN body, making it a template for application throughout the Third World—we were committed (in some ways a little reluctantly, because we feared that what we saw as the tail others might mistake for the dog) to writing a brief report, primarily for the donors but also to act as an *aide memoire* for all the stakeholders who had taken part in the evaluation and who, as I emphasized above, would inevitably have responsibility for taking the process forward on our departure.

The first workshop was to be preceded by two days of orientation and fact find-ing. In the ideologically loaded eyes of Fr. Peter and Br. James, this meant an ini-tiation-by-immersion into the street. We quickly realized that our credibility was at stake. Commitment is such a strong value in these organizations, overriding all others, that to refuse to enter as deeply as two days allowed into the reality of life on the street was to admit to an ontological and therefore heuristic gap between us as facilitators (which title we preferred to consultants) and our clients. It was only when the three of us had individually walked through smoking rubbish tips and sat with the garbage pickers; when we had been held at knife point by drug-crazed youngsters; been caught up in a police raid on a gang of drug-pushers (and assumed to be involved in the same trade); had rats run up our trouser legs as we walked past the recumbent forms of the sleeping children in the street; faced exis-tentially the question of where to sleep when a rainstorm makes the ground too wet to lie down; only then would we be accepted, in however provisional a way, as coworkers.

For us this was a steep learning curve indeed, but whatever its value in the eyes of Fr. Peter and Br. James, it brought home to us two impressions that were going to be crucial in the way we planned and executed the evaluation. The first was a heart-knowledge of the demands of work on the street. Courage, compassion and persistence of the highest order—an order usually only found in religious com-munities or those drawing their inspiration from them—were required of young fieldworkers whose task was to immerse themselves in the harsh world of the street day after day, until they could merge into the background and yet tell by fingertip feel when a child-porter (kayayo) was ready to accept the help the refuge offered or when a teenage prostitute was worried that she was pregnant or suf-fering from some STD. We realized, then, that we were dealing with a most unusual collection of people, "mini black Mother Teresas without the Catholic baggage" as one of my colleagues put it.

A corollary of this was that these people had been selected—and were now select-ing their colleagues—based on those virtues of courage and compassion rather than any formal qualification or intellectual accomplishment. Some were gradu-ates in social administration, some were graduates of the (low-level) Government School of Social Work. Most were neither. They were young men and women with, usually, some post-primary education but not necessarily much capacity for abstract thought and almost certainly no awareness at all of organizational theory or even organizational practice. (For the vast majority of the 30-plus field staff, this was their first real job.)

If the educational level of the staff was such that they would derive little from the normal appreciative inquiry workshop as we have developed it after many trials in our own culture, that of the clients, the street children themselves (arguably the largest and most important group of stakeholders), was non-existent. That did not surprise us and we had planned the final three-day data-analysis seminar with that in the back of our minds. What we had not taken into account were three things that revealed the depths of our naiveté. First, the children are usually so sleep starved that if they get the opportunity to sleep, they take it. However stimulating and participative a seminar might be in our eyes, for them it would be an ideal time to sleep. Second, many of them, especially but not only the boys, are on drugs, some soft, many (and increasingly) hard. This would not be conducive to constructive participation in the seminar. Third and perhaps most important of all, for a variety of reasons the attention span of street children is unusually short, even for uneducated youngsters. Because they are constantly on the go, hassling for work, keeping an eye open for predators or income-earning opportunities, they are simply not used to calm, sustained reflection on a single theme.

By the end of the second day of our street immersion, then, we were faced with the need for a complete redesign of the process. We had pre-designed it on the assumption that the fieldworkers would all be graduates; that the street children would be able to take part in at least some of the activities in the second seminar (possibly with some careful accompaniment by the fieldworkers); and that some of the background theory of appreciative inquiry would be both relevant and interesting to the fieldworkers and other stakeholders who would be attending the first workshop. All these assumptions were revealed as unjustified. We had also accepted at face value the claim that this was a democratic organization, well used to participative styles of inquiry and collaborative decision-making. Our time on the street had not stripped us yet of that illusion; that assumption, then, remained in place.

Overnight, we decided on three principles of design. First, we would focus more sharply than ever on story as the key data category. While this might jeopardize the participation of some of the non-fieldworker stakeholders (who could not be expected to have many stories of direct involvement in the life of the street), it would give voice and, we hoped, ownership to the fieldworkers themselves. Second, we had to accept the overwhelming advice we were getting that to plan on the participation of the street children in the second (data analysis and action planning) seminar would be counter-productive. That meant that the week for fieldwork would be the only indirect input available to the clients and had to be redesigned accordingly. Third, we would jettison most of the theoretical material, minimize talking heads, and maximize small group work with intensive facilitation of the small groups. We designed questions or exercises, or both, for these groups to be as direct, concrete and experienced-based as possible, and we learned as we went along (especially by the time of the second seminar) the value of mobilizing the right brain rather than the left brain.

At this stage we were still hoping for significant participation from a wider group of stakeholders. This was an issue we had discussed in detail with Fr. Peter at our early meetings in the UK, and he had assured us that he would do what he could to include them. We had in mind a very diverse group—from representatives of the donor community to people from the key departments of national and local government to those more directly involved with at least some aspects of the lives of street children such as shopkeepers who allowed them to sleep in their doorways to police who, at least in theory, enforce some degree of law in the squatments. (In fact, it turned out that some of the worst predations on children, especially girls, come from the police and local authority guards.) In the event, very few non-staff stakeholders showed up. A senior and rising figure from the Department of Social Welfare, a representative of each of Peter's and James' communities, and a junior staffer from the UN body concerned comprised the tally. The absence of anyone from the Advisory Committee was a major hole: the public health doctor who had promised she would attend had to attend a family funeral in a neighbouring country. That was, of course, an unfortunate coincidence, but it set alarm bells ringing in our ears for reasons already sketched above.

The great majority of the participants of the first workshop, then, were the 30 or so fieldworkers themselves. We felt justified in angling the style and content of the workshop more firmly in their direction, while still hoping to maintain the interest and participation of the few other stakeholders present.

After the formal preliminaries (Bengo institutional culture is surprisingly formal and the appropriate bureaucratic rituals have to be followed scrupulously) and some explanation of the timetable and process, we started by asking the participants to brainstorm on how they felt when they first started working for Street Children's Home and the Mothers' Refuge (hereafter SCH/MR.) We wanted to introduce the notion of feeling as a prelude to getting the group to focus on generative questions that they could use in their week of fieldwork. We were surprised by the negative tone that came through this exercise: words like uncomfortable, surprise, amazement, suspicion, rejection, fear of the unknown, doubt, fatigue, tense, frightened and insecure dominated the list, almost obscuring more positive feelings like excitement, sympathy, acceptance and challenge. The group was evidently prepared to be honest about its feelings and was not diffident about sharing the negative ones with each other. Without hitting them over the head with it, it was thus possible to suggest, in a very preliminary way, that we as individuals and, by extension, we all as a group are more energized and excited by the positive feelings that we experience than by the negative ones.

This idea was deliberately left hanging as we prepared to move into a simple practice-interview using generative questions. We preceded that by distributing a one-page summary of the art of active listening, one we had in fact prepared for a very high powered international conference a few weeks earlier, which the fieldworkers had much less trouble taking on board than the international executives. For the former, it becomes almost as natural as breathing.

To us—and I hope to most of the participants—it felt an easy transition to move from stories of our own experience to a consideration of the ways we each construct our own reality. In our normal appreciative inquiry workshops we spend time on theories of social constructionism, making the point that the way we interpret our organizations is itself socially conditioned. Here the emphasis was rather different though the basic point was the same. We did not want to get into heavy social theory, not least because we were holding the workshop in a room in the refuge itself, with a high level of noise from the boys next door and frequent interruptions as participants needed to break up fights or deal with emergencies. But we did need to get the participants to step back from their interpretation of life on the street and recognize that other interpretations—e.g., those of the children themselves—had their own validity. In Bengo—as in most developing countries—the construction that is put on the street and therefore on street children is a key determinant of public policy toward the poorest. If the street is seen as a crucible of vice, violence and crime—the usual bourgeois construction—then the bulldozing of the shanties has a veneer of logic. Destroy the shanty and you destroy the vicious culture of the shanty. (In fact you do no such thing; you merely move it somewhere else.) At the other extreme, street children themselves value many aspects of street life. They enjoy the camaraderie of the base; they enjoy the freedom and independence from parental authority; they enjoy the sense of being responsible for themselves; and they value the opportunities (some of them immoral, some of them illegal, some of them neither) that life on the street sometimes gives them. No wonder some children return to the street again and again, despite parental attempts to hijack them back to their native villages.

Most of the fieldworkers knew these polar opposite interpretations of life on the street. What they saw much less clearly was that their own understanding of the street was itself no less constructed from their own experience and exposure to the views of others. We took the view that if they were to be able to listen appreciatively to the views of the street children on their own projects and the way they related to life on the street, then they had to come to a deeper understanding of the way we all interpret our own reality. This, we thought, would lead at least some of them into a deeper appreciation of the way they were seen by the street children themselves and allow them to build more securely on their own best practice.

That was the thinking behind the next phase of the workshop. We started with the familiar drawing of the half full/half empty glass of water (interestingly, no one in the room saw it as half empty) and then moved on to the no less familiar exercise of interpreting an abstract drawing. This produced interpretations as various as a sprouting fruit, the road to destruction, a mangrove swamp—and "a design in the artist's head." It gave us a convenient peg on which to hang a discussion of the way we see the world and the way a group shares its apprehensions of reality. It was not difficult to relate that back to the interpretations of the street and to get the small groups to reflect on the way they had, up to that point, seen the street. We were concerned here with the actual process of observation and reality-construction; only later did we get into the matter of substance (which turned out to be another nodal point in the whole evaluation).

Once we judged that most of the groups had grasped the main point, we moved on to the role of feelings, emotion and expectations in the way we behave as individuals and groups. In retrospect, I think I—who was primarily responsible at this point—could have handled this better by relating it more immediately to a fact that all the fieldworkers (as we were later to discover) know perfectly well: that street children often behave as they are expected to behave. If they sense that they are being despised as petty criminals and drug dealers, they have no compunction about picking pockets and selling dope. If—as in the refuge—they know they are valued, accepted and even loved, they are capable of remarkable behavioural changes. Instead of focusing hard on that component of the workers' own experience, I foolishly talked about the evidence for the Pygmalion effect (without using that term) and told stories, in an attempt to remain in narrative mode, about my own experience of expectations changing performance. Having resolved to keep talking heads to the barest minimum, we quickly moved on to a group exercise where we asked each table of four or five to pool their answers to two questions: Who has affirmed you as a person, as a student and/or as a family member, and what difference has that affirmation made to your subsequent experience?

The groups found these questions hard to handle, one admitting that it would have found the mirror image—who has criticized you and what difference has that made?—a great deal easier. In part, this may be a cultural variable. In Bengo child-rearing practice, affirmation does not play a major role, and in bureaucratic settings, the same is broadly true. The role of the superior officer is to point out the deficiencies of his junior, not to praise his accomplishments. In part, too, there may have been a reluctance to speak of success or improvement or even affirmation, even in the relatively safe environment of a small group of colleagues.

Perhaps the least successful of the many exercises we put the participants through, this did at least encourage them to think of the role of memory, emotion and significant encounters in determining the development path of the individual. From there it was a short step to the heliotropic principle. Short or not, many of the group were obviously uncomfortable in moving from a consideration of the individual to a consideration of the group, in this case of SCH/MR. Indeed, the whole notion of their organizations having a life or form that was open to study and intervention with a view to affecting the future was evidently hard for many of them. This of course is one of the handicaps carried by any charismatic organization: the workers tend to define their organizational reality in terms of their personal relationship with the charismatic leader. Emotionally, we are dealing, in Handy's terms, with a spider's web and it is hard for the employees to see the web rather than the spider.

We found the idea of organizational memory helpful here. By encouraging the staff to think of the corporate memories of SCH/MR, it was possible to show that one way of constructing the present and the future of the organizations was by building on the basis of the best of the memories. I think it was this interpretation of the heliotropic principle that finally made sense to them. It set the context for the leitmotif of the fieldwork phase for the evaluation: what does best practice look like? Or, to translate, what are the best memories we have of our work with street children and how do we recreate those circumstances?

By now the idea of generative questions—those that elicit emotion as well as analysis—was beginning to take root. While some participants still had difficulty moving out of routine questionnaire mode—where do you sleep? when did you come to this area?—many of them were beginning to see that stories that encouraged respondents to get into touch with positive feelings were likely not only to generate more data but also suggest ways forward for both the organization and for the individual. We therefore ended the first day of the workshop by encouraging each table to produce a set of generative questions about SCH/MR. Again some had difficulty with this, but with intensive facilitation and coaching, most managed to produce at least some generative questions. We put them all on the wall and asked everyone to vote for the four they found most stimulating. The four that received the most votes were as follows:

- Tell me a story about the best things your organization does for street children

- What is it about your organization that makes street children have confidence in it?

- Have you a story about the best thing that has happened to one street child in your agency?

- Tell me about your peak experience at work.

Notice that these questions were focused on narrative, on storytelling, and the essence of the stories thus elicited was as much feeling as it was fact. Words like best, confidence, peak experience were designed to draw from the respondent memories, in story form, about which they felt proud and were therefore happy to share. By rooting the conversation in their own experience, we were honouring their work on the street and giving them permission to move out of analytical thinking—with which some of them were not comfortable—into a form of intellectual engagement in which they felt wholly at ease.

Observing this process at work, we were struck by two things. First, after a diffident start, the energy and volume levels rose markedly. Within a few minutes everyone in the room was fully engaged, so much so that there were groans of disappointment when we announced that it was time to swap roles. Second and more surprising to us all, was the quality of information that came forth. Because their fortnightly staff meetings were usually cast in problem mode—e.g., "The local council is threatening to bulldoze the shanties at Karanti. What are we going to do about the children there?" or "The fieldworkers in the central market area are spending too much time with the local authorities and not enough time with the children. What are they going to do about it?"—the staff had had few opportunities to hear from each other the exciting and rewarding things that were happening on the street. Certainly they had never, as they commented again and again during the feedback session, told each other stories about their experience on the street and it came as a revelation to them how much encouragement they could derive from each other. That turned out to be valuable learning that was constantly reinforced throughout the evaluation and which became one of the means by which the evaluative process was embedded in the life of both organizations.

In view of this, it was hardly surprising that when we asked how the exercise felt, a very different set of adjectives appeared on the board by comparison with the same question about starting work with SCH/MR. Now we heard words or phrases like, "makes you happy with yourself;" "relaxed;" "confident;" "challenging;" "makes you think;" "educative;" "flexible;" "interactive;" "interesting to share." There were also some negative comments. Some people found it difficult and one person found it frustrating. The latter was, I think, an expression of dismay that we did not allocate more time to the exercise. With the wisdom of hindsight, we should have had sufficient confidence in both the participants and in the process to earmark much longer. We actually gave each interview about 35 minutes: an hour would have been barely enough and many of them would have easily sustained a conversation of 75 minutes. As I have already commented the quality of the learning—and the nodal part that that was to play in the rest of the evaluation—would readily justify so large an investment of time.

The following day we returned to the data that had surfaced from the interviews. Because we wanted the participants to see how the data they would collect on the street would be handled—and thus give them added motivation to collect stories based on the protocol—we introduced them to the process of organizing the data into themes and then drafting provocative propositions based on those themes. This was territory we knew we would revisit in the second seminar when we had the data from the street, and to that degree this was a dummy exercise. We did not, however, stress that at the time, for some valuable material about the organizations had already begun to emerge from the previous days appreciative interviews and would, we were confident, give us—and all the participants—useful insights into the themes that we needed to pick up in the evaluation.

The groups did not find the abstraction of the stories—so energizing and life-full—into themes, which seemed distant and academic, an agreeable process. Part of the difficulty was the very idea of themes. To people unused to organizational theory or even to thinking abstractly about the way their work is organized, it is a huge leap to move out of personal stories into the identification of central themes in organizational life. It might help to communicate the scale of this transition if I reproduce some of the findings that the groups put on their flipcharts. Thus:

Group 1: Awareness; shelter; sponsorship; acceptance; discover individual potentials.

Group 2: Confidence; patience; love; independence; freedom; hope.

Group 3. Care; the future; persistence and continuity; motivation; acceptance.

Group 4: (A quite different approach, unconsciously approaching the formulation of provocative propositions) SCH/MR offers protection for street children from dangerous and violent situations; provides street children education and skills for the future; is the parent to street children; provides the best environment for counselling the street children.

Clearly, there is here a variety of types of theme, from abstract values that the organizations hold dear, to programmatic elements, to project objectives, to quasi-provocative propositions. Distilling the kind of themes that would allow the participants to get a taste of the process of forming provocative propositions required considerable effort from the facilitators. We ended up by offering four, three of which were very clearly derived from the work of all the groups (there were eight in all), one of which was raised by only one group but seemed to the facilitators to drive so at the heart of one aspect of the work of the organizations that it should not be lost. (We saw ourselves as facilitators, not computers of the lowest common denominator.)

The themes that we identified were the following:

1. The emotional environment of the street and of the organization(s);

2. The creative possibilities of the environment of the street;

3. Core values of SCH/MR; and

4. Mutuality within the organizations, and between the organizations and their clients.

We asked the groups to work at producing provocative propositions based on these themes. Our experience is that groups of all sorts—and perhaps paradoxically those working in the NGO sector with high ideals—find it hard to be sufficiently provocative. They tend to produce unexceptional and therefore unexciting propositions which will command universal assent but no sense of being stretched. What we were learning of the group dynamics of SCH/MR made us all the more conscious of this tendency. We therefore performed a mini-mime, almost a clowning act, to convey the idea of someone reaching for, fumbling after, something that is just beyond reach. He can just about see what he is after, but not as clearly as he would like; and he can only reach it after much effort, thought, contortion, rearrangement of the furniture and concentrated stretching. At last he grasps it—and discovers that it is something even more valuable than he had ever imagined.

Despite these facilitative exertions—and the hilarity thereby induced—some of the propositions that came forward were bland; e.g., "SCH/MR enhance the welfare of the street children by providing projects and programs that bring the best out of street children." Well, yes. "Our organization gives the street children the opportunity to live in a healthy environment." And so on. At the time, the facilitators were disappointed with such statements that seemed so undemanding. After spending eight days intensively on the street, night and day, with the workers, we came to read them with new eyes. For example, to set oneself the goal of providing a healthy environment for street children sounds banal until it is read against the current environment of hunger, disease (including a high incidence of sexually transmitted diseases), abortion (mostly self-induced), drug-taking and trafficking, violence, predation and homelessness that requires children to sleep standing up during the rains. By seeing themselves as a healthy alternative to such a lifestyle the participants may not have been using florid prose, but they were stretching themselves in a way that was, we came to see, entirely consistent with the clowning we had offered.

Some propositions were more obviously provocative: "This organization seeks out all available avenues by which the protection of the street children may be enhanced;" "We create the best enabling environment for an effective learning process between the staff and the clients."

We put all the propositions on the wall and then introduced the idea of consensus building around them. We gave each participant four coloured dots which they could stick on the propositions they most favoured; the only condition was that selection should take place in silence. In fact, there was no need to spell out that condition. The atmosphere round the clusters of flipcharts was electric. For the first time since the start of the workshop you could literally hear a pin drop. For about four minutes no one moved. Each was totally absorbed in what he or she was reading. Slowly, very slowly and deliberately, people came forward to place one dot. Then more silent reflection.

A clear pattern emerged, perhaps because of a snowball effect (though we saw no obvious sign of that). Three propositions (including the two in the last paragraph) garnered votes from about 40 percent of the participants, a further four received around a third, and the rest secured a handful. Very few got no votes at all as one would expect. We then gave each small group a red veto dot, castable only if the whole group agreed that the proposition concerned represented a direction which the organizations should definitely NOT seek to move in. Only one veto was cast and that against the proposition that had received the most votes. It read, "SCH/MR are very much aware of the uniqueness of each street child with its hidden giftedness and potential. As such we develop our projects and programs by carefully and compassionately listening to what is alive in them." It turned out that the veto was cast on a majority vote (i.e., against the rules of the game) and was actually registering a protest about wording which was held to be patronizing, rather than about real substance. We have encountered this difficulty before when giving groups' vetoes: no matter how much facilitators coach groups in ignoring wording and concentrating on substance and direction, the power of the words to arose emotional reactions is overwhelming. On reflection we decided to drop the veto in the second workshop—when we would be doing it for real—and use another technique altogether. That is described below.

Having summarized the process the group had been through in the workshop thus far—the production of a generative protocol, the collection of data through appreciative interviews, the analysis of that data into themes, the writing of provocative propositions, building consensus around them—we moved finally into the beginning of the second phase of the evaluation. Thus far we had been introducing some of the leading ideas and processes involved in an appreciative evaluation and had, in the course of doing so, learned a great deal about the organizations and their staff in a way that was almost invisible to the participants and which they did not experience as threatening. Now it was time for the participants to draft the generative questions they would use on the street during the eight days of data collection from the street children themselves. We took the view that it was for them to develop their own protocol. It was tempting to do it for them in the light of all that we had learned, but we needed to reflect that our knowledge was still very partial despite the steep learning curve we were conscious of climbing, and that, more important, the fieldworkers needed to claim ownership of the protocol they would be using. The only way we could do that was by coaching them in the production of their own questions.

It will, perhaps, come as no surprise to the reader that energy levels were getting low by this stage. Heat, humidity, noise, interruptions and overcrowding were conditions the participants may have been used to in the normal course of their jobs, but that course did not usually involve the hard intellectual and emotional effort we had been demanding of them. Nonetheless, they rose to the challenge we now laid upon them—partly, I think, because they sensed, however imprecisely, that they were embarking on something that could bring major benefits to the work to which they were so obviously committed.

Perhaps because we had overloaded them or taken them through too much material too fast, there was some confusion about at whom the questions were aimed. Some of those that emerged from the groups were perfectly acceptable as questions to SCH/MR staffers or other stakeholders, but were not appropriate to ask of the children themselves. (We realized later that our facilitation was at fault here: we should have coached each group much more intensively than we did. The strain was beginning to tell on us too!) Nonetheless some good questions emerged and the now-familiar voting process, again taken with the utmost seriousness, threw up four questions which the group decided would constitute the protocol from which they would work. These were the following:

- What is it about life on the street that gives you hope and encouragement?

- Tell me a story about what led you to a life on the street.

- How do you obtain the best care for yourself when you are not feeling strong? (We were a little surprised by the popularity of this question, and questioned whether it was genuinely cast in appreciative mode. It turned out be rather a good onion question with many layers of meaning for different respondents. What it revealed was wide-scale abusive self-medication and an ignorance or distrust of the medical care offered by the refuges. It thus served a valuable evaluative purpose.)

- Tell me a story about what led you to use the SCH/MR refuges? What did you like about those places?

I suspect all three facilitators had some misgivings about these questions, and it was clear that some of the fieldworkers thought they knew the answers before they asked the questions. The facilitators decided, for their part, that they must honour the process but agreed to keep in close touch as they coached the fieldworkers over the first couple of days. If the questions were not working, we would have to revise them. For the fieldworkers who were claiming that they already knew the answers and so what was the point of asking the questions, we had sympathetically to urge them to honour the process, especially to stay in narrative mode and to listen to what was not being said as well as to what was.

We asked them all to keep careful notes of how the interviews went and assured them that we would be available for coaching and consultation over the coming week. We parted with the familiar mixture of excitement and apprehension.

Both emotions proved justified by events. The facilitators each spent the next two days working alongside a different fieldworker each day as he or she worked his or her way through the squatments visiting children he or she knew. By the end of the second day, then, we had between us observed six out of around 30 field-workers for a whole day and we had had shorter opportunities to watch the field-workers talking with children in the refuges. We were, of course, up against a serious language barrier. Most fieldworkers could operate in four local languages as well as pidgin, but even they were sometimes struggling when they found a child who spoke a language with which they were unfamiliar. None of us spoke any of the local languages; one of us had a reasonable grasp of pidgin. Although this was a serious constraint on the effectiveness with which we could coach the workers in the use of the appreciative protocol, we were surprised by how much we could learn by very careful observation—of the worker, of the children and of the people who often gathered round to eavesdrop on the conversation. After the conversation was finished, we naturally asked the worker for as extended a summary as he or she could manage. Inevitably some were more forthcoming than others.

Despite these operational difficulties, we were fairly confident by the end of the second day that too many of the fieldworkers had not really grasped the point of the appreciative mode and were operating in their familiar style. It was not difficult to see why this should be so. Among ourselves, we could immediately elicit seven reasons. Put shortly, these were the result of a seriously deformed pedagogy in school and tertiary education (take notes but don't think); very careful drilling in the techniques of inquiry hitherto used by SCH/MR; a confusion, for which we had to accept our share of responsibility, about whether the protocol was a set of examples or a schedule to be followed; the feeling, already voiced, that they already knew the answers; a need to conduct their own business with the children they met which tended to push the protocol into the margins or off the agenda altogether; a failure to internalize the learnings of the workshop (because we had tried to do too much too quickly); and in our presence, as if sitting on their shoulders, they were shy, nervous and afraid, so they stuck with what they knew best.

We shared our findings with the leadership of the projects. The Bengolese in charge of the mothers' refuge project were neither surprised nor alarmed. "It is new to them. They will learn. It takes time." Peter and James were much less casual. They had a lot invested in the evaluation and could not afford to have it go off at half-cock. They wanted to call all the field staff in to a full staff meeting and demand to see their notebooks. "Then we can see what they are up to. If they have not been keeping notes, we shall know they are not doing the job. If they have notes, we can check how far they are using the protocol."

For us this was a most illuminating reaction and reinforced some of our impressions about the use of authority in the projects. Collegiality clearly had serious limits. We were determined not to be drawn into that kind of pattern, but we were also clear that it would not do to carry on without some corrective action. We therefore arranged to meet the fieldworkers at their respective bases in the two refuges and give them a reinforcement seminar, perhaps more directive than we had been so far, stripping the central ideas down to their barest essentials and emphasizing the idea of best practice.

In the event, this turned out to involve significant tweaking of the appreciative protocol the fieldworkers had generated for themselves. After some discussion with the fieldworkers based on the boys' refuge, for example, we amended the questions to read as follows:

- What do you like best about the refuge?

- What do you like best about the mini-refuges? (These are huts spread around areas where street children congregate and staffed by fieldworkers who are available throughout the day for consultation, counselling, and so on.)

- What is your favourite activity at the refuge?

- Tell me a story about how you came into contact with SCH.

- Some days are better than others for you. Tell me what happens on the best days.

- When you are sick, tell me about the best thing you can do to help yourself get better.

On reflection, two issues emerge here. Perhaps we should have been more directive during the workshop, and refined and sharpened the protocol along these lines. Maybe we were overinvested in the notion that they should struggle with it themselves so that the questions reflected their experience and their level of understanding of the process. Looking back, that now seems a little purist and if we were doing it again, I am confident that we would opt for a more directive approach, although there may well have been some learning derived from the floundering of the first two days.

Second, this whole experience reinforced our conviction that we had tried to do too much too fast in the workshop and had over-easily convinced ourselves that the whole staff had internalized the process. The reality was that the best of them had; too many of them had not.

After this setback—and the mild demoralization associated with it—the pace quickened. Within two days, fieldworkers were expressing delight and astonishment at the level and quality of data that the new questions were eliciting, even from children that they thought they knew very well. It was no great surprise to us that, as their confidence increased, so their ingenuity and creativity with the approach took off. They began to ask "the stupid questions" that hitherto they would have thought it inappropriate to their status to put—and were astonished at the richness of information that such questions brought forward. One example will suffice.

A colleague was sitting in the dust with a group of girl porters in the central market area, awaiting the arrival of country buses and the opportunity to tout for business. A small child came up and started hauling off a black plastic bag. The owner, a girl porter, about 15 years old, jumped up hurriedly and grabbed the bag back from the child, berating him for having taken it. My colleague encouraged the fieldworker she was accompanying to ask the porter to tell what was going on. The fieldworker gave a look that suggested that my colleague must be even more simple than he had imagined but did as he was asked. The girl told a story about having managed to save enough to buy her own cup, which she kept in the bag, and her fears that it would get stolen or broken. This led on to her emptying out all the contents of the bag—her entire possessions—and telling how she had acquired each, what they meant to her, how they contributed to her life on the street and why she valued them. By the end of this exposition, the fieldworker was excited by how much he had learned about this girl's real life. He had thought he knew her well; now he realized how much he had not known and could see the SCH/MR projects through her eyes in a quite different light.

As the eight-day period of fieldwork came to an end, it was evident that most of the fieldworkers were delighted and amazed at what they had found. "It is like digging in barren earth—and then finding a box full of good things," one said. As we approached the second workshop—which we saw as the climax of the whole process and the means by which appreciative inquiry and its evaluative potential would be embedded in the organizations—it seemed sensible to capitalize on the enthusiasm of the staff for what they had been doing.

Dividing them rather carefully into different groups to those of the first workshop and trying to mix the ability ranges, we started by asking them to identify the most revealing question they had asked. This was an attempt to encourage them to reflect on the week's work and exchange stories about the way the new approach had opened up strata of data that had hitherto been closed to them. We also asked them to look at the kind of answers that came to the question which they had asked about what street children valued about life on the street. We saw this as a way of establishing a baseline against which they and we could evaluate the contribution of the projects. We did not need to spell that out, nor did we need to underline any conclusions. The sharper of the staff could see immediately that if the projects were perceived by the children to jeopardize or cut across the things they valued, they would either not use the projects' facilities or would use them instrumentally for what they could get out of them. In that case the change of consciousness which was the heart of the projects' work would never be achieved.

This analytical approach had its strengths and its weaknesses. The men were more vocal than the women: the well educated tended to dominate the less well educated. The Bengolese tended to defer to the expatriates. We needed another way of maximizing participation. Drawing on experience with training for transformation workshops in other African countries, we asked each participant to draw, individually, the answer to the central question: based on what you have heard this week what do you think is the contribution that SCH/MR make to the lives of street children?

There were, to our surprise, no groans of "But I can't draw," which is the response this exercise usually elicits in European contexts. On the contrary, it was as though a light had been turned on which illuminated hitherto dark or gloomy areas. There was a level of engagement, of absorption in their drawing, broken by an occasional giggle, that reminded us of the intensity of interest that had surrounded the voting for the provocative propositions in the first workshop.

Having asked each participant to share his or her drawing with the rest of the small work group, we moved to the second, and more demanding, phase of the process: eliding the individual drawings into one group drawing that synthesized the contributions of each. Each individual must be able to recognize his or her own idea or symbolism incorporated into the corporate synthesis, but that synthesis has to be a complete unity in itself.

Again, the level of discussion, argument, probing of each other's ideas, passionate advocacy and spirited defence showed that at last we were getting down to the pay off. Young women with no more than primary education and a halting grasp of English who had hitherto been almost entirely silent suddenly came to life in a way that grabbed the initiative from the verbally articulate or the natural leaders. It was as though they felt at home in the right brain in a way that they did not in the left brain. Or to put it another way, drawing put them in touch with their own affect and affective memories in a way that talking about them, even in narrative form, did not.

From our evaluative point of view, however, the real interest lay in the results of the drawing, duly put on the wall and explained to the whole workshop. Six of the seven were variations on the same theme: the fieldworker meeting the child on the street, befriending him or her and accompanying him or her to a better life of one sort or another. What was missing from all of these drawings—and which we can safely infer was missing from the individual drawings and therefore from the perceptions of the fieldworkers themselves—was an appreciation of the way in which the street child is set in a complex web of social relationships. The street is as dense a total structure as the village or the clan; indeed, it is more multilayered than either. To visualize the child, then, as someone who exists in a one-to-one relationship with the fieldworker, and is by implication free to leave the street if he or she so wishes, is a serious distortion of reality. From an evaluative point of view, it suggested a serious weakness in the training of the field staff, both in terms of their perception, but, more critically, in terms of their practice. By giving less than adequate attention to the emotional and social linkages of the child, they were not only failing to respond to the child's own reality, but were also greatly reducing their own effectiveness. That is a point to which we return below.

Before doing so, it is worth commenting briefly on the one exception to this rule—a picture that came from the group that I had mentally ranked as one of the weakest. This was an abstract on the theme of flowering or coming into blossom, highlighting therefore the hidden potential of even the most wayward street child and the role the organizations could play in providing an environment which nurtures that potential. This picture had a holism, a tenderness and empathy that impressed the whole workshop. It was greeted with spontaneous applause.

We were clear that we had now been given an insight into a crucial area on which the organizations needed to work, but how were we going to put that into an appreciative context that would allow the staff to embed any changes in their normal style of work? We gently pointed out the common features of the six drawings and awaited comments. They came fast enough. "But the child is not alone. Of course he is surrounded by all kinds of networks. But we do not just relate to the child alone. We know the minders, the gang leaders, the association people, the security guards. All of them. We know them."

That gave us exactly the kind of opening we needed. We could have them describe best practice in terms of their own work and list the ways in which the best of them relate to the whole culture of the street, and use those relationships to improve the protection of the child not just in the refuge, but also actually in the street.

We developed a way of encapsulating this best practice which used the right brain. Borrowing from participative rural appraisal (PRA) technology, we had the groups draw first social and then emotional maps for a child they all knew well. The object of the first was to put the child in a wider social context by asking who has power or influence over the child; and then making an admittedly debatable distinction between power and influence-for-the-better and power and influence-for-the-worse. If that seems very crude, the realities on the street are not thereby seriously misrepresented. Some children's minders, for example, do not exploit them and do give them a degree of protection and even a place to sleep. Other minders see the children under their care as free labour or free sources of sexual gratification, or both. In the same way, some of the mammies (for whom some of the porters or petty traders work) feed the child or pay at an agreed rate, or both. Others fail to provide food, withhold earnings or terrorize the child into submission.

It was a relatively short step from the social map to the emotional map. To whom are the children close? Do they have friends among their peers? How do they relate to members of other bases? What about their parents and other relatives? By building up an emotional map of the child's reality and comparing it with the social map, the workers can understand the total setting of the child and identify the forces that keep him or her on the street or begin to make it possible to visualize an alternative. As I have already said, it was clear that some of the best fieldworkers were already collecting this information and although they were not organizing it in this particular fashion, the social and emotional map would probably add little to their stock of knowledge or to how they operated in the field. The intention of suggesting that mapping become part of the standard routine of the organizations' field staff was to institutionalize this best practice and thus provide a benchmark against which all the fieldworkers could measure their own performance. It was also our hope that comparison of the social and emotional maps of different children, perhaps living in the same area or even belonging to the same base, would enrich the corporate understanding of the context of all the children.

In terms of our own procedures, this foray into PRA-style mapping was an unexpected diversion. It arose so naturally from the picture-making element of the data analysis, however, and contributed so directly to the central process of institutionalizing best practice that it seemed a sensible route to take.

To our relief it did not seriously interfere with the process of extracting themes from the data and forming provocative propositions from them. The participants were familiar with these steps after the first workshop's dry run and they therefore moved easily into them—thankful, in some cases, to be back into at least half-explored territory! We did, however, introduce a modification when we came to voting on the provocative propositions. It had become clear to us that the group was high on ideals—as you would expect of people who undertake such demanding work for a pittance—but much lower in terms of practicalities. Further, it seemed that the downside of their idealism was a reluctance to challenge or stretch the organization. To do so was an indirect way of admitting that the present was sub-ideal. We therefore needed a visually arresting way of making the point that for a proposition to be both provocative and implementable (even if in the longer run) it needed to be high in idealism, well removed from present practice and reasonably feasible. We therefore developed three scales, borrowing liberally from John Carter's work, reported elsewhere in this volume. Instead of asking for a straight vote on each proposition, we asked participants to rank four that they favoured in terms of those three criteria: consistency with core values; feasibility within present organizational parameters and distinction from present reality. (We deliberately left the middle term, feasibility, a little vague. We did not want to exclude propositions that implied substantial additional funding—which we thought quite possible to secure—but we did want to exclude blue-moon propositions that were clearly without any conceivable organizational development path.)

By scaling these characteristics on a one-to-five ranking, we could show that only those propositions for which a strong diagonal pattern emerged in the voting were serious contenders.

Thus:

	hi	highish	med	lowish	low
Ideal?	x				
Feasible?			x		
Present-reality?					x

After a false start, when it became apparent that some participants had not understood that they could only vote for four propositions and that they were to rank their chosen four on all three criteria, the system worked well. Again there was intense concentration while the participants read each others' propositions and considered the three criteria. If we had had the logistical capacity to do so, it would have been far better to follow Carter's example and distribute the propositions and the scales on paper to each participant so that they could sit and study them more carefully. Indeed, it would have been even more helpful to have one round of voting after individual reflection and then another after group consultation.

Despite our more limited approach, however, it was possible to show that some propositions which commanded much support did not pass the diagonal test and therefore had to be rejected. For example, a proposition read, "SCH/MR is an ambitious organization that recognizes the plight of street children and collaborates with other agencies to get them off the street." This secured more votes than any other proposition, but was very high on the present-reality scale and therefore had to be rejected. In the same way, a not particularly provocative proposition that read, "The agencies provide hope and encouragement to the street children by providing them quality shelter, counselling and learning," was characterized by a cluster of votes in the high column on each of the criteria—and none elsewhere. Not much sign of a diagonal there and so easy relegation.

It was when we went through the voting patterns, proposition by proposition, that the significance of the diagonal was most effectively communicated and the need to keep in mind the fine balance between safety (represented by a high present-reality score) and over-ambition (represented by a very low feasibility score) became apparent. That realization made the action-planning phase of the evaluation a great deal easier and more realistic.

At one remove from the immediate concerns of the participants, this exercise told us a great deal about how the staff (and rather few other stakeholders present) perceived their organization at the moment and how they assessed the feasibility of possible changes. For example, they saw themselves as doing a great job on one-to-one relationships with the street children they got to know, but they knew that they are much less good at collaborating with other organizations and especially with organs of local and national government. By gently pointing out some of the patterns that emerged, we were able to coach the participants in understanding their organizational strengths and weaknesses and introduce a dialogue that would continue long after our departure about the gaps between ideals and performance. Here, then, is another sense in which the evaluation became embedded.

Substantively, we wound up with three propositions that showed strong diagonality and a significant number of votes. They were the following:

- We create an environment where street children make their own choices.

- We learn from street children by accepting, protecting and caring for them. We thus change their consciousness and make it possible for them to move forward.

- SCH/MR works as a team (sic) which demands of itself an absolute priority for the protection of all street children and a chance for them to transform their lives. (This was the result of a little judicious editorial elision of two propositions that were substantively similar.)

I am again conscious of the fact that the Western reader, unacquainted with life on a Bengolese street, will be tempted to dismiss these as undemanding mom-and-apple-pie type statements. Without entering a long defence, it is worth just reminding ourselves that, for example, to speak of a street child making his or her own choices, in a social and economic environment where they are the butt of everyone else's agenda, pawns in everyone else's game (including that of older street children) is an exceedingly ambitious target to set. In the same way, for an organization with the full (if somewhat distant) weight of the Roman Catholic Church behind it to declare that it seeks to *learn* from street children, when most Bengolese regard them as beyond both contempt and redemption, is to challenge the construction of street children by society at large. What the propositions represent, then, is a typical Bengolese cultural habit: to say tough and demanding things in the gentlest and most unthreatening way. *We* might read them as too gentle and too unthreatening; Bengolese themselves would see the iron within the velvet.

Procedurally, we were now in a position to enable the group to test their aspirations against their resources in a more systematic way than had been achieved by the ranking of feasibility. The resources of the organizations are nearly entirely confined to their staff; they have no financial resources apart from what they can raise from donors, no technology (not, at least, in the normal sense), and rather few networks of collaborators. We therefore decided to introduce a corporate stock-take of talent. We asked each of them to write on a piece of paper the one thing at which they think they, as individuals, excel. The papers were folded up and placed anonymously in a hat. One of the facilitators then pulled them out one by one and read them aloud, passing the slips to two colleagues who pinned them on a large board. Unbeknown to the participants, they had mentally divided the board into four categories, corresponding to the four core skills needed by any organization working in their field: interpersonal/caring/counselling; administration/organizational housekeeping; finance/fundraising; and networking with other NGOs, government and local authorities, both formal and informal.

As the slips were pinned up under the appropriate category, two patterns emerged; one expected, the other totally *un*expected. There was a huge cluster of slips under the first head and hardly any under administration. None came under finance; one (which we knew to be Peter's) under networking. So much was predictable—with very serious implications to which we shall have to return in a moment. Less predictable was the significant number of returns that mentioned some kind of creative activity—singing, dancing, drumming, drama and theatrics.

This surprise gave us a splendid, if unexpected, opportunity. One of the things we had noticed was how little creative and engaging activity went on in the refuges. Sure, many of the children wanted to sleep and that is a most important service the refuges provide. But most of the children for most of the time are gazing at foreign videos, usually of violence, of which they understand next to nothing of the dialogue (which might be just as well). For an organization that puts the transformation of consciousness at the heart of its objectives—as reflected in the three provocative propositions above—this seemed to us a less than satisfactory state of affairs. We had now uncovered, to everyone's surprise, a wealth of unused creative talent that could be put at the service of the street children, not just for their entertainment but as a way of reaching them at levels far deeper than sympathetic chat about life on the street ever can. A child who can learn to sing or dance or drum is a child whose self-respect is on the mend, and the one who shares those skills with him has a chance to touch some of his deepest, and perhaps some of his sorest, places.

We did not need to spell this out in any detail. Some of the staff themselves were dissatisfied with the activities in the refuges: all we needed to do was to offer a positive alternative, based on an appreciation of the skills already available, for a radical change to become unstoppable—unless opposed by the heavy hand of the leadership.

The stock-take, however, showed that the leadership had plenty of other things to worry about. Three central functions were seriously under-resourced; and one, the financial and fundraising, currently the province of James and Peter alone, had no corresponding talents, even those of James and Peter themselves. Here we had a graphic representation of what we intuitively felt to be the case: Peter and James had talents they were not using, because they (probably rightly) did not trust any of their Bengolese colleagues to do the job. But they were equally determined not to hire anyone who could make up the deficiency because of the primacy of the ideology of the street. When in discussion, Peter floated the idea that some of the fieldworkers should be trained in financial management or fundraising, or both, it was obvious that he was still dominated by this kind of thinking: only those who had come to know the street viscerally were fitted to work behind a computer on behalf of the agencies. It was not for us to contest that view; it was for all the stakeholders to decide whether they could continue to run an ever-growing and increasingly expensive operation with the pattern of resources the stock-take had revealed.

(Skeptics might argue that by asking each person to name only one talent, we had prejudged the outcome. There might be some truth in that charge, and the next time we work with such a group, we might well ask people to identify three skills, writing them on three different slips of paper. For what it is worth, our common view was that, however crude our methodology, we had identified a crucial area of organizational need, and done so in a way that was wholly consistent with the spirit of appreciative inquiry.)

Given what we had all learned of the talents of the group, it was not surprising that the participants made heavy weather of the action-planning phase of the workshop. Their skills were in interpersonal relationships, not in organizational development. With intensive facilitation which focused on questions of who? how? what? when?, some plans did emerge.

For example one group instituted a system of mutual accountability and training, setting aside agreed times to meet to learn from each other and to follow through on some of the learnings of the evaluation.

Another group bravely tackled a hot potato, the creation of a network of night shelters for children who have nowhere to sleep. This issue is hot because it runs counter to government policy. That policy is based on black-hole thinking: that if you provide for a seriously felt need, you increase the scale of the problem. The more shelter there is at night, the more children will migrate to the street from the poverty-stricken rural areas. Hitherto SCH/MR had gone along with this policy, well aware of the fact that the children are most vulnerable at night, and especially during the rains. Now, committed by their own provocative proposition to give an absolute priority to protecting children on the street, they had to grasp this nettle. To say that they had, by the end of the workshop, a detailed action plan for doing so would be wrong. They did, however, have a range of options to discuss with their advisory board, with relevant government departments and with each other. These ran from the informal renting of unstaffed, unsupervised shacks in the shanties, which would be made available to identified bases (especially those of young women), to a fully fledged night shelter with an array of support services, including feeding and medical care. No one underestimated the difficulties, but at least the issue was now firmly on the agenda and specified individuals accepted responsibility for taking it further.

By now the strain of the three days' work was beginning to show and it might well be that we should have finished at that point. We were, however, anxious to enlarge the vision of the group. Again we noticed an almost pathological introspection, a foreshortening of horizons, a generalization of the fieldworker/street child bubble originally revealed by the drawings. The group had difficulty, it seemed, conceiving of its work—and by extension of its organization—in a more rounded set of relationships. Partly this seemed to be a kind of residual paranoia: "everyone despises street children—and they despise us for working with them, so it's no good trying to involve a wider world;" and partly it was the result of the pressures under which everyone in the organization works. If a child you care about is constantly being raped by her minder, it is hard to get too excited about a meeting at UNICEF or a seminar with government bureaucrats. However understandable, this introversion exacts a heavy price and even makes the work unsustainable in the long run.

Given the ambitious nature of some of the action plans, we judged it important to enable the group to see that while they certainly had opponents and even enemies out there, they also had allies and potential friends and supporters. We therefore introduced them to the familiar force-field analysis, using the less pompous title of "Headwinds, Tailwinds." Building on our experience to date in the workshop, we suggested that they *draw* the winds they identified, using colours to denote the emotional tone of the respective wind. The results were presented and shared in the normal way.

It proved to a powerful way of reminding the group of their need to work more intentionally at building alliances and networks, even at the much-resented cost of time on the street. It also showed us, as evaluators, how hard this would be to make happen. Very many of the drawings were concerned with the individual psychological or spiritual head and tail winds of the staff—apathy, fear, lack of commitment; enthusiasm, courage, perseverance. Here again we were presented with evidence of a thorough-going introversion. We had done all we could within the brief time span available to us to enable the organization, as an entity, to confront that. Here the group could identify it for itself. It would have to work on it as part of the embedded reflection on the whole experience of the evaluation.

We wanted to end the workshop and our work with the whole staff with a ritual that would be fun, relevant and memorable. Thanks to the initiative of an Afro-American volunteer from Harvard working in the boys' refuge, we ended up forming a close circle, all facing the back of the person next to us and then trying to sit on each others' laps. Bizarre as it may sound in cold print, it can be done—and the millipede can actually rotate—so long as, but only so long as, each has total confidence in the person behind him or her. It is thus an acted parable about trust and interdependence, a theme central to our appreciative evaluation. Perhaps it was not totally coincidental that each time we tried it, we ended in an undignified pile on the floor. Behind the laughter, there lurked an important finding.

5. Conclusion

I have sought to show how appreciative inquiry can be used to embed self-evaluation in an organization by highlighting the organization's own best practice and allowing all practitioners to assess their own performance against that benchmark. Here, the picture was complicated by four issues, none of which is intrinsically uncommon. First, there was the contrast between the rhetoric of democracy and participation on the one hand and the reality of an authoritarian style of leadership on the other. Second, there was a great diversity in the formal education and training levels of the participants. Third, there was a kind of lopsidedness to the organization that gave it great potential in the caring and counselling role, but left such a gap on the administration and finance functions that it was not possible to speak realistically in these areas of best practice. And fourth there was what I have called a kind of corporate introspection that arose out of a sense of being permanently under attack from other sections of the community, not excluding the NGO and donor communities. It might be helpful if, by way of summary and conclusion, we ask how successful the evaluation was in addressing these four areas of organizational need.

As far as leadership style and authority structure go, there is no doubt that the process gave voice and confidence to many of the staff who were conscious, perhaps for the first time, of having the opportunity to share their own experience and present their own ideas. Naturally some responded to that opportunity more vigorously than others. Some still saw Peter and James as "the boss" (sic) and were clearly nervous about expressing open disagreement. How far the process shifted the centre of gravity is hard to say. What is clear is that James was sufficiently worried to try to close down any further discussion for two months, possibly in the hope that the ideas being generated would evaporate as dew in the sun during that period. Our own assessment is that that would prove exceedingly hard. Enough of the well-educated (graduate) staff had the bit between their teeth. Attempts to silence them would be unavailing or disastrous in the sense of alienating them from the organization for good.

Second and related to that, we had been dealing with an unusually wide spectrum of educational and experiential backgrounds. How far did we successfully include them all in? The answer to that has to be mixed. Even by keeping the talking heads to a bare minimum and maximizing the participatory work in small groups, some participants had clearly struggled hard to understand what was going on and even what they were being asked to do. In retrospect, it was the shift from left-brain to right-brain activities that made the most difference, and perhaps, the formality of the voting procedures (which, as it happened, was highly topical as Bengo was about to have a rare election). Did we get the balance right? Almost certainly not in the first workshop, where we were still operating in the shadow of the misapprehension that all the fieldworkers were graduates or at least diplomates. The attempted role play was only partially successful, but the drawing exercises seemed to engage everyone in a way that nothing else did. There are, however, limits to how much can be drawn and it is possible that we exceeded those limits.

As for the lopsidedness of the organization, this bore directly on the whole future development strategy, what I called in the first section the transition to institutionalization. Did the process make that any easier? Did it persuade the key players that it was necessary? I suspect our intervention may have proved double-edged here. On the one side, we exposed the need to face the transition and the mismatch of present resources for that transition. On the other hand, one of the by-products of the intensity of the experience was a tighter bonding of the staff to each other and to the ideology of SCH/MR. If the way forward is to grow into a mature NGO with a proper institutional backbone, that may prove an asset. But that is not the only form of the transition on offer. It might be better to split into a number of small, light NGOs, each with its specialty and its own capacity for speedy response. In an unfriendly political climate and a not especially supportive regime among the large donors, there may be a great deal to be said for that hydra-headed approach. To that extent the bonding and the sharing of common dreams of what the organizations might be able to achieve *may* have made the future more problematic rather than less.

What finally of the corporate introspection, the sense of being alone and unloved with the hand of everyone in authority raised against their clients and themselves? Here I am confident we can claim significant success. By the constant emphasis on best practice and the exchange of stories that illustrated it, the participants were eventually able to internalize the fact that they—as an organization and often as individuals—were achieving remarkable results under almost impossible conditions. Perhaps that change of consciousness among the staff and other stakeholders—a change not wholly unlike that which they seek to enable the street children themselves to make—is the most long-lasting effect that this evaluation will prove to have had. With that, we would be well content.

Chapter 13
Multicultural strategy building

This is a case study of the appreciative approach in the context of an organization approaching—but arguably not yet in—crisis.

In section 1, I shall explain the organization's task and structure and in the next section I shall lay out some of the difficulties with which it was beset. In the third section I shall finish the scene setting by examining some of the dynamics within the group which experienced the inquiry. This will then clear the way for a detailed account of the process. The last section looks at some of the wider implications for the use of this approach in organizations of this type.

1. Sigma as an organization

Sigma, as I shall call it, is an international development organization, drawing voluntary and government funding from a wide variety of rich countries, including some in the Far East, and spending those funds in a large number of poor countries in ways that straggle the waterfront—from traditional child-survival programs to much less traditional income-generating projects, community-organizing programs and international awareness building and, more discretely, direct political campaigning around issues of particular relevance to the life chances of the poor of the world.

I was to work with the West Africa regional group of senior executives, all expatriate and few of them African. They are led by a West Africa regional director, responsible to the Africa vice president (based outside the West Africa region) and through him to the president based in North America. It is important to emphasize from the start that the countries in which the team works are not easy. They include some of the poorest countries in the poorest continent where human resources are limited, infrastructure of all sorts inadequate and the climate—meteorological, political, administrative—as hostile as one is likely to meet anywhere in the Third World. This makes planning any kind of development intervention hazardous, with unpredictable delays, cost overruns, high staff turnover, political interference (usually as attempts to appropriate the rents associated with development work) and creaking administrative machinery the norm.

Now into this complicated, shifting and wholly unpredictable environment the parent organization had placed a set of management systems which were extremely demanding in terms of information, timeliness and comprehensiveness. The question had thus come to be asked, especially by the regional director who in some ways saw himself as being caught between the international system and his regional staff, whether these complicated and demanding management systems were designed for the primary task of the organization—serving the poor—or for servicing the subscribers and their political representatives. To put it at its crudest, the question was: Management for what? For more effective delivery of goods and services to the clients (the poor, especially the distant rural poor)? Or for providing the headquarters and the money raisers related to it with huge wads of data which could be used to defend the organization against every charge of failure, incompetence or directionlessness?

In fact, the dynamics were a little more complicated even than that. For the regional office and its country-based partners (referred to hereafter as field offices) are dependent upon funds raised in rich country offices of the same organization. Because they hold the purse strings, the funding offices (hereafter support offices) are in a strong position to call the tune for information and management systems from the field offices.

There had thus developed a pathological love-hate relationship between the field offices and the support offices. The former were crucially dependent upon the latter for the their operational budget (and for their salaries.) They therefore needed the approval and even enthusiasm of the support offices. At the same time they increasingly resented the power wielded by the support offices, not least because the latter acted as a gatekeeper through which the field offices had to pass if they wished to approach a major donor, e.g., a governmental bilateral aid program.

At the same time, it was—and was acknowledged to be—a symbiotic relationship in the sense that the support offices needed good stories, good PR, exciting field visits and high-quality reportage if they were to continue to raise large sums of money. As support offices tend to rank themselves—and be ranked by the organization as a whole—in terms of how much money they raise, their appetite for the kind of material that excites potential donors is almost insatiable. (Conversely their vulnerability to even the merest breath of scandal, misappropriation or incompetence by the field staff hardly needs emphasis.)

There is one further bit of background that needs to be sketched in. West Africa is not an appealing area for the vast majority of Sigma's private or official supporters. The organization is almost non-existent in France and weak in the UK. Colonial linkages are therefore feeble. In the countries in which the support offices flourish, French is not commonly spoken, nor is Islam much practised. Although the environmental story of the drying of the Sahelian zone has some appeal, its force is quickly displaced by more recent or more dramatic environmental catastrophes. By comparison with East or Southern Africa, India or Bangladesh, West Africa is a poor relation indeed.

2. Institutional anxieties

If the close-up picture of the organization suggested both conflict and strategic muddle, the big picture showed why there was so much anxiety in the middle managers who were to mount the appreciative inquiry. It was not hard to identify nine causes of individual and/or corporate anxiety.

First, the global organization had just appointed a new president. This had come after a search lasting more than a year, during which the eventual appointee had been acting president. The long delay in confirming him in the top job had underlined the lack of confidence in him evidently felt by some members of the board, fed by some of the senior staff worldwide.

Second, the global organization itself was in turmoil, following the work of a committee to review its worldwide strategy. The details need not detain us here; suffice it to say that there had been a battle between those who wished to maintain the maximum central control and those who wished to spin off as much responsibility and accountability to the national offices as possible. A compromise had been reached, but it was unclear how the new structure would work and how the final distribution of power between the centre and the regions would settle down.

Third, at the time the appreciative inquiry was conducted, it was becoming clear that fundraising was becoming harder. Some of the major fundraising (or support) offices were seriously under target and both government and private sources, hitherto abundant providers of finance, were showing signs of extreme aid weariness.

Loosely and indirectly related to this, some of the major support offices were themselves in deep organizational disarray. Two had had to have emergency treatment from the centre, two were undergoing painful re-engineering, and in one personal and organizational relationships had deteriorated to the point of multiple resignations. Given the dependency of the field offices—my client group—on the support offices, a certain spillover from the former to the latter, in terms of anxiety and emotional disturbance, was inevitable.

Fifth, there was anyway an increasing question mark over the long-term sustainability of the structure of the organization. In brief, the existing model was that the support offices accessed governmental and international funds and passed them, plus the revenues from private fundraising, to the field offices. Increasingly, however, the official sources were inclined to want to relate directly to agencies in the field, thus bypassing the support offices. This left the support offices with less funds, less influence and more commitment to private fundraising. It also gave field offices every incentive to relate directly to official rich country agencies, thus conflicting directly with stated organizational disciplines.

Sixth, even at the field-office level, major changes were underway. The organization in general, and especially in West Africa, had elected to organize its work in the field in the form of large, multisectoral development programs which were, in pursuit of sustainability, to move forward to self-management and self-sufficiency as locally registered NGOs. The implications of this were much greater than originally foreseen, not least because it meant a drastic shrinkage of staff at national headquarters and the relocation of surviving staff to the operational areas, usually in much less favoured regions. Many of the national office chief executives were thus in as much a state of shock as were their support office confreres for roughly analogous reasons.

Seventh, both in the support offices and in the field offices the stresses had taken their toll. Many of the symptoms of burn-out have been touched on tangentially above: others were obvious enough in the staff who assembled for the appreciative inquiry. One absentee had recently burnt out in spectacular, if embarrassing, fashion. Interestingly, his name was not mentioned in the five days I was with the group. Nor was the topic of burn-out raised in any form. It was hard to resist the notion that at some levels the group was in the depths of denial.

Eighth, one form that that denial took was a reluctance to recognize that high executive turnover had led to the promotion of people, usually but not exclusively African, well beyond the limits of their effectiveness. Maybe many of the individuals concerned *did*, no doubt painfully, recognize that they were being asked to perform to a level they could barely aspire to, and maybe that semi-conscious acknowledgement helped account for the tendency to retreat to the comfort zone that came to be a mark of the group as a whole. Certainly it contributed to a general awareness that the team (as they tended to call themselves after a period of intensive team building that preceded my joining the group) was already seriously stretched in terms of executive capacity.

Last—and most difficult to judge with any degree of confidence—was the effect of the largely accidental withdrawal from the group of some of the key players. The representative of the German support office cried off for reasons that were never properly explained. The Canadian support office person could not travel to the venue because she was heavily pregnant. The Australian was new to the job and had much still to learn. The US support office person had been given extra demanding responsibilities and could therefore not focus on West Africa. One of the most experienced and able of the expatriate field office directors was struck down with an undiagnosed high fever and spent the time at death's door in hospital. This incomplete catalogue of personal inconveniences amounts in aggregate to a serious weakening of the group, but more than that it symbolically represented a draining away of the lifeblood of the group. It came to be interpreted—perhaps misinterpreted—as a diminution in the commitment of the group to its own future role and even survival. It was as though the group was internalizing the absences as evidence of withdrawal of loyalty to the group, or even, more revealingly, as a rejection of the group's existence and purpose. We shall see later some of the impact of these unconscious processes.

3. Appreciative inquiry in a traumatized organizational setting

In the foregoing sections I have suggested that there were signs that the group as a whole was anxious and conflicted, but that those largely unconscious emotions were rendered the more problematic by the organization's habitual denial of negative emotion. In this section I shall make more explicit the grounds for those fears, and conclude with some reflections on the implications for the appreciative process.

It quickly became apparent that there was much deep-seated unease about the direction in which the regional director was trying to steer the group. Faced with the fundamental disadvantages of the whole global system that I have described above, the regional director had begun to think of turning the weaknesses of the region into strengths. Precisely because the region is unimportant and unattractive within the politics of Sigma as a whole, why not free each field office to make whatever deals it could with any donors it could find, whether support offices in the organization, other official or non-governmental donors or private individuals wherever they may be found. The attractions were obvious: the field offices would be free of much organizational top-hamper; they could take direct responsibility for their own funding; they could decide their own priorities relative to their own programs without having to respond to the priorities of support offices; and they could have far greater freedom to develop those programs in response to perceived needs, subject only to the constraint of their own fundraising energies and skill.

If this was the regional director's vision, the reaction from those above and below him in the hierarchy was initially somewhat similar. In a word, no one—or nearly no one—liked it. The one major exception was the field director of a country in which the organization's program was anyway so outside Sigma's normal parameters that the field director was having extreme difficulty with the organization's accepted mode of operation. Apart from him, the common reaction was essentially two fold: how would the West Africa region fit into the rest of the organization, and how could the organization at all levels tolerate one major region sidestepping the well-established organizational procedures?

Behind these concerns there lurked, of course, quite different fears and anxieties. For the senior management of the organization, this initiative looked like a unilateral declaration of independence, an attempt to escape the controls of the organization, which were in place as the result of bitter and hard-won experience. More especially, Sigma had a public image to protect, and that public image could be compromised by an unwise or ill-considered action in any part of the world. Joe Public could not be expected to understand that things in Mali or Chad were somehow different: a mistake there could jeopardize the organization's work anywhere in the world.

So much for the PR fears. But behind those again there were questions of competition for scarce resources. If the field offices were to be allowed to solicit both within and outside Sigma for funds for their programs, would that not lead to resources not going to where the need was the greatest, but to the most silver-tongued or Midas-touched field director? And—now to the real bone—what role would senior management have in controlling the flow of funds, and therefore the overall balance of Sigma's work? If there was to be an openly competitive bid for resources, how could there also be a serious long-term strategy for the work of the organization as a whole?

The fears and anxieties of the field staff were in some ways the mirror image of these. As I met some of the field staff in West Africa well ahead of the key meeting, I was struck by how much anxiety there was about their own capacity to absorb more change. The nature of the work of the organization had indeed shifted in a major way over the last five years, essentially from a child-survival strategy to a more holistic area development program approach, based on the felt needs of local populations.

With that had gone, too, more emphasis on local training (traditionally hard to fund from overseas donors) and less on the provision of large-scale imports of food aid and medical supplies (traditionally relatively easy to fund, especially from US and European food-aid and goods-in-kind programs). Now the field directors and their expatriate staffs were being expected to fundraise, to determine their own development strategies, to fashion a wide variety of new and threatening alliances with other agencies, both official and voluntary. This looked an exciting but deeply disturbing world, especially in those countries in which the field directors were, perhaps rightly, most critically aware of just how thin was the veneer of local management competence. It was no surprise, therefore, to hear one (newly appointed but much experienced) field director say, "Sure I'll go to the meeting. But I shall play dead dog when I get there."

Organizationally, then, we were faced with the familiar symptoms of incipient revolt from a team who feared to march in the direction the leader was pointing. The regional director had evidently chosen an appreciative approach because he intuitively felt (so far as I am aware he had had no direct experience of the approach) that it would cohere well with the corporate denial of negativity and yet allow the team to face some of the real issues before it in as non-threatening a way as possible. If that was indeed the hidden agenda, then the process would have to be designed in a way that not only allowed a full expression of different opinions but also ensured that dissent was properly heard and honoured. The corporate habit of denial had to be challenged, albeit within an appreciative context.

That that was going to be difficult within the culture of this organization was already obvious. It was going to be made much more difficult by the fact that the regional director wanted to combine training in the appreciative approach for all his colleagues with the strategy-formation process. In other words I was both to expose the whole team of around 20 executives to the theory and practice of the appreciative approach and facilitate the use of the approach in strategy determination. My previous experience of combining training and application was not especially happy and I expressed my concern at the (very short) planning meeting. I did not get the impression that this concern was heard. As we shall see this complicated the design of the process quite extensively, but there is little direct evidence that, apart from that, it had the negative impacts I had feared.

To summarize this compressed introduction, Sigma was at a major crossroads. Its past pattern of work, certainly in West Africa and possibly elsewhere in the world, was being called sharply into question and a new model was being proposed experimentally. That new model raised, albeit in covert and low-key ways, deep questions about the distribution of power and responsibility within the organization and about the confidence and competence of second-level managers to deliver. Its most powerful advocate was the one person in the whole structure who would arguably be least affected, and yet whose privileged position within the organization gave him a unique insight into the shortcomings and possible unsustainability of the existing model.

Perhaps paradoxically it was he who had been most vocal in calling for an appreciative approach to the discussion of future strategy and it was he whose position within Sigma would become much more difficult and perhaps untenable if progress toward his vision of unilateral declaration of independence (UDI) proved impossible. Yet he was determined to down-play his leadership role, to leave his colleagues as free as possible to make up their minds whether they wanted to accept his vision of the future. (From private conversations, I knew he had other exciting employment possibilities lined up if they refused to follow him.) As we shall see, his low-key, laudably democratic approach came within a whisker of putting him in an unviable position.

4. Appreciative inquiry in action

In this section I give an account of the process itself, highlighting the particularities of the design in response to the needs of the group.

For it was clear from earlier planning meetings and private briefings with many (but by no means all) of the participants that as the facilitator, I was faced with what looked like a double-decker sandwich. On the outside were the two overt tasks: to teach the participants the elements of the appreciative approach so that they would be encouraged to introduce the approach in their own work areas; and to take the group through a critical strategy-determining process. In the middle of the sandwich were, first, denied *anxiety*; second, a team that was *danger-*

ously weak in some areas; and third, a layer of *resentment* at demands laid upon that team by an able and ambitious regional director.

In contemplating the task before me, I was aware, however, that we were in danger of putting ourselves in a false position. For many of the key stakeholders were not to be present at the appreciative inquiry and their views would, in the somewhat strained atmosphere that was operating beneath the surface of *bonhomie*, almost certainly go by default. This would have been a matter of concern in any case: in the particular circumstances of this organization, it was doubly unfortunate. To take only three quick examples, the communities with which Sigma works were not represented, yet one of the key goals of the organization is to maximize sustainability by being as responsive as possible to the communities' own preferences. Those were simply not going to be stated.

Second, Sigma's main board clearly had a direct interest in the regional director's strategy as it marked a considerable modification to existing corporate structure. For the middle and senior managers at the workshop to commit themselves to that strategy without even hearing the views of the board was dangerous and could be counter-productive.

Third, the donors themselves, both official and private, might be thought to be interested parties to the discussion. It is their money that drives Sigma and they therefore have critical questions about cost effectiveness that need to be heard. They would not be asked in this forum.

So concerned was I at the potential imbalance between the group that was present and the stakeholders who were absent that I planned to organize a simulation of the likely input from these stakeholders, with the group themselves role-playing the missing voices. For the reasons that we shall explore below, that plan had to be abandoned. Some of the objectives were partially met by a presentation of findings and discussion with a large number of key executives of the US support office, but the lack of proper representation of such a wide and significant bunch of stakeholders has to be seen as a major flaw in the design of the process, at least in its strategy-formation aspect.

Once it became clear that, in the absence of any input from other stakeholders or even their simulated proxies, whatever strategy emerged from the appreciative inquiry would have to be regarded as one step along a much longer road, it became more appropriate to concentrate directly on the needs and pathologies of the participants in the process. How could the process be redesigned, on the wing, to begin opening up the areas of denial; allowing opposition to be given proper voice; alternatives to be formulated and tested that were consistent with both the needs of Sigma as a whole and the constrained capacity of middle management? Above all, how could the suppressed corporate anxiety be brought to the surface, faced and made tolerable?

One way I approached this was by emphasizing the role of memory and narrative in my introduction to the formulation of appreciative protocols. What I was hoping would happen was that the executives would hear about best practice in each others' experience and thus begin to see that, although the demands of the future are indeed severe and unpredictable, there is within the organization, even within the West Africa region, a huge reservoir of experience, of history of adaptation and change that can be drawn upon in the future. Given the high rate of turnover of senior executives in the region, to which I have already referred, corporate memory tends to be short—a shortness reinforced by the regional and national structure of Sigma, since most executives will know in detail only the history of Sigma within one particular country.

By encouraging the exchange of stories of peak experience or best practice, or both, I was hoping to take the denial of anxiety in the flank rather than confront it directly. The event transcended the plan. For many people (though not for all), the storytelling proved so powerful that they tended to get locked into that with the result that the questions about the future, calling for the use of imagination, tended to get lost. By the end of the first day, then, we had some fascinating and sometimes deeply moving history, but we had precious little idea of the possible shape(s) of the future.

Now it may be argued that this refusal to face the future in the appreciative conversations was itself one more example of the semi- and unconscious anxiety of the group. If you are terrified of the future, it is tempting to dwell in the past. I do not wholly discount the possibility that that was operating for some of the people. Having eaves-dropped on many of the conversations, however, I can only report that that was not how it felt at the time. It seemed to be more the case that, as paired conversations moved into a more natural engagement with a real person talking about his real history, often in extremely difficult situations, the tone shifted from detachment to involvement in recapturing some of the sense of excitement, of achievement, of creativity, of adventure. As one participant put it after the first round of conversations, "Incredible. Wonderful. I've had the time of my life. I'd no idea we had such amazing *stuff* in Sigma. We never hear this." Now this *may* be a cloak for denial, an excuse for not facing some of the negative *stuff*: all I can say is that that is not how it seemed to me.

Nonetheless, there was clearly a problem in that the group as a whole had not adequately focused on the kind of material that would be helpful when we moved to the preparation of provocative propositions. On further reflection on what I had heard of the first round of appreciative conversations, I came to the conclusion that much of the skewing of the shape of the conversations could be traced back to insufficiently rigorous or clearly focused protocols. These had been prepared in the work groups of eight (as representative of the whole gathering as they could be made) after some introductory remarks from me. I had deliberately *not* given the groups sample questions for the protocol for fear of biasing the inquiry, but had explained carefully their nature and function. Having listened to the discussions that preceded the preparation of the protocols in the work groups, I had been struck by how general and unspecific they were, but I had allowed myself to assume—based on work with similar groups in the past—that the actual discipline of conducting the conversations would sharpen the questions and push the participants into a firmer engagement with them.

This turned out to be an error. With the wisdom of hindsight, it may well have been the case that I had been infected by the regional director's extreme caution and his determination not to place himself in a position where it could be said that he had pushed his colleagues in a particular direction. If that was operating unconsciously, at the conscious level I was aware of how hard the work groups were finding it to work together and I was reluctant to put them under greater pressure by constantly goading them to sharpen their protocols. The result was now a mess, not that the participants, or the great majority of them, were not excited by what they had been discovering, but that they were seriously under-prepared to make the next move.

There was therefore a strategic decision to be made. I had only been allotted three full (very full) days for the exercise and if we were to go back two steps, the simulation of the roles of the other stakeholders would have to be jettisoned. On balance that seemed the lesser of two evils, and so we reached a compromise whereby we had a plenary discussion of the nature and viewpoints of the other stakeholders but did not formally include them in the process as originally planned. What emerged from the discussion was that the group as a whole had a far better and fuller understanding of the ramifications of their organization for the other stakeholders than I had expected. Indeed, they identified nearly 20 relevant other stakeholders, and while it is true that some were more important to some members of the group than to others, it would have arguably been both false and distortive to include some—as indicated above—and exclude others.

Even more important now that they were getting into the swing of the process, the participants as a whole were very reluctant to *simulate* the other stakeholders. "That isn't fair to them," said one senior African executive. "They should have the opportunity to go through the process in the same way that we are doing so that they can draw on their own experience. We may think we know what they think and what their interests are. But that is not the point, is it? What we need to hear—what they need to hear—is their best experiences. We do not know those and so we can't speak—and shouldn't speak—for them."

Equally, the group had no difficulty in accepting that the process would be seriously incomplete without the other stakeholders' input. The same African executive went on: "That's OK. We know this is going to take time and will involve many meetings and much discussion. We may have thought before we left home that we could get it all sorted out in the week we are here. Now we see how foolish that is. If it takes longer, well, we are used to that. Everything in Sigma takes twice as long as you originally expect. We can live with that."

Slightly to my surprise, then, it did not prove difficult or disruptive to change course fairly dramatically and take the group back to looking again at their appreciative protocols. They accepted it as part of their learning process, and interestingly were themselves critical of their own protocols now that they had had experience of both interviewing and being interviewed. The result was a much sharper and more finely balanced set of protocols and consequently a quantum leap in the quality of the second and third round of interviews in which the work group members interviewed participants outside their own work groups.

I want to pause here to emphasize the causal link between the quality of the protocol and the quality of the interviews based upon them. Any social scientist is trained from the cradle to recognize the link between instrument and result, yet in using the appreciative process the assumption sometimes seems to gain ground that the protocol is only a means of identifying the general areas that the conversation based upon it will cover. *Of course* it is not and should not be allowed to become an interview schedule, to be slavishly followed, as though by a Gallup researcher. And yet like any open-ended interview process, the more thought that has gone into preparing the questions and foreseeing likely answers and further sets of questions based upon those answers, the more illuminating and satisfying the conversation is likely to prove to be.

And so it proved in this case. The second and third rounds of interviews did not produce less stimulating and in many cases surprising results as a result of being less spontaneous, more carefully planned and more tightly focused; if anything, as reported by the participants, the reverse was the case. The difference was that the interviewer and the interviewee were now much more aware of the need to move more creatively between the three modes of memory, narrative and imagination, rather than allowing themselves or their partners to become bogged down in the past.

5. The provocative propositions

The way was now open to move to the formation of the provocative propositions, the area both the regional director and I knew would be the most sensitive. Would the three work groups spontaneously buy into the regional director's vision of an essentially independent regional organization with the lightest set of bureaucratic links and institutional accountabilities to the rest of Sigma? Or would they signal to him that that was not a direction in which they wished to travel by highlighting quite other, and less demandingly controversial, issues as their own visions of the future? Wisely or not, the regional director decided to continue his self-imposed discipline of near silence, limiting his interventions in his own work group to answering direct questions from other members but eschewing any overtly leadership role.

From my own point of view, the formation of the provocative propositions would confirm or deny many of the impressions I had been forming about the health of the group as a whole. Were the tensions between the various dichotomies—white/black; field/support; anglophone/francophone; ideologically committed/skeptical; whole-organizational oriented/my-patch oriented—going to act as a stimulus to the creative thinking that the group so clearly needed; or were they, more predictably, going to lock the group in their shared anxieties and fears about the rate and nature of change?

I decided that in my briefing on the formation of the provocative propositions integrity to the group demanded that I emphasize only loyalty to the data. It was not my job to anticipate the dynamics that would be released by preparing the participants ahead of time. But it was my job to give them the tools by which they could make the most of the process in which they were engaged. I therefore sought to help them see the interviews as data—a strange concept to some of them who had been trained in a rather narrowly technical notion of the analysis of social science data. The scheme I used was simple, perhaps deceptively so. I told each work group to ask itself, in as systematic a way as they could manage, the following questions:

What have we heard about

1. the sources of energy that are shaping Sigma?—*and how* do we better plug into them?

2. the values of Sigma that give all our stakeholders life?—*and how* can we extend and honour them?

3. the quality of our work that makes Sigma special in the marketplace?—*and how* can we strengthen that quality?

4. what we are called to become?—*and how* can we better become it?

In guiding the data analysis like this I was seeking to build a common purpose around the conversations that had taken place and thus lift each participant from a narrow concern with his or her preformed judgements and sensitivities. By stressing the "…*and how*…?" part of the analysis I was trying to recall the groups to a serious engagement with planning the future. How provocatively they did so was, in the final analysis, up to them.

My field notes read, "The work groups got down to work with great enthusiasm and seriousness. The whole pattern of conversation shifted very interestingly—the field people became much more vocal. In two of the three groups they immediately homed in on provocative propositions to do with the need for development workers at all levels of seniority to be close to the projects. This they see as essentially life giving. Analogously, they regard genuine ownership of projects by the communities as the key both to the sustainability of the projects and to their own satisfaction in facilitating development."

So far so good. But there were already some worrying signs. The groups were clearly more comfortable sharing best practice—their own or those they had heard in the appreciative conversations—than in addressing the central issue of the provocative proposition: how do we make that universal throughout the organization? My field notes remark succinctly: "They are having real problems shifting from data to provocative propositions." And so it continued.

Before the next session started—a session which was merely a continuation of the attempt to distil provocative propositions—I gave a brief presentation on the kind of variables they might consider when thinking out some of the wider implications of the provocative propositions that were beginning, painfully, to emerge. I decided to limit it to three. I highlighted style, structure and strategy. *Style* was a way of hinting that they needed to look more consciously at the implications of any changes for the very delicate—and often deeply conflicted—relationships between the various structural components of Sigma. Currently, much of that conflict is subsumed under a slightly triumphalistic group loyalty to Sigma. It may not be a glorious way of dealing with it, or perhaps even a sustainable one in the long run, but at least it works tolerably well, and, in West Africa, perhaps best of all. If that was to be challenged, it had to be clear that other, better ways of dealing with intra-group conflict were in place.

Structure spoke for itself at one level. At a deeper level, the implications of structural change in West Africa for the rest of the organization needed to be borne in mind. (This was the stakeholder point in another guise.) In pointing this out, I hope I did not dampen whatever enthusiasm there was developing for structural change of a fairly radical kind. My intention was merely to remind the group that if their provocative propositions were going to survive the acids of organizational corrosion, they must be able to withstand probing from many different directions.

By highlighting *strategy*, I was making the obvious point that no change exists in a vacuum. Virtually any change of current practice has effects elsewhere, some of which may be much more severe, in terms of the energy needed to manage them successfully, than the original disturbance.

How this intervention was received it is difficult for me, as an outsider, to guess. In fact only one group, which incidentally came up with the most provocative proposition of all, used these concepts in any coherent or systematic way to test their propositions. They said they found it a very useful—and paradoxically encouraging—discipline. The others had so much trouble distilling any provocative propositions at all, that they had neither time, energy nor creativity to consider them adequately. And it is to their struggle to fashion provocative propositions that we must now return.

I noticed that the three work groups adopted very different approaches to the task. That in itself is not surprising; indeed, it is a commonplace that three teams will adopt three ways of solving the same problem. What struck me here was that the group processes were, in each case, counter-intuitive. For example, a group that was richly endowed with facilitation skills was by far the worst facilitated, as four semi-professional facilitators vied for dominance and in the process shut the African members out of the conversation almost entirely. Another work group that had some very creative minds in it quickly elected to follow a dumb voting procedure around lists of propositions that were individually generated and never properly discussed. The third group, led, it is true, by a highly skilled facilitator, worked immensely hard and systematically, sifting and categorizing all the data they could assemble, sorting it into topic areas, and then sequentially searching for provocative propositions that came from the data. Of course they could find few, for provocative propositions do not present themselves out of the data, like shrimps in a net: they have to be created by the shared vision of the group, *inspired by and tested against* the data.

What I had feared most was happening: groups were coming up with provocative propositions that were anything but provocative. What was going on? I suggest three things.

I have already mentioned the difficulty Sigma as a whole has with conflict. Part of the corporate culture is to reward conflict minimizers and penalize conflict facers. My field notes, scribbled as I listened to the groups struggling with the provocative propositions, read thus: "These people are so used to finding lowest-common-denominator-type statements to keep as wide a constituency as possible on board, that they are locked into that. It's a kind of PR approach both within and without the organization." To put it shortly, it was so counter to the ethos of the organization to *be* provocative that, when invited to be so, few indeed knew how.

But there was something much more malign at work, too. For reasons that need not detain us, one of the participants had been allowed to bring his wife to the workshop. By common consent, she entered as fully into the process as any other member. When her work group was struggling with how provocative it could be, someone turned to this lady and said, "*You* be radical. Your job is not on the line." In some ways, this was the crux. Sigma is, rightly or wrongly, *perceived* by its middle and senior staff as both so hierarchical and so conservative that any new thinking will be received by the hierarchy as so threatening that dismissal is a real possibility. In such an organization it takes either courage or desperation to put your head above the parapet. Or to put it in more analytical language, the anxiety that I had detected under the surface all along now had a clear name: it was fear of a deeply conservative hierarchy.

There was, however, a third issue that was more pervasive yet much more subtle. I have mentioned above the emphasis that had been given, primarily by the regional director, to team building, as though he was not confident that he had a team (despite all the rhetoric). When I observed the work groups from a process point of view, the one thing that struck me was how *individualized* were their patterns of work. There was, despite the close bonding that had arisen in the appreciative conversations, little sense of hearing each other, empathizing with each other, helping each other develop a line of argument. One work group did not even pretend to do so. The instruction from the facilitator, as recorded in my field notes, was, "Everyone write down one provocative proposition and then we can all vote on them.... Get something on paper so you don't ramble too much." It is too easy to burlesque this approach; yet it is, I believe, deeply significant because it points to a corporate culture where cooperative tussling with the deepest issues is, for whatever reason, at a discount. That is dismissed as rambling. What matters is speed, efficiency, clarity, (bogus) consensus built around a pseudo-democratic voting procedure. Behind that, again, I suspect, lurks fear of conflict, openly and forcefully expressed disagreement, and, even more fundamentally, a (deeply American) sense that truth is finally the product of the individual mind rather than the outcome of collaborative effort.

In the end, 10 provocative propositions were produced. These were presented to the plenary by a spokesperson from each work group, and questions of fact and interpretation were put from the floor. About process, two points are worth making. The first is that some of the propositions were, despite all that I have said above, very far reaching in their implications, but were presented in such anodyne terms that their full impact was not, I am quite confident, appreciated by most participants. In the subsequent consensus-building, they therefore tended to be ignored.

Second—and this will come up again below—wordsmithing tended to be taken too seriously so that form began to dominate substance. This manifested itself in a tendency for participants to try to redraft propositions from the floor to make them, as they thought, more acceptable to the group as a whole. This had to be firmly resisted from the chair.

Most interestingly, two propositions bore directly on the concerns of the regional director for a virtual UDI. One, from the work group in which he had participated, spoke of Sigma in West Africa as a "network of diverse entities energized by the (central) Sigma mission, working free (sic) from current Sigma systems and structures; supportive of the discovery of new and effective practice."

Ignoring the clumsy wording, what this proposition was about was precisely what the regional director had been working for—freedom from a bureaucratic load that was counter-productive and inefficient, and experimentation with new structures that would by-pass many of the established power centres. So at last the real issues were on the table.

Their presence there was complicated, however, by a second proposition, from a different group—the one that had had so much difficulty working together, not least because of an *embarrass de richesse* of facilitation. This group now produced a proposition that called for the full integration of the work of the field offices and the support offices. Behind a bland exterior there lurked a bombshell, for the suggestion was that the central dichotomy between fundraisers and program implementers be scrapped and that each side accept full responsibility for and involvement in both aspects of the work.

The contrast between the two propositions needs a moment's clarification. The first, associated most closely with the regional director, was for the independence of the field offices. They wanted to be given their heads and allowed to fundraise as and where they wished, with or without the say-so of the support offices. The second stood that vision on its head. It looked for a time when the support office staff would have a role in program implementation in the field *as well as the field staff having a role in fundraising*. Instead of a UDI by one group from the other, it saw both field and support staff working more closely together on the output as a whole. Perhaps unsurprisingly, the former was the product of a man who had spent all his working life in the field, and the latter was the brainchild of a woman who was intensely frustrated by her role in a support office.

I spell out the inner logic of both propositions primarily because I am still uncertain how far it was really appreciated by the workshop as a whole when we came to build a consensus around those propositions that seemed to command the widest support. Certainly in the presentation of the two propositions, there was enough grey fog in which to lose a couple of battle fleets, and, interestingly, no one, not even the regional director, seemed especially keen to clarify the real issues. (It has to be said, though, that the group presenting the second of the propositions, on integration, was the only one that had considered carefully the implications for style, structure and strategy and was prepared to spell them out in the plenary.) I fear we were back to the lowest common denominator again, and as facilitator of the process, I have to accept my share of the blame for allowing the group to fudge the issues in this way.

6. Building a consensus

With 10 provocative propositions on the floor, some much more comprehensive and challenging than others (but nearly all wrapped in surprisingly bland language), it proved difficult to facilitate a plenary discussion that would allow a smaller number to emerge as the core propositions around which a consensus could develop—although all participants were becoming aware of the speed with which the presentation to Sigma's president and the most senior executives of the US support office was approaching. It was clearly going to be necessary to go through some formal voting procedure to allow the leading half dozen propositions to crystallize out.

Crude voting, however, threatened the tyranny of democracy, so the following scheme was devised. Each participant had five votes (i.e., half the number of propositions), weighted from five to one. These were to be written on the appropriate sheet in silence. Then, without further discussion, the work groups were to meet in the plenary hall, surrounded by the propositions with the votes written on them. This would give the work groups a rough idea of which were emerging as the most popular and which had attracted few votes. The work groups were each given three super-votes, worth an absolute value of five each: two were plus five, one was minus five. They could only be used if the group was unanimous. If one proposition received two minus super-votes it would be eliminated no matter how many positive votes it had achieved. Thus, no single work group had the power of veto, but two-thirds of the whole number of participants acting unanimously did.

The rationale behind this voting scheme and procedure is obvious enough though it took the participants by surprise. It was designed to spread the propositions along a long continuum, making clear any bunching. The expectation was that there would be a group at the bottom which could be quietly forgotten, a group at the top on which further work could be done, and a group spread along the middle as dirty noise which may or may not demand further attention. The super votes gave each group some capacity to push an individual proposition along the spectrum in a desired direction, but the requirement of unanimity in the group was designed to ensure a much more thorough discussion than had been achieved in the plenary.

In the event, the participants had no difficulty with their individual choices. In the great majority of cases they gave their top three votes to the propositions emanating from their own work groups, a testimony both to the amount of bonding that had occurred in those groups and to the generally slow speed at which propositions from other work groups had been assimilated by the rest of the participants. The other individual votes tended to be cast either for very nitty-gritty, easily understood propositions or one or other of the radical but mutually exclusive propositions discussed above. The expected tail appeared, comprising four propositions, which included some of the blander apple-pie propositions, inviting the response: "So what?"

To my surprise, the determination of the distribution of the super-votes nearly caused a riot. At last, corporate inhibitions and anxieties were cast aside and people committed themselves passionately to arguing real cases. Before unpacking that a little more, however, two prefatory comments are needed. The first is the issue of wordsmithery. Perhaps because Sigma is the kind of business it is, too many participants seemed to think that tinkering with the wording would solve the problem. Sometimes there were real issues of substance behind this editing approach, but the tendency was to deal with the substance editorially rather than grappling with the fundamental issues. For example, the phrase in the "UDI Proposition" about being "free from current Sigma systems and structures" was hotly contested, not because it was a radical break from existing corporate disciplines but because "it sounds anarchic and adolescently destructive."

Second, there was—as I should have foreseen—too much Tammany Hall-type politicking with the super-votes: "If we use our minus vote on X and they use their plus vote on it, we've both wasted a vote. So let's agree with them that neither of us will vote for X." Clearly with quite a complex voting system, a number of prisoner's-dilemma situations arise, evidenced by a demand from the floor that groups be allowed to discuss across group boundaries how votes would be cast. (I ruled against that. If time had been available, it might well have been worthwhile to have a second round of super-votes where that was permitted. My hunch, however, is that it would have affected the outcome only marginally, perhaps in reinforcing the bunching.) There is nothing wrong about this obsession with micro-politics in itself. It risked becoming, however, a distraction from the real business of the session—which was not about casting votes but about understanding the issues raised by the propositions and testing that understanding against other people with very different experience of and responsibility within the organization.

As I have already indicated, however, some of that did take place—*con brio*! The heat centred predictably on the UDI and integrationist propositions, although few if any of the participants saw how finally incompatible they were. It was around these propositions that the majority of the super-votes were cast—or not, in the end, cast at all because one of the work groups was so split it could not agree to use any of its super-votes!

The final voting pattern defined well enough the four propositions that had received scant support. By contrast, the most popular proposition was well differentiated from the rest (it was essentially a restatement of current policy about communities becoming self-sufficient), but the two contending UDI/integration propositions remained very close (at three and four), even though one minus super-vote had been used against the UDI and one positive super-vote had been used for integration. This had put integration ahead, but hardly by a convincing margin.

It was hard to resist the conclusion that the group had crystallized its position very well. It was committed to the principle of sustainability by making communities with which it works self-reliant; it had various staff concerns which needed attention; and it was highly dissatisfied with the present structure, both global and regional, without a clear idea of how to advance from that dissatisfaction. The regional director had permission to be bold and innovative, but not along the lines of an unsubtle UDI. He needed to find ways of carrying the support offices with him, either by offering their senior staff a much closer involvement in programming and implementation, or by forming very close alliances with selected support offices and his region—which would amount to much the same in the longer run.

7. Action planning

Time did not permit us to explore these conclusions in the depth they needed. As a training exercise we moved on to action planning, to emphasize to the group that when they use the appreciative approach in their own environments, the derivation of provocative propositions is justified not by the propositions themselves, but by the action to which they lead. Here, we split into functional groups for the action-planning sessions and it was immediately striking—though perhaps unsurprising—how much faster the functional groups became effective than had been the case with the cross-functional work groups. Much more surprising was the way the functional groups saw the radical implications of even the bland propositions in a way seemingly denied to the work groups. Action—or plans for action—does indeed speak louder than words, and now that action was in the air, the functional groups found themselves stretched to comprehend the demands laid upon their parts of the organization by what was being proposed.

We did not have time to take this phase too far, but we did run a consistency check in the final plenary. I find this a very useful device not only to ensure that action planning is free of mutually defeating inconsistencies, but also, and in some ways more fundamentally, to ensure that the interpretation of the provocative propositions remains a shared set of meanings. Even in the limited exercise with the Sigma group, there was a noticeable tendency to *reword* the propositions when they came up against the hard reality of organizational change. Here it was explicit; often it is implicit and sometimes even devious. In either case such rejigging of agreed objectives can lead to mayhem when action begins to be implemented. Hence a systematic check of the consistency of plans at each stage may not be hugely exciting but proves again and again to be a sound investment.

8. Conclusion

The appreciative approach to strategy formation for an anxious, conflict-avoiding, cross-cultural and highly diverse group had met the demands placed upon it. With some glitches, it had enabled a high level of participation and collaboration; none of the 24 participants had been marginalized. By the final sessions, even the most timid Francophonic African was arguing passionately for or against some of the propositions. Although both the conflict-avoidance and the anxiety remained present throughout as subtexts, they had not stood in the way of a genuine struggle to find a way forward from a system that, in their hearts, virtually all the participants know is in serious need of radical overhaul.

The real achievement, however, was that the group avoided buying the regional director's plan and showed him, in an unthreatening and undemeaning way, that there was a wiser, more inclusive, more enabling way forward. What precisely that will turn out to be is still uncertain. It will need much more work and even more creativity to establish. The effort will be worthwhile because when it is found, it will have the support of the whole group who will see its genesis in this workshop. And seeing it thus, there is a good chance that their fear of change, their anxiety about the future of Sigma, their diffidence before a dominating hierarchy—all of these serious inhibitions to corporate evolution—will be the more containable. That is a good return for three days' work.

Chapter 14
The roundtable project

John Carter and Pamela Johnson

1. Background of rapid growth

Appreciative inquiry was still in its early stages of development when a long-term client of John Carter & Associates agreed to use it as an intervention in their organization. The site was a Big Eight accounting firm in Canada, which we will refer to as Alexander, Konstanz and Greene. AK&G was the oldest accounting firm in Canada, founded before Canada became a nation, with a historically strong presence in the French Canadian province. During the 1970s, AK&G had ranked seventh in size and significance within the Canadian market. To counter this and increase market share, they had engaged upon an aggressive strategy of growth and restructuring. In the period from 1979 to 1987, 22 separate mergers had added almost 150 new partners to the practice. The firm had wisely invested a great deal of time and attention in managing the dynamics of merger integration, and developed an industry-wide reputation for success in its merger activities.

Focusing on people enrichment as a key benefit of the mergers, the firm had created a separate human resources function at the national level. Performance review and planning processes were introduced for staff, and a partner development process was created to provide valuable feedback and career planning for partners. Several new training programs were created to help both partners and managers enhance their skills in managing people.

Q   *Do you think there was something special about AK&G that made them almost uniquely suitable as early users of appreciative inquiry?*

A   Yes, the managing partner of the firm believed in bringing out the best in people and put significant energy into the firm, seeing itself as a group of winners.

Believing that people who feel like winners project this image with clients and competitors, the firm had renovated their office facilities and eventually moved into new upscale offices. In 1977, major investment in new information technology had begun. In the 10 years that followed, they purchased a new mainframe computer, developed software to enhance service delivery and developed programs for training and computer support. Ultimately, their investment made possible expanded service capabilities with an availability of one computer for every two people in the firm.

Development of an aggressive marketing strategy was signalled by the creation of a national client service and development group. While the client base had expanded because of the mergers which had occurred, as well as through acquisitions by their existing clients, a new target account program had been introduced. Marketing AK&G services became a major priority for every partner.

Finally, AK&G had engaged in a four-year process to define an integral statement of intent for the firm. This effort was a long-term consensus-building process with every partner involved in its development. The result was a multipage document with a statement of mission, principles of partnership, and national objectives and strategies in 10 different areas. The statement of intent reflected essential values shared by all partners. These values included a sense of obligation to one another and a commitment to building AK&G for the long term.

The combination of these strategies had achieved considerable success. By 1985 AK&G had positioned itself as third largest of the Big Eight accounting firms in Canada. By 1987 there were 340 partners, and in 10 years to 1988 the net revenue had more than quadrupled.

2. Governance issues

In 1981 AK&G had changed its governance structure by separating management from policy and creating a unique system of shared leadership between a managing partner and the chairman of the board of directors. It soon became apparent that a significant change of leadership would occur in the mid to latter part of the 1980s. The chairman of the board and the managing partner of the firm were potentially due to leave their respective roles at the same time. Attention began to be directed to the leadership succession of the firm. Of particular importance was the development of younger partners who were regarded as having the talent, knowledge and ability to assume the leadership of the firm and maintain a willingness to manage change creatively. Further, even in the midst of the growth, turbulence and change of the last 20 years, there was felt to be a need to affirm the fundamental strengths, values and competencies that had sustained the firm over its long history. In response to these needs, by 1987 the roundtable project had been created.

The name roundtable was chosen to suggest leadership without hierarchy, shared resources, and cross-functional networks. In his address to roundtable participants, the managing partner of AK&G explained:

> What is the roundtable? Roundtable is having you discover, explore and become missionaries for what is strong and good in the firm. The roundtable has to do with strengthening the culture of the firm and the partnership. The roundtable is working with each of you as potential leaders. When we first

envisioned the roundtable, we said, "We want the next tier of potential firm leaders to ask questions such as:

- What is it that makes us successful?

- What are the special features of the partnership which are critically important and which must be retained?

- How do we deal with each other as partners?

- What are the key underpinnings of this firm that are critical for our continued success?

- How can we have these emerging leaders understand and be aware of what they can and must do to build continuity into what we have as a partnership?"

3. Early stages of the roundtable project

The above questions were framed to guide the roundtable project by February of 1987, and the structure and design of the project began to assume greater form and substance in March. There were a number of assumptions and desires that undergirded the project and that closely reflected the views of the managing partner. Among these was the desire for people to have a vision and be able to talk about it, and especially to create a network of individuals in the firm who shared a common vision and could use it in a powerful way.

Q *This suggests a high degree of coaching! How much time did you spend with senior management, introducing them to appreciative inquiry before the roundtable got underway?*

A We spent four years looking for the right interventions to accomplish the desired outcomes of the managing partner and top leadership group. Once appreciative inquiry was introduced as a possible approach, it took less than three days over a three-month period to get the tacit buy-in required. We as outsiders never spent any time with the senior management on buy-in; it was all done by the top leader. The five-year window we started with was closing, and now we faced a now-or-never situation.

We wanted to create awareness of the relationship between stability and change, to identify life-giving forces within the firm and create a catalyst for enhancing and giving focus to these life-giving forces. To understand and reinforce culture, we knew we needed to heighten the capacity for vision of deepest possibilities, passion as the integration of logic and emotion, integrity which was consistent and focused, and love reflected in the ability of members to care enough about each other that they would not allow anything to get in the way. We hoped that the participants would take both vision and passion back into the firm, with a network on which they could rely for both support and collaboration.

Q *These are certainly powerful values and the last is surely unusual in this kind of context. Where did it come from? Did it cause any embarrassment or is it a reflection of the best of partnership? How would it go down in a more traditional corporate setting?*

A Love of one's work and one's partner emerged out of the data as important to those interviewed. It is a reflection of the best of the partnership. The agreement between the firm leader and the outside consultant was that absolutely nothing, including the death of one of us, would stand in the way of this project being completed.

The stages of project implementation can be seen in the following figure. Early stages were spent resolving many issues of design and logistics, such as how the affirmative topics would be determined and who would be involved.

Q *Who were these? How were they chosen? Did anyone check how those who found themselves excluded felt about it? This has a very elitist feel to it. Did that get in the way of the appreciative mode?*

A The 40 people chosen were seen as future leaders of the firm by both the current leaders and their peers. Since all partners were interviewed and everyone ultimately was involved in the process, there was little expression of in and outness. Most people looking at those chosen would have perceived the group as an equitable and fair microcosm of future leadership and not inclusive or exclusive.

A decision had been made to involve the 40 roundtable participants in all phases of an appreciative study of the organization. This meant that decisions needed to be made about who would be interviewed (especially, how to ensure that present and former leaders, history carriers, unique individuals, and those who embodied the firm were interviewed), how to educate participants in conducting an appreciative inquiry interview, how the interview protocol would be developed, how the management committee would be kept appropriately involved and informed, how the larger partnership would be engaged in the project, and so on. The managing partner and the management committee identified 40 individuals who would be participants: all were visible within AK&G as emerging leaders and had been identified as potential candidates for positions that would become available in the next three to 10 years. By April, enough of the initial plans had been solidified, and an announcement of the project was made in AK&G.

Q   *Corporate memory-holders are a particular interest of mine. How did you identify them?*

A   There were individuals recognized as being the embodiment of the firm and these individuals also happen to be the storytellers, carriers and creators of myth.

Q   *Who is this management committee? How were they chosen? What were their terms of reference? To whom were they accountable?*

A   The management committee in this firm consists of individuals selected by the managing partner and appointed by the board of directors to oversee the daily operations of the firm. They are accountable first to the partnership and second to the managing partner.

Q   *This strikes me as a large number. Is this usual in your experience?*

A   The number of identified future leaders is unusual. The belief underlying leadership succession was that there should be at least three individuals being trained for every critical position of leadership in the organization.

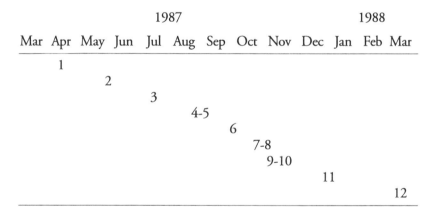

				1987						1988		
Mar	Apr	May	Jun	Jul	Aug	Sep	Oct	Nov	Dec	Jan	Feb	Mar
	1											
		2										
			3									
				4-5								
					6							
						7-8						
							9-10					
									11			
												12

1.   Structure and design of roundtable takes shape
2.   Announcement to firm
3.   Affirmative topics determined
4.   Interview format designed
5.   Interview protocol and instructional videotape sent to participants
6.   Collection of data: participants conduct interviews

7. As interviews are completed, they are sent to the consultants and data are analyzed

8. Summarized interview data are sent to participants to read

9. Logo for roundtable project is developed

10. Roundtable session is conducted

11. Report to firm partnership: entire partnership consensually validates provocative propositions created during the roundtable session

12. Participants send short stories to the managing partner about what happened, what was new and what was different after the roundtable

To identify affirmative topics for the study, the managing partner designated a group consisting of himself, the chairman of the board, the human resources director, the human resources manager, the consultants and others. We asked this group three questions:

- Think back to peak experience in your professional life in the firm, a time when you felt most alive and excited about your work. Describe the key elements of the situation: Who was involved? What was happening? What was the firm like?

- As you think about the firm in general, what is it that represents the most life-giving force?

- If you could bring into the firm anything you wanted, what would you like to see more of?

- After listening to the peak experiences of members, stimulated by these questions, we asked them to identify topics that generated energy and excitement, ones they would like to study in some depth. Fifteen topics surfaced; they were presented to the management committee for their input and buy-in, and were finally boiled down to the following six affirmative topics: (1) partnership; (2) determination to be winners; (3) diversity; (4) consensus decision-making; (5) possibilities and positive thinking; and (6) conditions for people to excel. All of the preparation was now complete; the timing was right to get the roundtable participants involved in the process.

4. Middle stage: Data collection and analysis

In June, the 40 participants were formally invited to participate in the roundtable. The objectives of the program were described thus:

"The short-term objective is for the younger group of partners to learn about the rich tradition and the ingredients of success in the firm. It is hoped that through this process they will become a missionary group which will work to multiply those success factors in the firm and in their offices. The long-term objective of this program is to operationalize the statement of intent through the practice of appreciative inquiry."

And the intended outcome was put like this:

- "Develop a common vision among participants based on the statement of intent and the results of appreciative inquiry."

- "Provide the proper tools for participants to work toward making the firm's vision a current and future reality."

- "Create an environment in the firm that supports pragmatic means of putting the statement of intent into action."

A qualitative interview format had been developed around the six affirmative topic areas and this protocol was sent to participants with an accompanying videotape that demonstrated the techniques of conducting an appreciative inquiry interview. In addition, each participant was paired with another participant, and the two were required to interview each other as soon as possible. This gave them some practice and feedback in conducting appreciative interviews before interviewing other partners. Each of the participants was assigned nine to 10 partners to interview and they were told interviews should last between two to three hours. Every partner in the firm was interviewed.

5. Data management

A key to management of data in this project was detailed instruction about how the data were to be transcribed and delivered for data analysis. Interviewers were instructed that completed interviews should be typewritten and submitted in hard copy or on floppy disk. The generation of large amounts of data (the first 75 interviews alone generated over 700 pages of text) and the need for prompt turnaround of the analysis made attention to detail in preparing the data for analysis a critical issue.

Responses were first subgrouped according to similarity of theme within an affirmative topic area. Next, a method of analysis was chosen for the subgroups to enhance validity and reliability. Analysis was done by two external analysts who had no prior knowledge of the process. In addition, interview data for each affirmative topic was run through a computer program which counted the number of times different words occurred as part of each response, and ranked these in order of frequency.

Q   *How helpful do you find this kind of computerized discourse analysis? Many people from linguistics and literature would argue that it obscures more than it reveals. What is your experience?*

A   Word count and other computer analysis provide little useful information. They indicate potential directions for inquiry and exploration, and sometimes confirmation of findings.

Raw data, edited to preserve anonymity and representing responses for 80 interviews, were provided to roundtable participants by the end of August. Participants were instructed to read the data, as a microcosm of the full set of interviews, in preparation for their attendance at the roundtable session in mid-September.

When they arrived at the session, participants also received summary materials that contained information covering each of the six affirmative topics as well as two others; namely, experience in the firm and a typical day. For each of the topics, a word and content summary from the computer database was provided. For example, on the affirmative topic of partnership, the following list of words, ranked in order of frequency, was provided for the question, "List factors that heighten responsiveness, trust and partner support?"

1. Success generates success, confidence and solidarity
2. One partner, one vote
3. Team spirit, pride
4. Partner performance feedback system
5. Quality management
6. Demonstration of integrity and justice
7. Fair play
8. Remuneration
9. Growth philosophy
10. Collective decision-making
11. Communication between partners
12. Common goals and objectives
13. Acknowledgement and announcement of accomplishments
14. Open and honest management committee
15. Open and honest board of directors
16. Delegation of administrative tasks
17. Firm's support for the partners
18. Supervision from the management
19. Office and partner assistance when needed
20. Contribution from each partner

Following the word and content summary for each topic, a two- to three-page interpretation and commentary was provided to add greater depth and context. There was no intention for the summarized information to represent the final word; rather, we hoped that the material would spark the participants' own provocative propositions about the firm and contribute to an enjoyable as well as profitable roundtable experience.

Q   *Could you give some indication of the additional insight this commentary provided?*

A   The commentary allowed us as outside consultants to heighten awareness of the obvious in the data that sometimes represented the unspeakable, like love and integrity. It supported making things people take for granted real and alive versus silent and dead.

During this phase of the roundtable project, there were three points we wished to emphasize. First was the emphasis we placed on multigenerational learning; in this we had been influenced by the work of Margaret Mead. From her anthropological work, she had become aware that to develop communities capable of learning required the involvement of three generations: the elders to provide wisdom based in lessons of the past; the middle-aged to provide responsibility in response to the challenges of the present; and youth to provide vision, hope and optimism in anticipation of the future. In this inquiry, younger partners were engaged in learning from each of the other two generations, even as they were being encouraged to develop their vision for the future responsibility of the firm. An underlying metaphor might be, "The deeper and stronger are the roots, the taller and more far reaching are the branches." Following the roundtable session, we intended to use images of the future of the firm created by these 40 partners to promote dialogue among all the partners and across generations.

Second, because each of the participants had actually conducted the interviews, they each owned and could represent a significant portion of the data available in the partnership at large. In contrast with an inquiry where the client generates and owns the data, here, the participants were the data: it was inside them. Individually and collectively, they were a microcosm of the partnership at large.

Last, we gave much attention to images and symbols that could integrate value and fact, reason and emotion, and create an integrative or contextual framework for the roundtable project. Two particular examples were important. In early September, a logo was created for the project. The logo comprises, first, two horizontal, outward-pointing arrows which represented the national, coast-to-coast scope of the project; they also represented the direction of future leadership and focus. The second component was two vertical arrows pointing inward to a centre point. These represented receiving input and feedback. The logo was used on all materials. It was explained to all roundtable participants, and was later introduced at the annual partners' meeting for the entire firm. Even language acquired a symbolic significance. For example, the very term *roundtable* became part of the connective language of this group of partners, and continues to be present for many partners today, despite massive changes and restructuring in the firm.

6. The roundtable session and application of appreciative inquiry in large-group settings

The AK&G roundtable session had five objectives. Each of these will be discussed below, along with the actual session design and the methods we used to accomplish the objectives.

I.   Reaffirm affirmative topic choices and create a common base of data for all participants

The AK&G roundtable was a 3 1/2 day design. The initial challenge was to transform individuals, each of whom carried some part of the data with them into the session, into a community of inquiry with a common set of data. As we have already seen, before the roundtable, participants had received raw data from 80 interviews and later received word-count analysis and summarized interpretations of the data from the consultants. This was no substitute, however, for sharing their personal experience of the interviews, the understandings, surprises and insights they had attained.

To achieve this, we facilitated a discussion around the following four questions:

1.   What one word best characterizes your experience of the appreciative inquiry interviews?

2.   What was the most exciting, surprising or humorous thing that occurred during your interviews?

3.   Based on the interview data you have, what would be the most important outcome or message for all partners from the roundtable session?

4.   What do you believe is the essence or life-giving force of the firm?

The effect of those discussions was that both the objective data and the subjective experiences of the participants were now available to the whole group. However, the leadership of the firm also needed an opportunity to add to the mix, to talk about their interpretation of the data and contribute their perspectives, especially in the context of current organizational dilemmas and challenges. The initial discussions of the data were therefore followed, the next day, by the current managing partner talking about what he wanted from the roundtable project. Consistent with our effort to generate dialogue rather than talking heads, we then created a fish bowl of the management committee. Grouping them in the middle of the room surrounded by roundtable participants, we asked them to talk with one another about what personally excited them in the data and what they saw as possible outcomes. They engaged in an animated conversation which illuminated their values and hopes for the continued integrity of the partnership and the future strength of the firm. There was an opportunity for roundtable participants to add their observations and to ask questions after this conversation.

Q *I am interested in what appears to be a privileged role in this process for the leadership of the firm. Did you not find that this cut across the principles of co-inquiry?*

A In the words of Ken Wilber, there is always hierarchy. This was our way of acknowledging the leader hierarchy in the room without allowing the leaders to exercise any control over the dialogue. It was also our way of forcing the issue of buy-in, since the management committee at this point had still given only tacit buy-in to the intervention.

At this point, both the voices of individual participants and current leadership were present in the room. This enabled us to test whether the affirmative topics which had been determined in May after discussion with the management committee were still applicable. There was also a possibility that new affirmative topics were implicitly or explicitly suggested by the data. We wanted to give participants the opportunity both to affirm the relevance of the topics which had been selected, and to create new topics if that seemed warranted. Knowing that the topics selected would govern the provocative propositions to be created, the goal was to grant the participants, future leaders of the firm, full ownership for a vision of the future they would collectively create.

From these discussions, all of the topics were re-affirmed by the participants and two were added. Since the design called for each group to focus on one affirmative topic for the remainder of the roundtable, the next step was to decide which groups would work on what topics. During the two-hour lunch break, the roundtable staff talked with a designated representative from each group who explained the nature of their discussion, which topics had generated energy and why, and made a case for the topics which most interested the group. Based on this data, the staff made assignments so that the groups could begin work on their affirmative topic in the next phase of the roundtable. At this point, the roundtable participants had full ownership of the topics of inquiry and sufficient common ground to make possible discussions about prospects for the future of AK&G.

II. State provocative propositions about the life-giving properties in the firm

In terms of writing provocative propositions, the task assigned to the groups was to discuss the ideal organizational embodiment of their assigned affirmative topic.

As so often happens, the groups at first found the process of writing provocative propositions awkward. Affirmational writing requires that the propositions be written in the present tense even though they may not fully reflect the present reality. They require language in the present tense, and use of words that generate effect and inspiration. This is in stark contrast with concise, objective writing that most use in normal business transactions, and groups are often somewhat conservative in the statements they eventually produce. It must be recognized, however, that, from the point of view of their creators, these statements are often highly radical. They often represent a large jump from the *status quo*, even though all of the propositions are grounded in best of present practice. It must also be stressed that the dialogue that occurs in the groups as they create the propositions is at least as significant as the propositions they produce.

Groups were given the opportunity to present their provocative propositions to the full roundtable. They were encouraged to do this in creative ways to spark the imagination of others and convey their excitement about the vision of the ideal they had created. For example, they could do this with a panel, a skit or role play, as "ten commandments," and so on. The purpose was to educate and inspire others about what was possible. There was opportunity for other participants to ask clarifying questions, but not to argue or debate any of the propositions. A few of the propositions roundtable participants created for the topic of partnership are shown below:

1. There is an attitude that strives to have the principles of partnership consistently applied to partners and staff alike.

2. The partnership is committed to a management style that is inspirational, directive and consultative.

3. The concept of shared ownership demands that each partner be responsible for the success of the firm and its future direction.

4. In recognition that we are in a knowledge business, leaders direct and partners accept responsibility for significant relevant self-development, including personal, professional and people-management skills.

5. Each partner is responsible to leave a legacy in terms of building firm assets, including people, clients and services.

6. Partners in the firm who cease to have the leadership positions are retained in substantial roles to ensure their contribution.

We have found that the experiences of creating provocative propositions, of freeing a group to think optimistically and hopefully about building a future vision based on the strengths of the present, are enormously uplifting for participants. The quality of this conversation does transcend differences and build bridges. Individuals begin to discover, sometimes to their astonishment, that others seem to share similar values, dreams and hopes, and that there is much common ground between them. In our experience, this process of discovery continues during the remainder of the workshop. It is highly affirming to the participants, building resilience in the group to deal with the differences that inevitably arise.

Q *Yes, but they are often very conservative, as you recognize below. Do you have any general comments on the paradox this represents?*

A Realizable provocative propositions will be conservative; idealized provocative propositions should not be conservative. Conservative propositions are an indication that accountability, goal setting and strategic planning have become more the focus than innovative and creative thinking that are focused on the best of the best.

When the groups present their provocative propositions the night before, we ask them to print each proposition neatly on a flipchart page and numerically order them. We also ask them to write the propositions in the same order on a piece of paper. After the session ends, the staff tapes these to the walls of the room and attaches the scales we will use for consensual validation the next day. Also, we have already formatted a computer disk with the scales so that all that needs to be added are the propositions; accordingly, one staff member takes responsibility for typing the propositions into the format and creating a document which is, in effect, a questionnaire for participants to complete the next morning.

At the roundtable, we validated the propositions using two scales. The first was an ideal-state scale (I) which asked, "To what extent do you believe that this statement is important as an ideal to be pursued by the organization?" The second was a present-state scale (P) which asked, "To what extent is the statement actually reflected in practice?" The rating for each question was on a seven-point scale, where one indicated *to a very little extent* and seven indicated *to a very great extent*. In other words, a participant who marked one for the ideal-state scale would be saying that they absolutely disagreed that the proposition reflected a valid ideal for the firm while a seven indicated absolute agreement that the proposition should be an ideal for the future of the firm. Likewise, a one in the present-state scale indicated that the proposition was never realized in the present state, while a seven meant that the statements reflected what was always true in current practice. Examples of two propositions created during the roundtable illustrate how they would be prepared for validation.

The leaders in the firm are role models for positive thinking: motivators, listeners and risk takers.

	1	2	3	4	5	6	7
I	☐	☐	☐	☐	☐	☐	☐
P	☐	☐	☐	☐	☐	☐	☐

The firm supports people in the development and use of their imagination, creativity, determination and vision.

	1	2	3	4	5	6	7
I	☐	☐	☐	☐	☐	☐	☐
P	☐	☐	☐	☐	☐	☐	☐

Each provocative proposition created by groups the night before is in hard copy with the appropriate scales for individual participants to complete the next morning. The same propositions surround participants on the walls, organized according to affirmative topic. Most participants are somewhat stunned when they walk into the room the next morning, seeing their work of the day before made almost larger than life and central to the remainder of the session.

The first task of the morning was to instruct the participants to go through the document which had been prepared for them, and ask them to answer the questions for each proposition by placing their individual ranking in each of the scales. We do this individually first so that participants can think about their choices privately and make the appropriate response.

We then began to construct a group scattergram. Each participant had been given sheets of variously coloured Avery dots sufficient to the number of propositions. Group members were asked to take their individual responses and move to the propositions on the wall. For each proposition, they were asked to place an Avery dot on both the ideal-state and the present-state scales which reflected their private responses. We told them to use a red dot for their I-scale response and a blue dot for their P-scale response because this heightens the visual impact of the gap between the ideal and the present state. Because everyone was moving at once, at their own pace and in different sections of the room, it was almost impossible to see where people placed their dot. The result was a completely level playing field that was not influenced by the articulated opinions of others perceived as being of higher status or greater power.

Q   *We have often found what we call an agglomeration effect, i.e., people tend to go with the flow. Is that your experience?*

A   It is a serious risk with any large group process and needs to be managed. If the focus is kept on common ground and common compelling pictures of the future, rather than attempting to problem-solve conflicts, this risk is minimized.

When they were done, group members were asked to walk around the room and look at where the dots have been placed. Without photographs, it is hard to describe the visual impact of seeing the gap between the ideal and the present state so graphically and colourfully depicted. The impact on participants is usually one of surprise: either there is more or less agreement about the ideal state than they expected, for example. There is often surprise about the extent of the common ground which exists. Also, there may be outliers which trigger the curiosity of some people who have placed their dot on a three or a four when the greater number of dots is on the six and seven. People are sometimes intrigued by how large the gap between the ideal and the present state is; alternatively, they may be surprised at how narrow the gap is.

Q   *On reflection do you regret that—as you imply below?*

A   Critical analysis is important to appreciative inquiry and problem solving. I do not like the term appreciative mode because most people equate it with simply looking at the positive without any discipline.

During the roundtable, there was not much time for discussion of the ratings before moving to the second part of consensual validation. In our work with subsequent organizations, we allow more time for plenary discussion of the data which has been generated. Sometimes, people will express their curiosity about outliers and ask if the persons who placed their dots in those positions would be willing to discuss their response. Usually, participants frame their question as an inquiry with the effect of reducing defensiveness, and very often people will respond, talking freely about their perceptions and the rationale for their response. Sometimes, they are responding to the phrasing or word choice in the statement, but at other times it reflects a substantive difference of perception. At these times, most participants are careful to listen fully to the individual's perception and to state their differences of opinion openly, as a difference, without disparaging the view of the other. There is more emphasis on sharing meanings than searching for a single truth.

One important mechanism for insuring open dialogue is a technique we use for letting people know how others are responding to them. It often happens that we do not know how people are responding to our statements, and this can be particularly disheartening when one is speaking at a level of deep values and understandings. We believe it is important during the discussion to allow people to see where the consensus is in response to individual statements. Each participant is given an index card and asked to fold it into a tent. On one side they place a red dot, and on the other a green dot. When anyone is speaking, a green dot indicates agreement with the speaker and a red dot indicates a point of conflict. It is possible for the speaker then to ask those with red dots what their reservations or reactions are to what has been stated and to reveal this information for discussion. Surprisingly, we have found groups highly receptive to this technique. When there is laughter or great agreement, people sometimes wave their green dots in the air to emphasize it; this likewise happens with the red dot when intense disagreement is felt. It makes each person responsible for articulating their consensus or their difference, and grants each speaker the opportunity to make the appropriate inquiry.

7. Force-field analysis

The next step in the process was to begin to examine current realities which would affect the capacity of the organization to generate movement toward the ideal. To do this, we instructed the groups to conduct a force-field analysis by exploring the forces which could hinder or support creation of the ideal organizational state as represented by the provocative propositions they had created. This can be done quite simply on flipcharts, with facilitating forces (tail-winds) listed on one side and hindering forces (head-winds) on the other. Groups usually like this part of the process because it feels familiar, using more of their accustomed analytical skills.

Groups were then asked to return and to give a 10- to 15-minute presentation on the forces they had identified for their propositions. Before they proceeded, however, we assigned a different group to watch each presentation very carefully so that they could prepare a rebuttal. This was done to reduce the possibility of blind spots in the group's analysis and of group think. This is consistent with Argyris' (1985) theory of organizational learning in which the principal goal is to generate valid and confirmable data, thus reducing the possibility of defensive routines. After the group presentation, each group was given about a half hour to prepare a five-minute rebuttal to the group they had been assigned to point out inconsistencies and challenge assumptions. By the time these presentations were concluded, the entire group had a very clear idea about environmental contingencies and current realities, the opportunities they created and the dilemmas they posed in moving to the ideal state.

Q *Do you ever find that this devil's advocacy process jolts the group out of the appreciative mode and pushes them back into the old paradigm?*

A Dialogue is the cornerstone and most important product of appreciative inquiry. Every design compromise which undercuts individual, interpersonal and group dialogue significantly undermines the potential outcome. The ideal would be to have a paperless process with enough dialogue that what is deemed important becomes institutionalized through dialogue.

The force-field analysis represents a bridge to the problem-solving side of the process, but we did not shift the focus of the session to problem solving at this point. Conducting a force-field analysis uncovered some of the problems which would need to be solved to achieve the desired future state. However, any problem solving would happen after the event, spurred by the energy and commitments of participants. At this point, the force-field analysis grounded participants in current realities and enabled them to create realizable provocative propositions in the next phase of the design. We know that provocative propositions which are too ideal or which represent too much of a stretch from the current reality can be demoralizing for the participants. At the same time, if the ideal has energy and commitment of the members, it will make movement possible in spite of obstacles. The key is to produce a provocative proposition which is an appropriate stretch for the organization, neither too comfortable nor light years from possibility. The intent of the force-field was to help participants reveal and challenge each others' notions about current realities so that they could eventually make decisions about how to rewrite the provocative propositions.

8. State realizable provocative propositions

After being brought face to face with the constraints and opportunities implied by their construction of present reality, groups returned to write provocative propositions which, while remaining a significant stretch, would be more realizable for AK&G. Specifically, they were asked to rewrite provocative propositions for each affirmative topic so they would represent what could realistically be achieved and which group members believed they and the rest of the partnership should commit themselves to working toward. They were then given the opportunity to present these to the roundtable.

Since our work with the roundtable, we have experimented with various processes to create more possibility for dialogue around this activity. For example, we sometimes add a third scale in both the provocative proposition document and on the wall. This scale is for answering a question about the achievability (A) of the statement: "To what extent do you believe that this statement is achievable given current organizational and environmental realities?" Again, a one would indicate that the statement is absolutely impossible to achieve, and a seven would indicate that the statement is absolutely certain to be achieved. This question is asked after the force-field analysis. Participants are once more asked to respond first on their questionnaire, and then place a green Avery dot on the A-scale for each proposition. The results are very revealing and reflect the group's perception of the impact of current realities on the ability of the organization to move toward the ideal.

The relationship between the scales is significant. For example, if people strongly agree that a statement does reflect the desired ideal-state, and there is a large gap between the ideal and the present state, a group may decide to rank the working on propositions with moderate to high achievability. On the other hand, some people are impassioned by the difficulty of a challenge and will rank those statements which reflect a deeply felt ideal where the relative achievability is low. If the gap between the ideal and the actual is not large and the achievability is high, the group may lose energy because the statement is not really provocative: there is not enough dissonance to catalyze additional effort. Data generated through the use of the third scale can be used to stimulate dialogue about what would be necessary to rewrite provocative propositions so that they are more achievable, even while they retain some of the tension and risk which create a stretch and impel action.

Q   *Do you ever find that this encourages excessive wordsmithing?*

A   The devil's advocate process is an input process, not focused on input to determine a particular outcome or to micro-manage the work of others.

In subsequent work we have found that people sometimes have input, advice or reactions to provocative propositions for affirmative topics other than the ones they have been assigned to work on. These data need to be made available to groups who will be rewriting the propositions. At a recent retreat with one department within a major hospital, we dealt with this in two ways. First, we placed a flipchart sheet below each provocative proposition on the wall and asked participants to use that sheet to write any reactions, opinions or input they wanted to influence the group's discussion. Also, we gave each person an index card, telling them that if there were any provocative propositions they thought were missing or needed to be added, they should write it on the card and give it to a staff member. Whatever method is selected, the purpose is to get any input the group needs to consider before rewriting realizable provocative propositions.

9. State personal commitments and plan next steps for acting on provocative propositions

At this point, there had been much discussion about the strengths of the present, the possibilities of the future and current environmental and organizational realities. Participants had gotten to know each other better than they ever had before, to explore each other's deepest values and hopes for the firm. The roundtable session had by this time revealed common purposes and shared meanings, and it was possible to begin focusing on personal commitments individuals would make in response to the provocative propositions and the roundtable event as a whole.

Roundtable participants were asked to state their commitments to the entire group, and these statements were audiotaped to be transcribed and published in the documentation to participants after the event. The consultant who introduced the process framed it in the following way:

"What we want to do this evening is to have each of you, as participants, be willing to state some particular goal that is important to you, we hope either emerging from or supported by the information that has been generated by the provocative propositions, and having to do with something you want to act upon over the next year. It should be one that you're willing to take some action on in the next seven days, and definitely do something before the partners' meeting [a month away]... It can be as simple as having a conversation with someone about your particular goal, or some particular steps that you want to take so you are more public and can build the support you feel you need to move forward.

For some people in this room, committing themselves to a particular action to achieve a publicly declared goal in a group of people this size can be pretty anxiety-provoking or frightening. Questions arise like, What if I don't deliver on it after I've made it public to 53 peers here? What if I change my mind? What if I don't actually have a goal that I have some passion about or really care about in a way that I'm willing to put out to this group at this particular time?

These are legitimate questions. It's okay to say, 'I really don't have something I have a passion about at this time, but here are a couple things I'm thinking about.' And it is legitimate to put something out here and later to come along and say that things have happened and that you've changed your mind about that particular goal. But then you have to be willing to put out what's taken its place or what you have arrived at that you've really invested in."

By introducing the activity in this way, following an enjoyable dinner on their last evening together, the consultant made it possible for individuals to talk about goals and commitments that were still tentative or being formed. He also created an environment of safety, which he then reinforced with some personally revealing stories about times he had experienced the power of profound commitment. Examples of the personal commitments made by three individuals are shown below.

"The two concepts that clearly have interested and excited me and aroused my passion are leadership and the concept of legacy. I think those are important concepts that can provide some exciting frameworks for some of the work we should be doing and that I'd like to do. So my goal for the next year is to have the concept of leadership and legacy understood, accepted and evident in a stronger way in my office partners... In terms of action steps in the next seven days, I clearly intend to get leadership and legacy on the agenda of my partners' meeting next Friday. I would hope we could reach agreement that this is an important topic to become a theme for ongoing discussions throughout the year so we can begin to flesh it out in terms of some action plans."

"The action step that I had in mind, because I have a lot to learn to understand the office environment that I'm going into, is to spend some time between now and the partners' meeting with each and every staff member. I think that will have a lot of impact on my personal learning. I think at the same time, if I go out of here with the enthusiasm that I came in here with, and take the opportunity to talk to each of those staff members to share some of the values and excitements that are coming out of this conference, I will have covered little bits and pieces of a number of the provocative propositions. While I'm doing that, of course, the other thing is that within the next two weeks, I will also address the issue of how to put a more formal, more structured communication plan in place in my office."

"I looked at the interview data and the messages that the partners have told us or that I've read things that are important to the firm and things that would allow me to do my job better. I'm looking at areas like improved communications, listening better to partners and staff, sharing our plans, sharing our visions, asking more about and listening to their hopes and aspirations in a sense, being more supportive and positive to the staff..."

The personal commitments, aspirations and values expressed capped a session in which new relationships and understandings had been forged. The statements were symbolic of the trust which had been established and would become the basis for the trust which would remain after the conference.

Q   *How was this follow-up received by the roundtable participants? Did they see it as a welcome proof of the continuing interest of senior management or did they see it as unwelcome pressure from on high?*

A   They welcomed it and actually wanted more. It was perceived as support for their agenda and what they wanted to see happen as part of the desired future. It also supported them keeping themselves focused in the midst of very powerful competing organization agendas.

Six months after the roundtable, the managing partner sent a memo to all of the participants and asked them to send him a short story of what had happened, and what was new and different after the roundtable. Most participants responded, and all stated how they had acted on their commitments of that evening and how those commitments had shifted because of other pressing business contingencies. In several cases, there were samples of newsletters and communication strategies which had been developed after the session. About two months after he received the responses, the managing partner had copies of all of the responses distributed to all of the roundtable participants so that they could see the activities which had been catalyzed in those personal commitments. In addition, he continued to follow up with participants at six-month intervals, asking them for reports on their progress around commitments they made, and this continued for a period of 18 months.

10. Long-term impact

After the roundtable in September, the provocative propositions created by participants were prepared for presentation and consensual validation by the full partnership of the firm. The partners' meeting took place a month later, in October of 1987. All 350 partners were provided with the entire set of raw interview data, edited to assure anonymity of the respondent, as well as a set of summarized data. Presentations about the roundtable project and its significance for the firm were made by David Cooperrider, John Carter and the managing partner. All of the partners then broke into groups of 50 to validate by consensus the propositions, using an identical process to the one described earlier. Most of the propositions were supported, and the process had the effect of collectively re-energizing the partnership around their shared values and commitments. It was also successful in expanding the impact of the intervention throughout the firm.

Q   *I am interested that you write "re-energized." Does this imply that energy was flagging? I ask because some of the organizations with which we are familiar have told us that they find they need another appreciative inquiry shot in the arm after about two years. This slightly bothers us, because it suggests that the appreciative mode has not taken root very deeply after the first intervention. Perhaps we are naive to think that it should or could.*

A   Shared values and common commitments are largely part of the context and ground in organizations. Without periodic or constant individual and group interventions which heighten collective awareness, these important reference and contact points cease to be part of the compelling picture and lose their ability to mobilize energy.

It is now five years after the roundtable, and it continues to have significant influence in the organization. The real impact was less the roundtable event itself than the fact that people continued talking about their experience, how the roundtable had influenced their values and the things they eventually began to act upon in the organization. Even more significant, many aspects of the theory, concept and methodology of appreciative inquiry attached to the roundtable experience continue to be used. Participants were empowered to use techniques such as scattergrams, use of provocative propositions to envision a desired future, and acting from an appreciative stance with meetings of their office partners, and sometimes with office managers and staff, often leading to enhanced communication and participation within the firm.

Since then AK&G has been through an international merger which doubled the size of the partnership in Canada. Without the roundtable, it is likely that the organizational culture of AK&G would have been extinguished. Instead, it caused people to be clear about what they valued and wished to preserve in the new organization. Further, roundtable participants continued to use the theory, concepts and techniques they had experienced in their individual offices to help build the culture of the new firm. From a multinational perspective, the merger was actually a takeover of AK&G. In Canada, because of the strength of the AK&G culture, the situation has actually been closer to a reverse takeover. Even more surprising, the partners from the other firm have been pleased about this because it addressed many of the problems and issues inherent in their culture. Merger dynamics are difficult in any organization, but the roundtable project is recognized throughout the merged organization as being instrumental in ensuring successful management of the merger in Canada.

11. Key insights and conclusion

There are four propositions about what is necessary to institutionalize change which reflect our learning from this intervention. By institutionalizing change, we mean perpetuating core values and principles that are integral to the culture of the firm and the integrity of its business practices. Change is institutionalized when it has deeply affected the hearts, minds and guts of individuals involved so that, when appropriate, they tend to recreate their learning. It is institutionalized when it is perceived as responsive to relevant business needs within the context of client service. It may seem counter-intuitive to talk about institutionalized change, especially with the current focus on turbulent or chaotic change and the ability for any organization to be able to turn on a dime successfully to respond to global challenges. However, in the midst of change, continuity must also be managed, and this can mean the continuity of best business practices which will make an organization more successful in the future.

1. The most powerful change is that which strengthens the best of the existing culture.

    A change project is paradoxical in that its power lies not in loosening the cultural grip to bring in the radically new, but rather in strengthening the best of what already exists. Many cultural change efforts tend to throw the baby out with the bathwater in their zealousness to move toward something new. Many organizations and consultants may ignore (and thereby negate) the best of what made them successful in the past. In doing this, essential elements of the very culture which could help the organization realize its preferred state may be irrevocably lost. The discovery and celebration of the core values and principles which have made an organization successful in the past may be the most critical aspect of developing a compelling vision of the future which inspires energy and momentum.

2. Institutionalizing change is easier when: (1) there is alignment and commitment to the mission and superordinate values of the organization; (2) people are deeply responsible and accountable for acting on their commitments; and (3) change is seen as enhancing business objectives.

In AK&G these conditions were especially well met. The statement of intent had been developed with the input and involvement of the full partnership. It represented a statement of shared values and commitments which established common ground for all of the partners. Further, partners experience themselves as highly accountable owners of the firm, and key stakeholders of its success. Many partners see their role as participating in a way that leaves some future legacy for the firm. There is no compromise on professional values, the integrity of the practice or the desire to do high-quality work which will ensure that business objectives are achieved. Because of this uncompromising commitment to shared values, there is willingness to do whatever is necessary to ensure continued integrity in the practice which includes changing habits, behaviours and attitudes as necessary to ensure continued success.

3. Institutionalizing change requires structures and processes which ensure rich dialogue and a basis for establishing a group will be based on a chain of consent rather than a chain of command.

Again, we stress the distinction of dialogue as the communication of shared meanings mentioned earlier. The roundtable event offered the next generation of firm leaders an opportunity for sustained dialogue around superordinate values and goals. Afterwards, participants created a number of meetings which provided others in the organization with a significant forum for open discussion, dialogue and debate. Such meetings allow organizational members to have voice and enhance collective commitment to decisions which provide the basis for mutual action toward change goals.

4. When you are strengthening the culture to change it, we suggest that the following principles, processes and structures will be helpful.

   • Seed the organization with those values, norms and practices that are strongest. Organizing powerful but isolated events to institute such values, norms and practices are less important than their gradual dispersion and implementation.

   • Promote cross-generational learning. The elders point to the best of the past and provide wisdom; the middle-aged point to the reality of the present and provide discipline; and the youth point to the possibilities of the future and provide inspiration.

- Involve the best and the brightest of potential future leaders in the best of what has shaped the firm. This will perpetuate the best of what is and hold out promise for the best of what might be.

Q *This again feels very elitist. Maybe the less bright have important things to say. Indeed, one of the real kicks we get out of doing appreciative inquiry in many organizations is precisely giving voice to people who do not usually have it and finding that they have really significant things to say which the leadership needs to hear. And I wonder how consistent this paragraph is with the next one.*

A Everyone has something to say and the process allows everyone to be heard and represented. Any organization that does not have the goal of having the voices of the best and the brightest significantly influence its future will not compete effectively in the global market. Everyone provides leadership by putting their voice in and making their pictures of the future public. Everyone will not be a leader, because being a leader requires followership.

- Create a critical mass for change. This is not a matter of getting the largest number of people on board, but rather those who will be the most influential in attracting movement toward change goals. In this situation, the group of younger partners who had emerged as future leaders of the firm became the critical mass. They had a collective experience of envisioning future possibility based on the best of the past. This experience then became a solid basis from which they dispersed the vision throughout the organization.

- Invite, influence and involve. Discourage boundaries or a sense of exclusiveness in defining the critical mass. The role of a critical mass is to permeate the organization, to act as a missionary group to influence key processes and systems, and to involve as many others as possible in their vision of possibilities.

- Design change events in which the event itself is the ground, and the value-laden activities which result are the figure. Here, organizational participants did not promote their attendance at the roundtable as evidence of enhanced status or prestige. This is contrary to notions of partnership. Instead, they went out to act on their commitments and infuse what had been learned into their practice and management of the firm. People should notice not who attended the event, but what activities were later initiated to support and enhance superordinate values, goals and practices.

- Design a structure honeycombed with committees, taskforces, training sessions, annual-planning processes, and other forums that provide opportunities for open dialogue, exchange of ideas, solicitation of advice and support, and dispersion of information. This provides an environment in which ideas can be shaped and influenced, and consensus ultimately achieved.

- Finally, focus attention on the positive image and on the big picture on all of the events and activities moving toward change and on success indicators that are benchmarks of progress.

We have stressed the need to approach organizations with a coherent theory, a conceptual framework, and a methodology which can activate the theory. Here, the theoretical basis was a deep understanding of appreciative inquiry, its roots in a social constructionist perspective which makes possible the idea that intervening in organizational cognition will result in transformative organizational change. The conceptual framework included notions such as the power of affirmative topic choice, provocative propositions, and consensual validation as elements of intervention into the social cognition of a group. The methodology included such techniques as the scattergram to consensually validate provocative propositions, and the force-field analysis as a way of testing provocative propositions and moving them into the realm of what would be achievable for the firm. Finally, it included structures and processes such as involving participants in the collection of data, the roundtable design, inter-generational learning, public airing of individual commitments and periodic monitoring of progress, and diffusion of the provocative propositions into the rest of the organization beginning with the partners' meeting a month later. Any one of these elements alone, we believe, would not have the power or impact that they have when there is a coherent theory to guide their implementation with supporting structures and processes in an organization. In the end, that was our most significant insight.

Chapter 15
Conclusions—and questions about sustainability

I have argued in this book that the appreciative approach has much to offer practitioners of social change in a wide variety of environments, from a small company to an international organization to Third World villagers to public service providers of all sorts. I have not explored the person-to-person applications of appreciative inquiry—e.g., in marriage counselling, career counselling or stress management—although there is a huge field here only just beginning to be delineated. Let's leave that whole area aside as we address the central question of this concluding chapter: what can appreciative inquiry contribute to the processes of sustainable social change? In one sense, that question has already been answered, though often tangentially. In nearly every case we have looked at the key issue of sustainability, from Healthco which was, at one point, looking into the abyss; to the Mauritanian villagers who were having to discover for themselves new patterns of survival; to Sigma which was facing an organizational crossroads which would determine its capacity to develop as an organization—or the reverse. Even the case study contributed by Carter and Johnson has sustainability as a central theme. For what drove the key players was precisely the fear that unless there was a common vision, widely shared and passionately held, of the future of the partnership, its reputation for quality work would slowly—or perhaps not so slowly—dissipate. In these last pages, let's try to take the discussion a little deeper.

I want to make four main points. I shall argue that the main contribution that appreciative inquiry brings is an assault on our prevailing social conditioning toward cynicism. In so far as it replaces cynicism with hopefulness, it is a *necessary precondition* of sustainability. Second, I shall ask how far the appreciative approach itself is sustainable. Is it not undermined and subverted by bitter experience, broken contracts, personal and corporate failure? Third, I will explore the implications of dashed hopes for the nature of relationships generated in and through appreciative inquiry. That will lead us, fourth, into a consideration of the sustainabilities of the community that is formed through appreciative inquiry.

1. Appreciative inquiry and the culture of cynicism

"You'll never get these hardened prison officers to look at what gives them life, energy and hope. These guys are tough, really tough. You'll just get rude or put-down comments. They wouldn't be doing the jobs they are doing with the people they are doing them with if they were interested in any kind of optimistic view of future possibilities." So we were told—and three-quarters believed—when we started an appreciative inquiry in one of Britain's most notorious jails. Working with lifers convicted of the most appalling crimes and their totally demoralized jailers, blamed universally for the break-outs and riots that had marked the recent years of the prison's history, what could we expect but a cynicism, on both sides of the bars, so deep laid and untouchable that it alone could keep both jailers and prisoners sane? Indeed, was it not that very cynicism, that refusal to give value and respect to both the present and the future, that was the psychic fuel that kept the regime going?

If that was true, then cynicism itself was a force for sustainability, and that implied that to challenge it, to seek to open minds and refresh spirits, was not only counter-productive but also deeply uncompassionate. Why raise false hopes? Why pretend there was an alternative future when the basic structure—some incarcerated, some tending the incarcerated, and the exchange of violence between them—was beyond change?

I will return to that in a moment. First, let's change the locale of that dialogue to a Sahelian village or an African slum or a threatened community of Amazonian Indians. Might it not also be argued that the denial of hope, the securities of cynicism about government, aid agencies and "the other" in general are what makes life possible for people in these extreme conditions? If they hoped, they would be doomed, and who knows the social and psychic penalties that frustrated hopes would bring? At the least a deeper cynicism; at the worst unchecked violence, most probably turned inward.

That argument cannot be lightly dismissed, and I want formally to recognize its power and its credibility. Yet I want, too, to put three weights in the opposite pan of the scale. The first is to argue that the culture of cynicism, which is in so sense confined either to the Third World or to prisons and their analogues, is itself so deeply destructive that it is an act of the profoundest social irresponsibility to leave it unchallenged. From the employer who abuses his employees because they are structurally weaker than he, to the government that manipulates its expenditure patterns to bribe voters at the next election, we are surrounded by the out-workings of cynicism that become self-feeding and finally seemingly self-justifying. Is that a sustainable pattern? In a formal sense, yes, of course it is. In a more meaningful sense, where sustainability acknowledges the essence of the human spirit, it is sustainable only by constantly denying that essence. And, as Sloterdijk has shown, that structured denial of human potential always, but always, contains within it the seeds of its own destruction.

Second, I want to argue that it is too late to put the genie back in the bottle. That is to say, most communities in most parts of the world—I would even say all communities in every part of the world, touched, however obliquely, by modern communications—have already seen a better future for themselves or their children. For good or ill, the revolution of rising expectations has already engulfed them. The operational question is how do we work with those rising expectations in a way that maximizes both their chances of success and their long-term sustainability? The answer surely lies in helping them form trusting communities that draw on each other's strengths, that mobilize each other's gifts and reinforce whatever steps are successfully taken along a long and hard road. I have already suggested—and will repeat below—that I believe that appreciative inquiry has a major role to play in this process.

Third, admittedly on a tiny sample, the empirical evidence is not that the destructive pseudo-sustainabilities of cynicism are ultimately *reinforced* by appreciative inquiry but that hopes are kindled, and energies are mobilized, for a realistic *change* that will challenge the roots of that cynicism. Return to prison for a moment. There we found the prior prognostications of disaster were entirely wrong. It was not that staff and prisoners were not cynical: most were deeply so. Rather, as we experienced it, the process of appreciative inquiry made it possible for the vast majority to review patterns of relationship and being and thereby identify the best even within a sad and punitive environment. By building on that *best*, prisoners were not expecting liberty nor staff an easy life, but they were hoping for a sustainable leap in the quality of life that everyone, from governor to newly arrived lifer, could enjoy. And they knew that the attainment of that vision would require work, discussion, revision, negotiation and renegotiation. But, as one prisoner put it, "Better to flog our guts out trying to make it work than to stew in our own miserable juices for the rest of our lives."[117]

2. The sustainability of appreciative inquiry

This takes us into the heart of the issue. As I have shown in the many case studies and bits of case studies in this book, the organizational impact of appreciative inquiry is to establish a community of people committed to change, enthusiastic about the possibilities of the future, and pledged, in one sense or another, to work for it. But what happens when they are disappointed? When a higher authority suppresses them? When the men of violence, opposed to any threat to the *status quo*, move in (as I have seen, to my horror, in a Bolivian context)? What is the sustainability value of appreciative inquiry then?

Or, to put it in another way, is the transfer of appreciative inquiry from the North American business scene to the Third World a mistake of categories? North American business culture may be ruthless in some senses, but it does not eliminate people who threaten the *status quo* and it does not ask people to risk their own survival in the cause of change. Yet that it is the common experience of people at the bottom of the heap in most poor countries—as studies of social change in both Latin America and the Indian sub-continent have repeatedly reminded us. If you get it wrong in North America, you lose your job. If you get it wrong in India, you lose your life. The higher stakes in the Third World make, so it may be argued, the sustaining of an appreciative spirit, so much more difficult as to be almost impossible.

Again, this is an argument that has to be taken seriously and perhaps is too readily dismissed by the incautious appreciative inquiry enthusiasts in the US. Even without the melodrama of physical attacks by those whose interests are threatened by change, it is of course true that many, small communities in the Third World are, almost by definition, isolated, neglected, deeply on their own. Reversals, disappointments, failures, human weaknesses (especially in terms of financial honesty) take a toll made the more unendurable by the fact that the community suffering these misfortunes is unsupported at the time it most needs support.

Two counter comments need to be made, one general, the other highly specific. In general terms, usually the better the original inquiry has been—that is, the more people it has involved, the more deeply they have invested in the process, the more wholeheartedly the entire community has bought in to the action proposals—the more sustainable is the energy that has flowed from the inquiry. That is why it is important to give the time, the expertise and the patience in the early stages of the inquiry. Skimping on them not only jeopardizes the immediate success of the inquiry: more significantly it makes it much less likely that, once the inquiry is over and normal working has been resumed, the effects of the inquiry will be sustainable.

More specifically, the concerns we are addressing here make it desirable—perhaps even mandatory—that any appreciative inquiry process should have built into the financial and time budgets a follow-up phase which enables the community to come together again around the main findings of the inquiry, address any weaknesses or disappointments, celebrate the achievements and successes and generally re-own the spirit of the process. Our own experience (inadequately reflected in part 3) has so convinced us of the benefits of this follow-up that, in our own consulting practice, whether in the First or Third Worlds, we now insist on the inclusion of such a phase. If we find it is not necessary, then it can be dropped. We believe that the option should be there, and that it is for the community itself to decide whether to exercise that option.

3. The relationships in the community

There is a half-true sense in which a successful appreciative inquiry could be represented as superimposing on the deep structure of an organization a shallow counter structure in which positions of authority and even power are temporarily reversed. We have encountered this many times in the course of this book, from the boss of the international organization who resented his staff taking responsibility for the future of the organization to the village chief in Mauritania feeling obliged to hold a village meeting for the first time, to the expatriate director of the street-kids' organization feeling threatened by the way the street kids and the agency staff were moving into strategic territory that he regarded as his own. The question then arises: what happens when normal working relationships are re-established, especially when the heat is on from other organizations or individuals who are opposed to change? Is it not possible, even inevitable, that the people really in charge simply walk away from the appreciative inquiry and wash their hands of its findings and dynamics?

Yes, of course that can happen. It would be disingenuous to deny it as a possibility, and as a possibility that is on occasion an actuality. But again the issue is fundamentally about how well the work of the inquiry was done in the first place. If the hierarchs have psychically stood aside from the inquiry; if they have actually been elbowed aside by either the facilitator or the work group, then it is relatively easy for them to disown the process when the going gets hard. And that will happen the more readily if the cardinal rule of the inquiry—that all stakeholders be included—has been ignored.

For an inquiry in which the hierarchs are permitted to keep a safe distance has within it the origins of its own undoing. That was very nearly the case with Healthco, as we saw. It was only because we had done some hard work in the pre-inquiry process whereby the board was locked into the inquiry that, in the end, they resisted the temptation to abort the process when it might have suited them financially and organizationally to do so. In the event they knew that if they did so, the morale of the organization would have been so destroyed that they would have been faced with the prospect of a large number of resignations, much adverse publicity and the incapacity to carry out their own plans. The sustainability of Healthco was in question.

It is not, however, that downside risk that I would want to emphasize in this connection. That is the old model. Rather I would want to emphasize that the object of the inquiry is to splice all stakeholders so firmly into the process that when pre-inquiry hierarchies are re-established, they are in fact qualitatively different. The old ground is simply unavailable. The organization—whether a village, a cooperative or a business—has entered new ground where the formal titles and organograms may still exist but where they are interpreted differently, where they are suffused with a new light that makes the exercise of authority a qualitatively different experience for all concerned.

We got a glimpse of this even in prison where we were in touch with both staff and prisoners long after the appreciative inquiry was finished. Formally, of course, nothing had changed or could change. Informally, on the ground, in the interstices of personal relationships, so much had shifted that in some cases (though certainly not in all) it would be difficult or even impossible to retreat into the old hierarchically determined relationships.

It is, of course, true that even that change of mode can be subverted, pushed back into the old routines. Questions about sustainability have to be faced again. It is to that that we return in the next section.

285

4. Sustaining the community

So far I have suggested that the key to sustaining the gains from appreciative inquiry in the community is doing the appreciative inquiry properly in the first place and then topping up from time to time as required. I want to take that discussion one stage deeper in these final paragraphs.

At the heart of the appreciative inquiry process is the discovery of a new community. In the first instance that is the community of the work group which normally bonds very closely and which skilled facilitation can bond even tighter. Later, in the sharing of the provocative propositions and in the building of consensus around them, the bonds of the work group are extended to a much wider circle, including all the stakeholders and/or the whole community. It is the quality of those two level of bonds—within the work group and within the wider arena—which will finally determine the *survivability* of the appreciative spirit within the relevant community. I wrote earlier about the deep structure of an organization (or community) and the shallow structure which appreciative inquiry superimposes upon it. That distinction is important and fair in one dimension, for no secretary is going to have the power of the CEO, no villager the power of a government minister. And in that sense the deep structure remains.

The question, however, is whether the shallow structure of the inquiry permeates into the deep structure, subtly changing it, not perhaps in outward form but in inner content. To change the metaphor, does the appreciative inquiry take—or is constant revaccination necessary? Is there a sense in which the community as a whole is so transformed by the experience that old ways of doing things, old ways of being (e.g., being the CEO, being the aid worker) are no longer appropriate or even necessary? Is it the case that, after the appreciative inquiry, no one *wants* to go back to the old ways because they have seen something, perhaps still in embryo, that looks much more rewarding, exciting and meaningful?

For me, those are still open questions. In some cases there does seem to be a process of transformation that is irreversible and in that sense self-sustaining. And the secret seems to lie in the wider community, in the way it relates to the inquiry, feels involved, feels energized and liberated by what seems to be going on. In others, there is less community buy-in, or a small but vocal group of dissidents, or a group who, for whatever reason, remain aloof.

It would be satisfying to me as author and to you as reader if I could list the steps that have to be taken to ensure that every case approaches the former and none the latter. Maybe one day that will be possible; maybe wiser heads than mine can already provide the secret formula. At the moment I do not believe we are there yet. What we can do—and what I believe to be infinitely worth doing—is to conduct the inquiry with all the sensitivity, rigour and creativity that we can bring to bear, trusting that in the end the process will *work*.

And that is a good place to stop. For again and again my collaborators and I have been near despair, near panic, in Reason's chaos, convinced that this is never going to work. The depths of cynicism, skepticism, self-interest and defensiveness have seemed too unfathomable for a few simple questions to touch. Yet in every case, so far almost without exception, we have come away saying to each other: "Trust the process." So do it as well as you can and then trust it—without reservation.

---

117 Alison Liebling, David Price and Charles Elliott, "Appreciative inquiry and relationships in prison," *Punishment and Society*, 1, 1, 1999, pp. 67-94.